THE SIMPLE GUIDE TO LEGAL *Innovation*

LUCY ENDEL BASSLI

THE SIMPLE GUIDE TO LEGAL *Innovation*

BASICS EVERY LAWYER SHOULD KNOW

Cover design by Tahiti Spears/ABA Design.

Printed in the United States of America.

24 23 22 21 20 5 4 3 2 1

Library of Congress Cataloging-in-Publication Data

Names: Bassli, Lucy Endel, author. | American Bar Association. Tort Trial and Insurance Practice Section, sponsoring body.
Title: The simple guide to legal innovation / Lucy Bassli.
Description: First edition. | Chicago : American Bar Association, 2020. | Includes index. | Summary: "Educational needs of practicing lawyers are explored with a practical guide provided. Details the legal ecosystem and how its complex, varied and often overlapping parts can and should be handled by practicing attorneys, alternative legal service providers and "non-legal" professionals"—Provided by publisher.
Identifiers: LCCN 2019048125 (print) | LCCN 2019048126 (ebook) | ISBN 9781641055871 (hardcover) | ISBN 9781641055888 (epub)
Subjects: LCSH: Practice of law—United States.
Classification: LCC KF300 .B377 2020 (print) | LCC KF300 (ebook) | DDC 340.068—dc23
LC record available at https://lccn.loc.gov/2019048125
LC ebook record available at https://lccn.loc.gov/2019048126

Discounts are available for books ordered in bulk. Special consideration is given to state bars, CLE programs, and other bar-related organizations. Inquire at Book Publishing, ABA Publishing, American Bar Association, 321 N. Clark Street, Chicago, Illinois 60654-7598.

www.ShopABA.org

Contents

PART I INTRODUCTION 1

Chapter 1 My Innovation Journey 3

A Journey That Redefined a Career 5
Sharing My Learnings 10
Plea to Innovate 11

Chapter 2 Legal Ecosystem Under Pressure 13

Law Firms 15
Corporate Legal Departments 18
Alternative Legal Service Providers 21
Industry Groups 28
Regulation 29

PART II FOUNDATIONAL TOPICS 33

Chapter 3 Legal Operations: What Is It and Why Is It Important? 35

Technology and Infrastructure 39
Business Strategy and Planning 42
Project and Program Management 45
Data and Insights 48

Chapter 4 Legal Education Landscape **55**

Quick Look at Law Schools 55
Continuing Legal Education: The Gap for Practicing Lawyers 58

Chapter 5 Legal Technology **65**

AI, Blockchain, and Other Buzzwords 67
Access to Justice and Technology 72
Competency in Technology 73
Jobs in the Legal Market 74
Model of Competency 75
Technology Implementation 76

Chapter 6 Women and Innovation: The Secret Weapon for Women to *Finally* Advance **79**

Why Women Make Great Innovators 80
Supporting Women as Innovators—Opportunity and Culture 85
Conclusion (a.k.a. the Final Pitch) 86

PART III JUST ENOUGH ON THE KEY TOPICS THAT EVERY LAWYER NEEDS TO KNOW **91**

Chapter 7 Talking Points on Each Topic **93**

Need to Know #1: Definition of Innovations **97**
Need to Know #2: Project Management **109**
Need to Know #3: Process and Efficiencies **123**
Need to Know #4: Automation **133**
Need to Know #5: Value and the Law Firm Managed Services Model **153**
Need to Know #6: Alternative Legal Service Providers **167**
Need to Know #7: Data **177**
Need to Know #8: The Modern Legal Workforce **184**

Need to Know #9: Outsourcing Legal **194**

Need to Know #10: Corporate Legal Management: Peek Behind the Curtain **209**

Conclusion 221

Appendix 223

Endnotes 239

Index 247

PART I

Introduction

CHAPTER 1

My Innovation Journey

How to Read this Book:

If you are methodical and like big-picture storytelling, read the book in the order it is written.

If you want to get to the main point and be ready for a cocktail conversation about legal innovation, then, after reading Part I for general background, skip to Part III for the meat of the book.

With countless articles and blogs on legal innovation, it is nearly impossible for attorneys to keep up. We're already stretched thin trying to negotiate deals, go to court, manage the business, build new client relationships, and stay abreast of the changes in substantive areas of law. And just as we think we're finally getting a grip on it all, the legal industry decides to wake up from its decades-long slumber, opening its blurry eyes to a rapidly changing economy that's being driven by a technology-powered workforce.

Should lawyers be expected to read every sensational article about robots taking over their jobs? Should lawyers become experts on blockchain? Or perhaps become certified in legal project management, or train to code software? Absolutely not! Such goals may be highly unrealistic, but every lawyer should be aware of these concepts. Lawyers need an appreciation of what is happening in the legal industry, who the key players are, the role that technology plays, and how these factors are changing the nature of legal services delivery.

Clients are demanding new and different services such as asking for project management assistance, alternative pricing structures, and lower cost resources. They want more value from their firms, and they want their firms to come up with ideas. Firms are responding by hiring a variety of professionals in other disciplines, including data science, project management, knowledge management, and solution architecture, as examples. Professionals in these fields are largely frustrated, however, because the practicing lawyers still need convincing about the benefits of their services. If, however, practicing attorneys understood the value and could articulate the benefits that other professionals bring, they would need no convincing and clients would be the beneficiaries.

Many lawyers are simply unaware of the revolution that is happening, adding further tension to the precious billable hour, with new players offering enticing solutions and technology playing a larger role each day. Unfortunately, many practicing lawyers continue to focus on their billable hours and rely on the personal nature of their client relationships, ignoring data, clients' needs (not stated wants, but actual needs), and the inevitable future of the law practice—a practice that has been largely unchanged for decades.

In this book, I explore the educational needs of practicing lawyers and provide a practical guide for lawyers who want to differentiate themselves. This type of education falls somewhere into a gap between traditional continuing legal education (CLE) topics, and the training and development that most law firms provide to their attorneys to develop professional (usually, soft) skills.

I explore in some detail the legal ecosystem and how its complex, varied, and often overlapping parts can and should be handled by practicing attorneys, alternative legal service providers (ALSPs), and "non-legal" professionals.

Lawyers are often unaware of the developing resources available, even if their own firm has them. They are not sure how to leverage these resources, when to engage them, for what kinds of work, or how to sell them to their clients.

This book has three main sections: introduction; followed by foundational chapters on the legal education landscape, the rise of legal operations (or legal ops), the legal ecosystem, women and innovation; and lastly practical chapters on the top concepts that lawyers need to know. It is targeted toward commercial attorneys at midsize to large firms, because it is written from my personal perspective and experiences.

The good news: lawyers can continue to learn well into their years of practice! With some updated vocabulary and a few real examples (the examples in this book come from my corporate experience, not consumer or legal aid services sectors) lawyers can learn to wow their clients, enticing them to try something new.

This book will help them on that journey.

A JOURNEY THAT REDEFINED A CAREER

So who am I and why should you care about my thoughts on legal innovation? I was a regular lawyer (just like you, reader). I'm not a coder or a Silicon Valley startup founder. I came to innovation through being annoyed with the inefficiencies and volume-based challenges I encountered in my work life—and by recognizing that there were better ways of doing things and that I could make an impact. I have experience in both small and large firms as well as in small and large corporations. I have background as a legal tech solutions provider, as part of a high-growth startup corporate legal team, and also as a consultant who was active in several parts of the legal ecosystem. This section details my journey and some key lessons I learned early on that helped me become an innovative lawyer.

My Innovation Journey

There is no better way to inspire others to change than to provide real examples of how someone else did it. I did not know that I was going to be an "innovative" lawyer when I graduated from the University of Houston Law Center. Actually, I had no idea what I would be . . . anything but a litigator or practicing something that has its own set of laws (tax or bankruptcy). As it turned out, I went into Bankruptcy Law and was in court regularly. I learned three valuable lessons at my first real job as a lawyer that have influenced and inspired my desire to innovate:

1. CONFIDENCE (or COURAGE). When a first-year associate is trusted to independently participate in a three-party negotiation mediated by a bankruptcy judge, there's no choice but to do your best. Honestly, I was not intended to take that lead, the circumstances at the small firm left me in that position, as all those senior to me had other commitments and, worse, a medical emergency. So, there I was, doing my best to not let my fear shine through. I had to demonstrate confidence and tap into all of my courage, regardless of my lack of experience. Being in this negotiation was unlike anything I had experienced in my short career to date. I took it as an opportunity to learn. To try something new and risk failure, you have to be confident in your ability to learn and adapt. To innovate, you have to risk failure and trust the process of learning from mistakes.
2. LOGIC. The owner of the firm had forty-plus years of experience and was well-known among the community of bankruptcy

attorneys around the country. He never acted as if he was constrained by conventional boundaries and norms of what "should" be done. He always led with logic and pragmatism. He didn't follow patterns and expectations, and always asked me what I thought we should do. Learning to trust your logic and go with what makes sense has been a key foundation. Often, innovation comes from the need to *do something better*; where the current way just doesn't make sense.

3. SUPPORT. Having the support of the owner and the other two lawyers in this tiny firm, I always felt empowered to stretch and encouraged to push my comfort zone. Having the right professional support is critical. Though everyone talks about mentors and sponsors, you also need those who simply encourage and support your attempts, while teaching you along the way.

Armed with these three key lessons, I was ready to conquer just about anything my developing career would throw at me. Before I knew it, a real opportunity landed in my lap. An opportunity that was ripe for innovation. So what really set me on an "innovation journey"? Simple, it was the work. The work I was doing lent itself to innovation simply because I could not manage the work the way it had always been done. There was too much work, too little time, and unreliable resources. Let's dive into a few examples of what I see as very simple versions of "innovation" or logic, as I like to think of it. Sometimes moving from old ways of doing things is a result of applying logic to doing things a better way.

Using Data

After the small bankruptcy boutique, I was fortunate to be recruited by a mentor and friend to join him at a great regional firm where I began to work on commercial contracts. As I was handling growing volumes of contracts for the client, I quickly realized that I needed to track huge chunks of work. Keeping track of legal work is not natural to the law firm lawyer, nor were the systems advanced enough at the time to enable good tracking of anything besides the billable hour. As the number of paralegals that worked on my transactions grew and the total number of transactions increased, it became necessary to understand how the workload was balancing. Who was working on which contracts? More importantly, how long did it take to review these contracts?

I began by creating a very simple table in Microsoft (MS) Word (before I learned to love Excel). Every lawyer reading this book likely knows how to use MS Word, but I bet its table functionality is not something that comes naturally to all lawyers. I used MS Word to create a tracking system for my own purposes, but more importantly, *I shared the data with the client.* It was important that they see the amount of work that we were handling and to understand the timeliness. It was one of my earliest lessons in realizing how something so simple could be helpful to the client. They didn't ask me for it, but it just seemed obvious to me that they would appreciate it. When I started receiving positive feedback from the client, I began to notice that what seemed so logical and obvious was actually novel for them to get from their law firms.

Asking a Basic Question: Why?

When toddlers ask "why" about everything, it can certainly become annoying. Apparently when a new boss does it, it also can be annoying, but there is a key difference. Toddlers do it out of curiosity. At work, we ask "why" because we are trying to understand the rationale for a particular approach and challenge if there may be a better way.

When I first went in-house to Microsoft, I adopted a centralized team of paralegals who were tasked with handling a certain type of work. I started asking them why they did certain things: such as starting with a particular template, or searching in a certain repository, or using sample language, and so on. In my efforts to explore how they accomplished their work, I noticed that every question was met with a very defensive response. They didn't seem to trust that I was not looking to criticize their processes, but rather hoping that together we could find better ways.

It quickly became clear that everyone was doing things their own way, and nothing was documented. How was a centralized team, servicing an entire department, supposed to deliver a reliable, consistent service without documented workflows or shared information? Once I learned that there was no solid answer for why things were done the way they were, I set out to gather some basic information and share it with the team. This was the beginning of our journey to standardize processes. I didn't know that process engineering was a "thing." It just seemed logical to write down the process and gather common documents in a shared place.

Apply Learnings from Other Experts

As I engaged with more project managers, change management experts, Six Sigma certified professionals, business analysts, and other professionals, I learned so much that I could use in my day-to-day work. For example, a project manager never starts a project without a charter. This document is much more than a piece of paper. It is a grounding mechanism that sets guardrails for any project and summarizes the basic information that anyone would need to get a general overview of the project. Preparing such a document is excellent training for a wordy lawyer to filter only the most important pieces of information to relay to others. Lawyers are accustomed to prose and lengthy detailed documents. Learning how to create a project charter is a transferable skill that I have used dozens of times for extensive projects that needed some organization of thought and ideas. Sometimes I used it to relay information to others, and sometimes I used it to orient myself and ground myself in a particular direction.

So how does a project charter help a commercial transaction attorney, without just adding administrative overhead? Each complex contract negotiation is actually a project. Each negotiation has a start and end. It has multiple stakeholders and exchanges of documentation. Most importantly for the business, it should have a clearly defined timeline. All of these characteristics are what makes an otherwise disjointed effort into a project. The project manager is skilled at keeping everyone on track, documents in order, and deadlines met. We assume that lawyers naturally do this as part of their contract negotiation experience, and in fact, they do have to manage the process—but are they doing it effectively? With the proper training or even basic access to certain project management aids and tools (not technical tools, but worksheets, templates, guides, and so on), any lawyer will become more effective.

A project charter template can be refined to apply to a complex contract negotiation. Imagine if every contract negotiation that was handed off to a law firm was handled by the law firm initially providing the client with a "negotiation charter." This one-page document would identify all of the stakeholders on both sides of the negotiation, a timeline, key principles of the negotiation, list of applicable documents (with links to a cloud-based collaboration site—dreamy, I know!), and even a potential budget for how much a negotiation like that would cost. This sort of visibility would be so refreshing to an in-house lawyer who is used to having very little transparency in the negotiation process until the law firm lawyer reaches out with a question or an update, usually based on a completely uncreditable schedule.

Aligning the Right Resources

As I evolved my commercial transaction practice after leaving the firm and going in-house, the volume grew. I began to have trouble keeping up with the people on my team doing the work. The full-time employees, a group of paralegals I was managing, were having a tough time adjusting to my need for data and process-driven decisions. They were balancing the growing workload and demands from our peers and clients for updates and status reports. Everyone wanted to know how many contracts we did and how long they took. While we worked on our processes, I began to expand my team virtually and added external help from law firms and temp agencies. I ended up with a mixed bag of external resources, each engaged in a slightly different way from different service providers. Then the natural problems started with absences, unreliable schedules, and unmeasurable quality.

It was obvious that I did not have the right resource model. At the time, I didn't think of it as a "resource model"—these were words I learned from program managers and operations professionals along the way. It was just not working well for me. I had to rethink how I was staffing this work. That is when the idea of outsourcing came up. I had heard about it in legal and was very familiar with it in the context of finance, human resources, and information technology. After all, my day job was negotiating with some of the world's best outsourcing companies. Surely, we could apply similar outsourcing principles to the contract review process that I was managing.

The outsourcing journey is its own story.[1] I raise it in the context of innovation because it was a very logical step in resolving my staffing challenges. What makes it innovative is that I did not turn to a law firm or a temp staffing agency. Nor did I ask for more full-time employees. I applied what I saw happening in other parts of the business to my own legal practice. I also took a leap of faith with a service that was accustomed to much lower complexity legal work (mostly in discovery and back-office work, like word processing or administrative support) and stretched it to do more complex work and replace the paralegals that I had strung together from numerous external resources. That leap of faith and some creativity is what made it novel at the time.

A Sprinkling of Technology

Prior to the fancy systems of today, we began with a fairly simple MS Access database, so we could track the volume of contracts. It was certainly a step up from my MS Word table at the firm, but even this was no rocket ship of a system. It was clunky, but it served a purpose. The reason I am proud of this system is that it was a first step in the right direction of data collection and automation, and it provided us with some great lessons learned when we set out to develop a more sophisticated system.

The real benefits of technology came when we automated the intake of the requests from our business clients. We moved from requests via email, instant messaging, and, heaven forbid, pop-ins into the office, to a fairly sleek system with a drop-down menu of help that they needed. Whether they needed a contract reviewed or had a general contracting question, they could use an online system and then track where it was in the process. At the same time, I was able to create reports on the data we collected. This allowed us to provide transparency to the business and have data to use with our external resources about the volumes we had.

We implemented a lot of other technology, and it all related to the workflow that was the most impactful to the business clients, and to our operations. The key message here is that technology is a ***part*** of the innovation journey—it is not the destination.

SHARING MY LEARNINGS

My journey over the course of thirteen-plus years at Microsoft was only the beginning. I learned so much and was eager to share my experiences with others. I was so inspired by so many other lawyers calling me for advice that I decided to start my own consultancy.

What makes this twist in my career relevant in a story of innovation is that it took exactly the same formula for innovation that I had learned in the start of my career, seventeen years earlier, that gave me the courage to leave the safety and comfort of a predictable job in one of the world's best companies: courage + logic + support. I had confidence from all the experience I had gained when transforming processes that had been unchanged for decades. I used logic to inform my decisions about what untraditional career options I should pursue that would leverage my experience. And I had lots of support—from family and friends who knew my passion for transforming regular work into work that I loved. Support came from industry peers who encouraged me to push myself and be creative in my next steps. It came from colleagues who didn't want me to leave, but knew what was best for me. Most surprising was how many people approached me to ask how I had the courage to make this change. Frankly, I saw it as crazy at the time. Then I realized they may be right—it did take courage to venture into the unknown.

So, after leaving Microsoft, I worked with law firms, taught an online professional education class at a law school, consulted for corporate legal teams, advised a legal tech startup, wrote extensively across various legal press mediums, and spoke at industry events. I was fortunate enough to touch almost every part of the legal ecosystem. I learned and was able to influence other professionals to try new things among very old practices.

I only wish the influence could happen faster. I witnessed industry players dedicated to innovation asking me to print, sign, and fax back a document. I saw too many lawyers still saving documents to their hard drives. I still find too many printed contracts with hand-written editing. There is still so much work to do to influence our profession . . .

Another Career Change to Drive Innovation

How often does an opportunity come up to create a function from scratch, a function that is completely focused on innovation and creativity? Not often! But it can happen. For instance, I jumped at the offer to create a new legal ops team at a hyper-growth startup called Snowflake Inc. The company was experiencing an unheard-of boom, and the legal team could not scale, or even keep up with demands. When the chief legal officer (CLO) asked if I'd ever plan to come back in-house, I said yes, for the right role. She then asked me about my dream job. When I described it, she said that's what I can do there. Hard to say no to that.

This proves that there are forward-thinking attorneys who see the need for processes, systems, automation, programs, and, most importantly, data, to run their departments effectively. When a CLO says that legal is no exception to the requirement for data-driven decisions (it helps when the corporation's business is a data business), you know you are in a department that will embrace innovation, not challenge it.

Before we explore what is happening in our legal industry, I want to address those lawyers who are early in their careers (or the managers of those new lawyers).

PLEA TO INNOVATE

There are opportunities to innovate in every corner of the law firm practice. Although it is likely that the law firm compensation model does not encourage efficiencies or innovation generally, there are small inroads that can be made without too much disruption. Associates at law firms can take the initiative to try new ways of handling work. These changes can start in the processes internally, and not be visible to the client, which may be better received by partners resistant of change. No law firm will openly (or at least I hope not) reject innovative ideas, but the ideas have to make sense within the law firm culture and infrastructure. Associates can begin to create some basic reporting for clients that shows clients trends or themes among bodies of work. Time spent on this may qualify toward business development credits. Associates can create ways to use their experience with consumer applications to apply to the systems already in place at the firms. The common experience of sharing updates via social media could be used to keep clients informed real time during critical events that impact the client (negotiation, trial, other meetings). Though these are just ideas, the purpose is to open up the minds of associates who may be so focused on reaching their billable targets that they can't imagine spending time to experiment. Experimentation is the only way to innovate. It must be encouraged and rewarded.

I am often asked what advice I'd give to attorneys just starting out. Here are my suggestions:

1. Explore what innovation projects already exist at the firm and find ways to become a part of them or offer help.
2. Identify partners who are interested in innovation and engage with them on client work that may lend itself to creativity.
3. Speak frankly with a senior partner who has offered to get you involved in more work or with whom you already do a significant amount of work and express your interest in innovation. Ideally, present some ideas that you have been considering.

Find the **courage** and have the **confidence** to identify something that seems so **logical** and seek out the **support** to do it!

CHAPTER 2

Legal Ecosystem Under Pressure

This is not the time to stifle creativity. It is exactly the right time to propose crazy ideas to the other partners in the firm and just go for it. It used to be you were happy to get the work and it was about getting that task done. I think this is the time for associates to question the "how," not the "what." This is the time to come up with ideas and whether there are better ways to do things.

—*LeftFoot* Legal Business Development Podcast, March 2018

In recent years, attorneys in various roles providing differing legal services have realized that they belong to a broader ecosystem encompassing legal service providers, regulatory influencers, customers with greater buying power, and other players that are forcing changes in the legal industry. At the same time, the legal profession is beginning to recognize that it is actually an industry, and not just a profession. The evolution into an industry implies that there are varieties of commercial constituents who provide various services.

Legal transformation pressures are forcing a re-evaluation of the entire ecosystem's functions and how the practice of law is conducted in the United States. Lawyers practicing in corporate legal departments are watching the evolution of their roles, as they are increasingly asked for advice that goes beyond purely legal advice. They must be able to provide advice that is business-minded and has a notable impact on the business of which they are a part. Those departments are also increasingly global and struggling to maintain consistency across the offices, creating redundancy and inefficiencies, if not addressed.

The rise of legal technologies (discussed in greater detail in chapter 4), especially in the context of artificial intelligence (AI), is shedding light on the lagging nature of legal professionals to adopt technologies, in contrast to their business partners. While technology advances at light speed, the workforce is changing the way work is delivered. Legal industry entrants want flexibility in their work and have different expectations of success than prior generations had. Besides generational differences, remote work is much more common these days, which creates new needs for employers to satisfy for their employees. Keeping up with information at the pace that modern business requires is increasingly challenging, and many in the legal profession are simply overloaded by information, seeking better ways to manage it all.

So, the commercial legal ecosystem is changing, and it is important to understand how the different players contribute to this evolution. Thinking about every part of the ecosystem that currently has an impact on the day-to-day practice and experience of attorneys, all of these parts are going through changes of their own while feeling the pressure to innovate. Some attorneys are adapting to these changes better or faster than others, some are more willingly accepting changes, but the pressure is undeniable as evidenced by the relentless amount of legal press coming at us daily.[2]

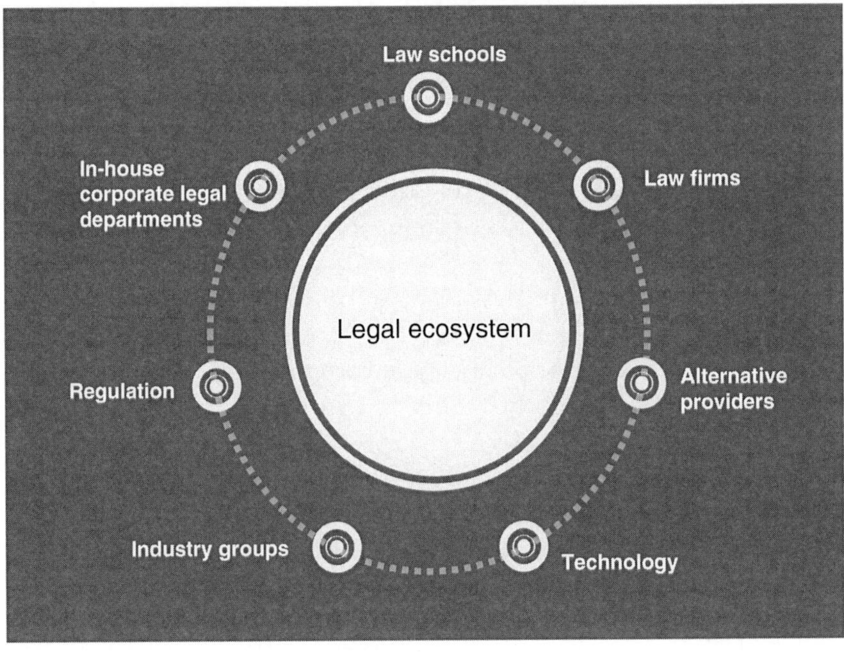

LAW FIRMS

The most discussed, well-known part of the legal ecosystem is the law firm. Arguably, the law firm is the one player in the legal ecosystem that is taking the most heat in this pressure cooker. In many cases, the law firm is attacked for a lack of innovation, antiquated practices, and general glacial pace of change. It is almost too easy to pick on law firms for their old-fashioned ways and inefficiencies, with their exorbitant hourly rates, millionaire partners, high-rise downtown offices, and their wining-and-dining client relationship activities.

Legal work is becoming more complex, and this complexity will only get, well, more complex. The world is becoming more uncertain and volatile. The issues are changing, as globalization and workforces are changing. So, the issues that in-house legal departments deal with are much more complicated, and, as a result, high-level legal advice is sought from outside counsel.

But law firms, as with law schools, remain mostly—and in many cases, stubbornly—unchanged. Law firms do get a bad rap for being unchangeable, rigid, and not willing to adapt. The reality is that the traditional business model of the law firms, built on that dreadful billable hour, is often unwelcoming to practices that may reduce the total hours worked, and therefore is not the most conducive to spurring innovation. It is not conducive to efficiencies and certainly not conducive to operationalizing the practice of law.

Many practicing lawyers are largely unaware of the seismic changes occurring across the legal industry. This is no surprise because they are so focused on the reliable (and simultaneously loathed) billable hour that it is hard to look up and see what is happening outside the building, or even their offices. Many are not even aware they are part of an ecosystem or an industry, but rather view themselves as members of a rarefied "profession."

Most firms still get much of their revenue based on the billable hour, even those who are doing alternative fee arrangements (AFAs). A deeper review of AFAs reveals that there remains some form of shadow billing or some sort of hourly basis in the calculation. This goes back to the business model. If the attorneys at the firm are still compensated based on the hours billed, it is hard to move the value that is offered in an AFA away from the hindrance of the billable hour framework.

But it's not just about the billable hour—it's also about the relationships. Relationships are based on past personal connections. They are based on what comprises the relationship, the person-to- person engagement, the connection between an attorney and an in-house client. Very little about the hiring process is based on objective standards, measures, or quality performance assessments. You know the adage: You don't hire the law firm, you hire the lawyer. That is still true, so there is no natural incentive or push for change until the client asks for the change. There is no better incentive than when the client asks for something to be done a little bit differently.

Law firms are also notoriously lacking in the ability to access data or create processes. Some law firms are making advancements in this area. I generalize for the sake of really getting at the bulk, the 80 percent perhaps, but certainly the majority of firms that can't access their data. They are actually sitting on quite a bit of data but they just probably don't have a good way to consume it or relay it to their customers, to their clients. And it is something the clients increasingly need.

To be more efficient, law firms must review their processes and then optimize to remove any waste from those processes. They are feeling pressure to drive down costs and, more significantly, they are feeling pressure from clients who want more value: "We want to get more from the same buck." Driving down costs is nothing new and is reflected in the annual negotiations of hourly rates. But recently, requiring more value for the same amounts spent on legal fees is the more common conversation. So, the pressure to drive down costs is changing from pure monetary savings to increasing value instead.

There's also pressure to provide additional related services, like project management and data analytics, including providing historical views, trending, and forecasting. These concepts are common in most other businesses and industries. But the legal industry has been slower to adapt while pressure from their in-house clients on law firms is high to bring this kind of value.

> There is an internal tension within law firms. There is a sort of battle between those who "get it" and those who "don't get it." It is not so much a generational issue, though there is something to that notion, too. There is a natural change that will occur as the current roster of senior partners retires and makes way for new generations.

More law schools are providing courses in business operations, finance, technology, and project management (though it's important to note that it may still be a minority, and is still debated by faculty in the schools with such new programs).

Those skills and knowledge areas will help the young lawyers be more efficient and provide value through related services. Law firms should target recruits with those skills and knowledge, but must also create new incentive models so they don't "beat the innovation out . . . by rewarding only the billed hours." As supply of these young attorneys with more business, technology, and project management skills rises, we should see more progress in law firm innovation.

Also, there is enough written about the millennial workforce and how they will influence the legal industry to embrace technology and healthier work-life balance goals.[3] Naturally, change will occur like it always does as new generations evolve. Perhaps this will be one of the more impactful changes in recent times, as the gap between the exiting partners' experience with technology, for example, is vastly different from the experiences of the incoming generation.

This tension is just as intense among those that "get it" and those that "don't get it," across roles, seniority, departments, and other variations. It exists in various combinations:

- Attorneys who get it and those who don't
- Business professionals who are tasked with innovation and the partners who manage client relationships
- Technologists and partners who determine resource allocation
- Practice groups more inclined to innovate their recurring work and those that claim to do only bespoke work

Are these different perspectives validated? Do people really not "get it" or are they just uninformed of the benefits and overwhelmed by the challenges? Why are some practice groups convinced that their work is so special that it could not possibly benefit from any of that innovation "stuff?"

It comes down to awareness and education. Unlike in-house lawyers who are often working closely with other professionals and can thus can pick up an appreciation for other skills and capabilities (like solution architecture, project management, and financial analysis), law firm lawyers often practice inside their own bubble of expertise and only engage with the clients' business from a distance. There is little opportunity for practicing lawyers to learn about the important skills that now are becoming common in modern legal practice. While they continue to expand their knowledge on specific areas of the law, there is little opportunity to learn even a little bit about other subjects. This lack of awareness, coupled with the traditional law firm business model restrictions, is simply a recipe for failure.

But not all firms are failing. Though it is easy to cast them all into one negative spotlight as the scapegoat for lack of innovation, there are pockets of progress. Many are trying to reinvent themselves, or at least enhance what they offer by adding new and valuable services and by being creative with their offerings. It is not the standard, nor the mainstream yet, but many firms are trying. A simple online news search will show dozens of articles and press releases. Firms are bringing in business professionals and seeking their skills and contributions (more on this point in chapter 7 about the modern workforce). Some are hiring technologists as they try to catch up with the demand of their clients.

Each firm is approaching the pressure to "get it" in its own way; and no two firms look the same, but over time there is hope that the various puzzle pieces will standardize and fall in place within each of the firms. Then the inertia will move the entire law firm community. So, give credit where credit is due: those firms who are actually doing something innovative for (and with) their clients. This is an old profession, engrained in precedent and history. The hints of progress within the firms are impressive. Those unique lawyers and law firm leaders who get it just need more support to move the masses along with them.

CORPORATE LEGAL DEPARTMENTS[4]

Corporate legal departments are key players in the legal ecosystem. Legal departments are forcing many of the changes to the ecosystem. They are creating much of the pressure that is happening across the ecosystem because they are feeling the pressure themselves. In-house departments have to justify costs and must optimize resources; they have to track data more effectively than ever before.

As corporations become more global and complex, entering different service areas that have never existed, legal departments are faced with new issues and simply can't do it all. They need help with optimizing, for example, the performance of repeatable, recurring work. Even with what is referred to as lower value work, it has real value to the company because it is necessary work. But it is work that may not require the costliest resources in-house or for law firms.

It is easy to maintain that without corporate legal teams forcing law firms to behave differently, law firms and other providers will never change. Although there is obvious merit to the notion that "money talks," it is too easy an out to place the responsibility on corporate legal teams. Though money is a natural incentive, many other incentives can put others in the driver's seat. Incentives like thought leadership, competitive advantage, and internal workforce changes play roles also. Still a lot of eyes on the corporate legal departments are waiting to see what they will ask for next, and are ready to reply with a "we can do it!" attitude.

It is time to bust some myths about the inner workings of corporate legal departments and disclose their limitations in influencing change.

Myth Busting in Progress

1. In-house lawyers are all innovative.

Everyone forgets this one. Most in-house lawyers come from the same firms they are procuring from. The training is the same. The knowledge about how firms work is the same. Nothing magical happens that transforms a law firm lawyer into an innovating machine by virtue of changing jobs and going in-house. To be fair, behaviors change over time as new in-house lawyers adapt to the sheer volume of work and the need to be more risk tolerant if they are to make any notable progress. But otherwise, the way they do their work remains largely unchanged. The appetite to accept risk may become somewhat more tolerant, but "that's the way I've always done it" still governs their approach.

The reality is that lawyers by nature and experience either have the curiosity and interest in innovation, or they don't. Innovative practices can be taught, but without an incentive to innovate, such as compensation models, why do it? In law firms we know that the business model penalizes innovation that results in less billable hours, so only those that truly want to innovate will allow that latent gene to flourish once they go in-house because the personal rewards of efficiency will be enough of an incentive. So, going in-house enables those inclined to innovate, and with great success. Those without that inclination move in-house and continue business as usual, unless or until forced to change.

2. Legal ops are naturally more successful in-house than in law firms.

Ask any legal ops professional, perhaps over drinks after a long day at yet another legal ops conference, and he or she will be the first to admit that the lawyers in their department represent the biggest hurdle to innovation.

The eye-rolling is obvious when legal ops pros have to respond to how they manage change in their departments and how they convince the lawyers. The big benefit of in-house departments is that the larger corporate culture helps to influence the general counsel (GC) and other lawyers that change is necessary. Legal ops can enlist the chief financial officer (CFO) and chief executive officer (CEO) as allies when pushing for data collection and metrics. So, there are more "tools" to deploy for change management; a sense of urgency also can be created when other departments are getting accolades while legal is treated as "special"—and not in a good way. However, convincing lawyers to change is just as hard in-house as at law firms. There's no reason it should take a year to get lawyers to allow electronic signatures for even a limited number of contract types, but this actually happens. Further, even at some of the best tech companies with the latest technology at their fingertips, lawyers hesitate to put documents in the cloud, count their workload, provide a service-level agreement (SLA), or measure their turnaround times.

3. Outside counsel panel programs are sure to influence the market.

Panel programs can have great benefits for pricing and diversity. To play in this sandbox, legal departments can demand certain basic features of the engagement. But, in reality, the general programs go only so far. They create great buzz and conversation, which in itself is valuable, but there is little measurable and visible progress for innovation. Innovation comes one engagement at a time, between a creative law firm partner and a similarly creative in-house attorney contact. It is that deep collaboration between professionals where magic happens. No corporate legal "program" can have the same profound impact as actual case studies, lessons learned from joint experimentation and time spent sharing and problem solving. Whether approaches by DuPont, Cisco, or Microsoft are viewed as examples of great steps to changing the nature of the relationships, I'm not sure that any one panel program has resulted in the sort of game-changing innovation we seek. Any game changers, even at those companies, came as a result of personal initiative and leadership support.

4. In-house legal teams are open to legal tech.

Ask any legal tech professional and he or she will say that once the lawyers are in the room it all slows down. Implementing technology in the legal department is just as much of a boulder up a hill as it is at law firms. The decision makers are lawyers, and technology-enabled legal practice is just not intuitive for most lawyers. They are not trained on the use of technology; rather, they are trained to identify risks and mitigate them. Although there is progress with implementing some infrastructure technology inside legal departments, any technology that is perceived to create a legal risk (such as the electronic signature) is often not embraced. More cutting-edge technology, such as AI-enabled contract review and analytics, is a hard sell for lawyers in-house who are worried the machine may miss something. (But what do lawyers miss on those days where they have not had enough sleep because a sick child kept them up all night and vomited in the car on the way to school, altering the entire course of the morning plan?)

In short, corporate legal departments have influence because they hold the purse strings, but in-house lawyers are just as challenged to change as lawyers at law firms (and professors at law schools, for that matter). Resistance to change is nothing new for lawyers, no matter where they work. Efficiency at the cost of increased risk is a process many lawyers are still not ready to pay. This is changing, albeit slowly. More lawyers with a tendency for innovation are now taking chances and pushing the needle in their organizations. That is how change will come about.

ALTERNATIVE LEGAL SERVICE PROVIDERS[5]

Thinking about where the legal industry is compared to where it was about fifteen to twenty years ago, the biggest change is the rise in numbers of ALSPs, or legal service companies.

ALSP is a more recent name for what was called legal process outsourcing or LPO for many years. As the field and work evolved and basic processes were no longer the only thing being outsourced, the connotation was too simplistic. This newer name was conceived to reflect the broader set of services being provided. Since law firms were the main and only provider of legal services for centuries, it made sense to call these LPOs "alternative" providers of legal services, and the ALSP was born.

ALSPs or LPOs encompass the various ways that legal resources are delivered across different levels, or the stratification of legal skills available. ALSP resources can range from a full-time practicing attorney, to perhaps someone who has a JD but has never practiced law. Or perhaps they are effective paralegals or other professionals who are capable of delivering certain parts of the legal service, but not the entire legal service.

For example, they became experts at document review, high-volume tedious searches through hundreds of thousands of boxes of old contracts, letters, and filings. They staff with lower cost resources and create a repetitive process and playbook for the searches. They could also more efficiently review stacks of contracts to extract specific terms and document it in a database for future use or entry into a contract management system.

Recent evolution in this taxonomy game has given birth to "Law Company" and "Legal Services Company" as these providers move up the value chain and actually compete directly in many cases with law firms. There's another variation: legal services providers or LSPs. Regardless of the name, they can compete with law firms because much of what law firms do is not technically the practice of law as defined by state courts and bar associations. As corporate legal departments look for more ways to be efficient and cut costs, these providers are becoming mainstream, and less alternative.[6] A recent report by Thomson Reuters found that 87 percent of law firm respondents said they were using ALSPs, up from 56 percent in 2015. At corporations, 74 percent said they used an ALSP, up from 60 percent over the same time period. So, who are they and what do they really do in the ecosystem?

There are a handful of very well-known strong players in this space, but it started with outsourcing (mostly to India) and to attorneys that are licensed in India at a much lower cost than U.S. attorneys. They mostly focused on document review and discovery but they have quickly climbed the value chain and will continue to do so. They are doing more in the contracting area and with the emergence of the General Data Protection Regulation (GDPR),[7] there is an increased need for this type of resourcing globally. Some of these alternative providers will play a key role and probably will displace law firms purely because of their price point. Quality is something that has to be monitored carefully, which is not necessary when sending work to a law firm. However, in-house teams are willing to invest in quality control measures to benefit from the cost savings and efficiency gains.

Also, law firms are reaching out to some of these alternative providers to do work behind the scenes and to pass those savings on to their clients. So, there are many interconnections.

It is not totally clear how LSPs are pressuring law firms. Many people remain convinced that only law firms can do what they have done for decades, and that the newer entrants into the market are focused on different types of service. Specifically, they are focused on low-value work that law firms don't touch anyway. The law firm leaders may look down at this work or not look at it at all, but this is a costly oversight in either case.

Although much of the work that the LSPs initially did was high-volume, lower complexity work, they are moving up the value chain.

Law firms should be concerned about LSPs for several reasons:

- Redefinitions of what falls outside the practice of law are a constant debate in state courts across the country.
- LSPs are hiring experienced lawyers and other experts.
- A broad range of LSPs' capabilities allows for a more holistic service to clients.

As legal services are disaggregated and unbundled, more processes are falling outside of the way regulators usually define the "practice of law." This allows more entrants into legal service delivery.

So, much corporate law department work does not actually require a license, and the LSPs are testing—with willing clients—just how far they will be allowed to go before they reach the threshold of providing legal advice or practicing law. For example, why is it necessary to be an attorney to review a contract? In fact, many companies have entire departments of contract managers doing 90-plus percent of the contract review and negotiation of a contract before escalating to an attorney. Similarly, document review for an acquisition by no means requires a licensed lawyer. One way in which the LSPs are finding more willing clients is that the roster of people at the LSPs is becoming increasingly sophisticated. Formerly mired in the old perception that LSPs hire lower tier lawyers from unknown law schools, LSPs are emerging as destination employers for successful attorneys looking for a different path or new ways of delivering legal services.

The talent pool within the LSPs is impressive and continues to expand. The LSPs provide a host of other benefits to legal departments that law firms traditionally have not been equipped to provide. LSPs track data, monitor performance, and embrace technology. They use expert project management and have business operations running through their DNA. Some of the work currently done by law firms (or that could be done by law firms if they were not missing this revenue opportunity) is simply done better by an LSP. Even more interesting is that the LSPs are

> *New entrants are a reality in the state court system already. It is happening formally in the state of Washington by creating a new licensed profession for limited practice areas in family law (the Limited License Legal Technician or LLLT[8]). LLLTs help fill out forms and explain legal procedures to clients. They may not represent their clients in court or in negotiations with opposing parties.[9]*

no longer just basic service providers. They are becoming trusted advisors and consultants on operational aspects of the practice of law.

In summary, LSPs are not to be underestimated or ignored as significant players in the ecosystem. They could be great partners for law firms who want to provide holistic solutions to clients, even for the work that they traditionally have not done. Guess what? That work needs to be done, and why should corporate legal teams have the burden of managing different providers? Firms can embrace LSPs and learn from them about process, project management and process efficiencies. Or LSPs can continue to climb the value chain on their own into work that had been squarely entrenched in law firms. If that doesn't convince law firms, consider that the LSPs have strong experienced leaders who understand the *business* of law and can take the client (a.k.a. customer) experience to a whole new level, because they know how to treat clients like customers. Delighting customers is a new concept for legal, but if we watch other evolving industries, everyone figures out at some point that . . . the customer is king!

What really is the "practice of law" today?

It is clear that the LSPs are testing the definition of the practice of law. As a commercial transaction lawyer in-house, I estimate that 90 percent of my job did not require me to be a licensed attorney.

In fact, my favorite clients were experienced contract negotiators who could get on the phone with an attorney on the other side and negotiate most of the contract without my involvement. When I was called in, for the last 10 percent perhaps, it was for the most nuanced legal concepts. Yet, most legal departments still have highly paid lawyers handling the contract negotiation from start to finish.

The LSPs have brilliantly disaggregated contract review, for example, to run the negotiation process through most of the journey, and then engage the in-house lawyer only as necessary. To be safe, that work is done by the LSPs "under the direction and control" of the in-house lawyer, so as not to get into trouble with regulators. I challenge just how much actual direction and control the in-house team provides beyond the playbook. The point of outsourcing is to be able to step out of that work.

So, a good playbook is the secret key to not being accused of "practicing law" and staying on the right side of the regulating bodies. But how long will that last?

Those who are willing to come together and help each other to deliver the ultimate in value to their clients are the ones who will end up succeeding in the end.

The "Big 4" and Legal Services

The Big 4[10] accounting firms are entering the legal space in the United States and globally. There are many reasons for this, such as historical developments, changes in regulatory restrictions outside of the United States, and the disaggregation of legal services. Setting that aside, what is it that makes the Big 4 appealing to commercial legal departments?

Having been in-house at a leading international company, I was a purchaser of legal services for ten-plus years. Although the Big 4 were a more recent entrant, it became clear to me that the characteristics of the services they delivered to other parts of the organization are applicable to the legal department as well and highly useful. There are several attributes of the Big 4 that make their services stand apart from law firms and stand above the alternative service providers.

These firms are many things to many people, including, but not limited to:

- ***Experienced Consultants***—The Big 4 have extensive business and management consulting practices, with highly capable professionals. They provide a perspective into legal services that is inherently grounded in

Personal Experience . . .

As I was beginning to build the legal ops function from scratch at the company I had just joined, I found myself in some, let's say, warm (if not heated) debates with finance about legal spend management. I knew I needed to implement a system, and had selected one, but Finance was firm that I still need to use the corporate purchase order system. I knew how it was done at my prior company but needed more examples and data points about inefficiencies and best practices. Before the rise of industry groups, I would start calling colleagues and peers at companies I knew. Instead, I did a few minutes of research on the industry groups' sites and found a beautiful survey that gave me the foundation to make a very factual and data-driven argument for my position. Who doesn't love charts and numbers? Especially in Finance!

business. They also tend to offer solutions to problems that anticipate the end business goals. They are experts in various operations and naturally focus on efficiency and practical application of theory. Even if I would not have known to ask for this perspective, the Big 4 will always provide it. That kind of experience is priceless for the legal experts buying these services, who may not know that they even need such operational insights.

- ***Process Engineers***—With an expertise in management consulting, Big 4 professionals will undoubtedly and inevitably identify process improvements. After all, managing is all about aligning resources and delivering outcomes, isn't it? In legal, we desperately need to rethink our allocation of resources. Much of what the industry is experiencing is about changing engagements with law firms, adding new professionals into the mix, and outsourcing certain legal work. As challenging as that is for legal professionals to consider and implement, it is easy for management consultants. Similarly, a focus on outcomes is never lost on management consultants, yet it is often lost on lawyers. Too many lawyers think that the outcome is the production of the legal advice, in whatever format. Helping lawyers focus on outcomes is another priceless benefit the Big 4 brings to every engagement.
- ***Project Managers***—There is no more beautiful deliverable than a piece of work product delivered by a professional project manager. Beyond just the actual deliverable, all work and engagements run smoother with a project manager involved. People are kept on track, timelines are strict, and action items are carefully tracked. The Big 4 are very comfortable with engaging project managers and make it a common practice in many of their consulting engagements.
- ***Established Trusted Relationships***—The Big 4 know how to deal with big enterprises. They understand the complexities and the *politics* of working with a matrixed organization with unclear decision-making authority and undefined processes. Beyond just understanding corporate culture, the Big 4 already have deep relationships with many large U.S. and global companies. They likely have useful contacts within the organization that may prove quite helpful when trying to accomplish a controversial goal or execute on an unpopular plan. Often these "outsiders" have contacts within the client organization at higher levels than those they are engaging

with in the client company on a particular project. Sometimes those connections help get projects over the finish line.

- ***Proven Results***—The Big 4's success in tax law services has set a foundation for expansion into legal services that is grounded in experience on complicated legal principles. Surely, if the Big 4 can become experts in tax law, they can deliver just about any other legal service.
- ***Scale***—The Big 4 have a presence in almost every country where business is conducted by multinationals. They can reach a scale that few other providers can compare with, and they have connections to experts on every topic of interest to their corporate clients, whether internally within their own employee base, or within an intricate and powerful network of related entities and affiliates.
- ***Quality and Reputation***—There is trust that is instilled with the Big 4, which is why so many large corporations choose to use them for a broad range of services. Trust seems to cover all the work they do, even in areas that are new to these providers. There is a history of high quality, and there are widely accepted expectations of continued quality work from the Big 4. There is little doubt or uncertainty in their ability to deliver on promises.
- ***Technology***—The Big 4 know how to invest in technology. They have sizeable research and development (R&D) departments and are comfortable setting aside resources for their future benefit. They have been around a long time and continue to evolve by keeping up with technology advances. They are also interested in legal tech, and with their ability to scale and investment resources, will have an easy time catching up to anything that is leading the market, and likely become the industry leader themselves. Those are baskets that many clients would be comfortable placing their eggs in!
- ***Predictable Pricing***—These are not low-cost service providers, but neither are law firms. What the Big 4 has, however, is predictability on pricing. Long gone are the days of pricing by the hour (at least in the Big 4's world), and instead fixed fees based on the project scope are the norm. More importantly, the Big 4 are accustomed to helping clients define the scope of work and can adjust their pricing accordingly.
- ***Sheer Size and Locations***—The Big 4 have many people located in the most remote corners of the world. It feels like there is no place in the world where they don't have a presence. There is nothing

more frustrating than hearing from a service provider that they don't have the people available when you need them. The Big 4 always have people available.

These are some of the attributes that make me confident about the Big 4 expanding into legal services. There is no question about their potential in this space, and it only makes sense that the *law firms*[11] and "*not-so-alternative anymore*"[12] *providers* should watch closely and learn.

Indeed, as I reflect on this list, I have to ask, why would a corporate legal department hire anyone else for certain work that is not worthy of law firm rates and is more complex than what the "not-so-alternative" providers deliver today?

INDUSTRY GROUPS

Industry groups such as Corporate Legal Operations Consortium (CLOC) are organizing around legal ops as a whole, as well as some of the underlying functions. They are coming together to share best practices and exchange information, such as:

- How did you innovate?
- How did you outsource that?
- Which law firm do you use?
- How do you assess the quality of the law firms you use?
- Which vendors do you like?

The legal industry community is growing and industry groups are creating a platform to discuss and to meet, and to push the envelope. If something works well in one legal department, another legal department will learn about it and want the same benefit. That's what is clear about legal ops: no legal department is doing all of the legal ops functions well or is excelling at them.

Every department focuses on what it urgently needs, whether it is technology, vendor management, or knowledge management; everybody is making progress. But industry groups are really increasing the pace at which that information is being shared.

If somebody has tried something and failed and tried again and succeeded, it is much more likely that this outcome will be passed along to somebody else, and they will then succeed on the first try. The influence of industry groups on the pace of change in the legal ecosystem should not be underestimated.

REGULATION

It is important to remember that the U.S. regulatory system for the practice of law limits other entrants who are trying to influence the practice of law but not actually practicing law. Because that is the ethical boundary. The unauthorized practice of law is the one great way that attorneys are continuing to maintain status quo and not letting others into our work. The restrictions of the bar associations make it very difficult for other service providers to deliver service that may be defined as the "practice of law" (see previous box, "What really is the "practice of law" today?").

PricewaterhouseCoopers has launched a law firm in the United States. The Big 4 are investing money in what they describe as legal services. This is very similar to ALSPs, but with the added benefit of significant research and development investments as well as excellent consulting and processing efficiencies expertise.

In the coming years, there will be increasing pressure on the regulatory scheme and what it means for the practice of law in the United States.

Two parts of the legal ecosystem are fascinating to study together because they have such opposing and contradictory perspectives, yet both are critical to the evolution of legal services. Industry associations that focus on the more efficient delivery of legal services directly clash with the existing body of regulation about the practice of law.

At their core, the two appear to have contradictory goals. Although industry groups like CLOC and

> As legal operations continue to push the envelope of all of the other functions and skills that are needed for the practice of law to become more efficient, there are more professions that are moving in and limiting the practice of law to the most specific, finite functions. This is an evolution to watch; eventually there will be pressures on the regulatory construct within the United States. We have seen this in the United Kingdom. It has an alternative business structure approach where professionals who are not licensed attorneys can have part ownership in law firms.
>
> ***(Note my refusal to use the term "non-lawyers.")***

ACC Legal Operations are focusing on new ways to deliver legal services and creative problem solving, regulatory bodies across the United States are focused on preserving the role of attorneys and the sanctity of what it means to practice law. Think of it as a battle between the practical and the philosophical.

Regulations regarding who can practice law in the United States are grounded in the philosophy that there must be minimal standards and rules about who can provide legal advice, and who can participate in the judicial system. This philosophy is based on the desire to protect consumers and ensure that the lay person has adequate representation in a complex legal system. The problem is that these rules do not distinguish between the practice of criminal law, family law, and commercial law, for example. Rules are to be applied similarly to a corporate in-house lawyer handling multimillion-dollar business-to-business commercial transactions and to a solo practitioner in rural America helping a couple with a divorce. Entire books have been written about the regulatory landscape of the practice of law. Let's look at how this regulatory restriction impacts today's practice of commercial law.

In a commercial practice, whether at law firms or corporate legal departments, there is mounting pressure to increase efficiencies and deliver faster, cheaper outputs. To accomplish these goals, attorneys are finding that parts of their practice or tasks can be delegated to others. This disaggregation of legal practice has been happening for decades as other players have entered the legal industry and taught lawyers creative ways of reconsidering their services.

Attorneys are learning how to rely on others, beyond the traditional roles of legal secretaries or paralegals, and are increasingly handing off tasks and processes. As attorneys continue to do this, it forces the question: What part of the lawyers' work is the "practice of law" as defined by the regulating bodies in the fifty states? Lawyers often take comfort in the fact that other people are not engaging in the practice of law as long as the attorney is overseeing the work. Why, though, do they need that air cover? Is the requirement that the attorneys have direction over that work just a way to preserve the long-standing goals of protecting the lawyer, rather than focusing on the work and the needs of the client?

Still there has been notable movement in the regulatory landscape in recent years, especially in the consumer law sector. In Washington State, the limited license legal technician,[13] or LLLT, is licensed by the Washington State Bar Association to advise and assist people going through divorce, child custody, and other family law matters. This is a special licensing process for people who do not have JDs, but can practice law in limited areas (hence, the descriptive name). This was a very encouraging step to opening the practice of law, but it took a long time to approve and is still extremely limited in application. It remains controversial years after deployment, with very few LLLTs operating in Washington, though there is talk of expanding their scope. If nothing else, it has shed light on this regulatory restriction that is keeping many people from accessing legal services in the United States in areas outside of the commercial practice of law. The commercial practice of law has been untouched from a regulatory perspective. So, we continue with governing laws that have not changed in decades, if not centuries.

Moreover, an argument can be made that current regulatory restrictions are hindering access to justice on a macro level. Just consider the barriers for a layperson to go through basic legal actions simply because they are not licensed to practice law in the state in which they live. For example, is it really necessary to have completed three years of law school to advise others on filing for a divorce or disputing an eviction notice? Certainly, these disputes can become very complicated and require attorneys' assistance, but often that is the result of attorneys over-complicating it. Surely, there are lessons to learn from the LLLT example in Washington to open up the practice and allow others to help with the complicated legal system—which was designed by lawyers, for lawyers!

On the other end of this spectrum is the growing number of legal industry groups that are pressing on precisely the topic of who can do what within the context of legal services, and asking about the difference between legal services and the practice of law and where they intersect.

The sheer number of people identified as legal innovators, disruptors, and futurists, coupled with the growing number of legal roles with the word *innovation* in the title demonstrate that these changes are a natural outgrowth of legal professionals seeking creative new solutions to age-old problems.

Industry groups are bringing together operationally minded lawyers with business and operations experts to gather and share ideas, and demand change in the industry. As corporate legal ops specialists have shared and adopted successful tactics and processes, there has been a seismic shift across the ecosystem. Law firms are hearing requests for similar approaches and efficiencies from different corporate clients. Legal tech successes and failures are now openly discussed and references from trusted colleagues are critical for successful implementation.

Thousands of corporate legal ops professionals are challenging the traditionally regulated practice of law by demanding change from law firms and bringing in new players without licenses but with skills that supplement lawyers in ways we have not experienced before.

If you've had enough introduction and background, Part II will dive deeper into a few key foundational topics that are contributing to the climate of innovation sweeping the legal industry. If you are ready to get to the real reason you started reading this book, skip to Part III.

PART II

Foundational Topics

CHAPTER 3

Legal Operations: What Is It and Why Is It Important?

Joke of the Day

Legal ops professional asks practicing lawyer: "Have you had any experience with a creative alternative fee arrangement?"

Practicing lawyer shrugs and says: "I had a fixed fee thing once, and well . . . you kind of get what you pay for. I was not very impressed."

Legal ops professional continues: "What was your governance model to manage the relationship?"

Practicing lawyer responds: "California was the governing law."

Legal operations, or legal ops, encompasses multiple functions. Topics related to legal ops are forcing new conversations across the ecosystem, leading the legal industry to pay close attention. Legal ops is also evolving as a strategic role within legal departments—front and back office—providing career options for many professionals who might otherwise not see themselves as succeeding in a corporate legal department.

It is time to redefine and "operationalize" certain aspects of the practice of law by, for one, adding a business operations mindset to the way law departments operate.

So, what exactly is legal ops? What is clear: there is no single definition. Many industry groups have made strides to define legal ops. For example, the Association of Corporate Counsel (ACC)[14] has a legal ops chapter and its own definition; and Corporate Legal Operations Consortium (CLOC),[15] an industry leader in defining legal ops, has a slightly different definition.

Each of these organizations has done a great job setting standards and providing resources for operationalizing the practice of law.

Legal ops is growing *and* also evolving. The more it continues to evolve, the more definitions will be tweaked and adjusted to reflect the realities of what is happening in the industry.

For now, a closer look at the utility of legal ops in law firms and departments shows an emergence of several widely accepted functions. I have separated them into four quadrants, or buckets, where the various functions reside, as shown in **Figure 3-1**.

People can choose the parts that are most important to their department and the functions that they are most capable of, and can focus on areas of improvement in their law departments. No matter how it plays out in any one company, what is common about legal ops is that this is the individual or team that focuses on the "how" of legal practice. Lawyers should continue to focus on the "what," but the growing crop of legal ops professionals are laser focused on "how" and often asking "why."

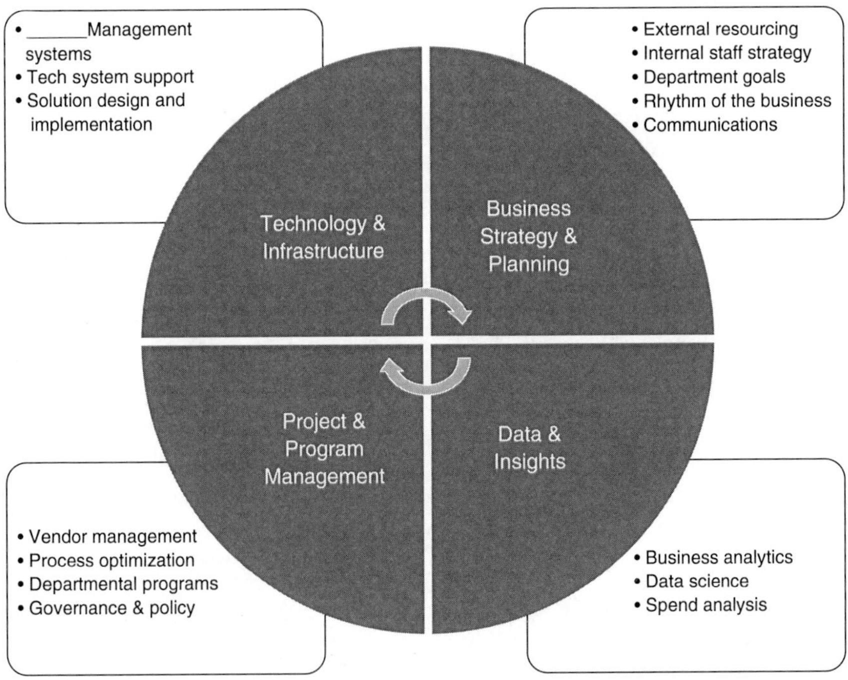

Figure 3-1. *Legal Operations Functions*

Back Office—Front Office: Two Categories of Legal Ops

Legal ops is exploding as a combination of functions bringing tangible change and benefits for lawyers, legal departments, and law firms. I see two categories of legal ops—back office and front office—that are at varying levels of maturity and acceptance. Both have benefits but have quite different characteristics regarding how each is evolving and who is leading the way.

Back-Office Legal Ops

The innovation occurring in the back offices of law firms and legal departments is what I refer to as "back-office legal ops" and covers a broad variety of functions. All of these functions have one thing in common: efficiency in running the office. The back offices of law firms have grown beyond pads of paper with time-recording grids and secretarial pools into high-functioning automated and outsourced processes. Some notable examples of back-office legal ops innovation are electronic billing/invoicing, online time-keeping systems, conflict management tools, outsourced word processing and administrative support, document management solutions, and matter management systems.

These necessary functions have advanced explosively in the last decade. Technology providers have invested in solving typical law firm back-office problems, such as the challenges of transferring written time sheets into bills ready to send to clients. Evolving from hand-written notepads listing entire days' compilations of six-minute segments, attorneys now click start and stop buttons right on their desktops, and enter descriptions into a little box on an app. Legal documents that are created in many law firms are now tagged and labeled by a system that gives them a clear home and the ability to access with ease. Gone are the days of starting to write a contract with a blank page. Invoices are issued electronically by firms and are received and processed electronically by in-house clients. Invoice inputs can be easily reviewed, and savings swiftly applied.

Front-Office Legal Ops

Great progress has been made in the back office, and it continues on a promising trajectory. But what about actual lawyering work, or the "front office" of legal practice? Have attorneys taken advantage of the innovation in back-office legal ops, learned from it, and applied similar concepts to the practice of law? There seem to be several reasons for the lack of comparative advancement in "front-office legal ops." The reasons are not new or surprising, and it is time for real change.

Risk avoidance, inherent in every lawyer's DNA (or at least in their formal training), plays a significant role in hindering innovation in the front office. Unlike the work of the back office, the work of practicing attorneys is grounded in risk mitigation and trusting precedence. The back office takes on very little risk when it automates an invoicing process or billing operations. Conversely, when the front office chooses different resources to get the work done, there is a risk that it won't be up to the standards set by the practicing attorneys who used to perform that work. Similarly, if there are steps in the legal work that are automated, there is the risk that the automation will not yield the same results as the work handled by attorneys. There is, of course, also the general risk that things simply will not work as they have before. Since legal practice is a client-centric profession, upsetting clients is not an option. So, the ability to assume risk is directly correlated to the appetite for innovation. Assuming there is some comfort with risks, innovation can begin.

Another big difference is how the back office has embraced other professionals and how the front office still resists that move by relegating all other professionals into the segregated bucket of "non-lawyers." Attorneys believe their legal work has to be handled entirely by attorneys. The thought of handing off even pieces of that work to someone without a license to practice law remains a major concern for most attorneys. In some scenarios, allotting portions of legal work is in fact a risk and significant training may be required. For example, handing off the drafting of pleadings to someone else requires training on legal terms of art and taxonomy and is not easily picked up by someone without legal training.

Conversely, lawyers are doing some of the work that other professionals are much better suited for. Realizing that a complex contract negotiation is actually a project that would benefit from a legal project manager is a huge step forward but one that many attorneys have not taken. They still plan and schedule the negotiation calls, gather the previously edited versions of the contract, compile other relevant documents, send meeting notes, and arrange the action item lists for all involved parties. An experienced project manager, familiar with the contract negotiation process, can and should handle these tasks. Embracing data analysts, project managers, operations experts, and myriad other professionals will help move the legal practice into the modern era. I'll have more on the terrible term "non-lawyer" later in this book.

Practicing attorneys should accept that change is coming, because the choice is simple: Lead the way to this way of working, or be left behind. There is a common belief that change will only happen by in-house legal departments that encourage the firm's attorneys to deliver services in a different way, or to deliver additional services. Often that demand comes from a legal ops function within the department. That is certainly a great catalyst, but change can come from many places: firms, legal tech providers, outsourcing companies, and so on. The key is demonstrating the value in doing things differently.

Change is constant and normal, but to initiate it, the value must be obvious. Besides value, the change has to be intuitive—meaning, don't expect attorneys to fundamentally change how they do their work. The innovation has to be subtle enough to naturally slide into the attorney's day-to-day work. Then, once hooked, attorneys can embrace innovation and will be more open to experimentation and even risk.

Now, let's take a closer look at what is going on in each of the legal ops buckets.

TECHNOLOGY AND INFRASTRUCTURE[16]

Starting in the upper left-hand quadrant of **Figure 3-1a** on the next page, the subjects that occur most frequently in legal ops technology and infrastructure discussions are technology, enhancements, automation, systems, and solutions. These are often the first places where a blossoming legal ops team will focus.

However natural this may be, this is probably not the best approach. Technology should not be implemented before existing processes are optimized, so that the technology can effectively enable those processes. Similarly, people's roles in a legal department should be optimized before technology is brought in to make those human resources even more effective. Only then should technology be brought in to enable and enhance the efficiencies defined and sought. Still, technology and systematic infrastructure are critical and here to stay. Some of the greatest advancements in operationalizing legal departments have been possible thanks to the new technologies that have made departments more efficient and capable of using data to drive results.

There are groups, departments, or teams who may decide they don't want to go through a process-mapping exercise because they think there must be a readily available technology solution that will simplify and help define the process. If the system is good and capable enough, it is certainly

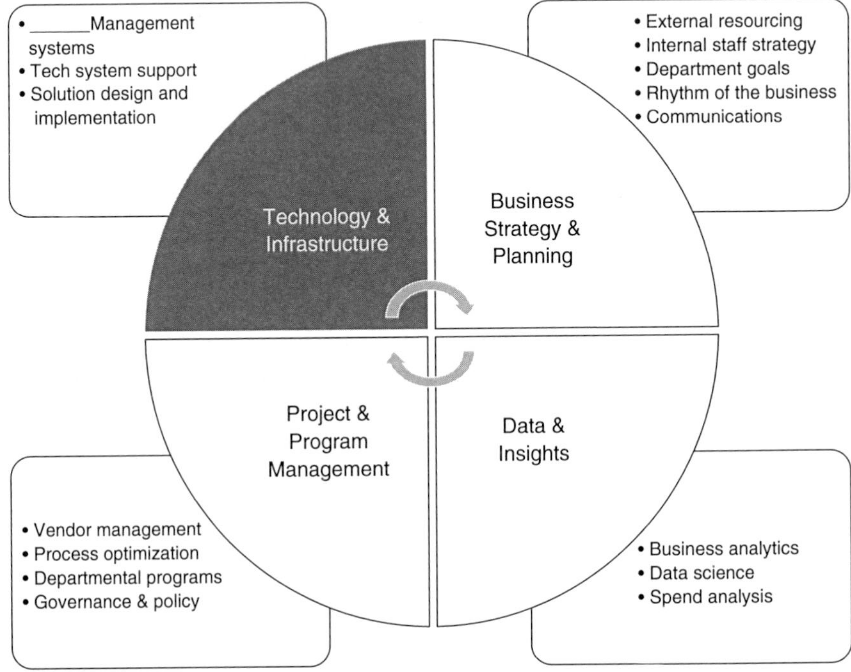

Figure 3-1a. *Legal Operations Functions*

a way of approaching it, but that is not the preferred route. There are some scenarios that make sense, especially when talking about a small department or a small team, or a team that has no internal resources dedicated to a particular function. That is likely the exact kind of area where a technology solution could help define the processes for the group.

So, what is within the technology bucket?

The first example from **Figure 3-1a** is a **"fill-in-the-blank" management system.**

The reason I call it the fill-in-the-blank management system is because it covers various systems, including document management, information management, knowledge management, matter management, spend management, and records management. Hence, fill in the blank. The list is probably longer than that, and could even include contract management, but that is worthy of a separate designation since it is so connected with actual lawyering work, rather than the infrastructure of a legal department. But the rest are very much infrastructure systems, or things that live more or less as part of the DNA of a legal department. They are used for different purposes to resolve different solutions to different problems, and they are not necessarily used by a department's lawyers or those that are actually delivering the legal service, as much as they are used to establish system organization, consistency, and access. Access to information is often what these various management systems are about, as well as workflow, helping to move things along, documents, artifacts, enabling—basically shepherding the process.

Another key function or skillset that falls into this area of legal ops is **tech system support.** This is not the tech support in an internal IT department. Rather, to the extent that there is a problem with any of the systems implemented in the legal department, there is almost certainly somebody within the legal ops team who is responsible for solving those problems. This isn't the person to call when your laptop isn't working. This is the person to call when you say: "Hey, the invoice is stuck in the e-billing system and I can't open it"; or, "I can't review the matter or the document seems to be erroring out every time I try to save it." The lists for that sort of thing can go on and on. It's about the technical problems with the law department's implemented solutions. Another critical role this function plays is often that of an advisor to lawyers who don't have the time, patience, or comfort with learning new technologies, and therefore rely on the technically inclined people to help them navigate new systems.

Residing side by side with these technical experts are **solution design and implementation** services. Within legal ops functions there is usually somebody who helps gather the requirements for the tech solution that is needed. The legal ops team is made up of enablers, often helping to serve and partner with the practicing attorneys or the other professionals in the legal department who are trying to accomplish their particular goals through technology.

Therefore, a solution design and implementation team[17] will often help in understanding the business problems, gather wish lists and requirements, along with those items that the ultimate users of the system are interested in automating while making sure these are features in the solutions that they propose. They are often the ones who are helping navigate the request for proposals (RFP) process and select a third-party system. Or they are working with an internal technology and engineering team that might help develop the system. These people are often very good intermediary translators between expert technologists and lawyers. They can translate the needs of the attorneys into specific features and capabilities that are necessary from the technology that is procured.

Corporate law departments, because they are always under pressure to do more with less, are eager to be innovative and typically are more comfortable accepting risks than law firms. They function every day in the world of having to prioritize and accept smart risks because they are so close to the business and the ultimate goal, that is, to get the task done. That relative comfort with risk allows corporate legal departments to experiment more with technology and handle the inherent risk of things being done in different ways. So, the opportunities for venture capitalists to recover on their investment in legal tech is growing as interest in technology continues to rise rapidly within corporate legal departments. Notably, investments in technologies marketed to law firms are also on the rise, but the risks associated with automation in the front office of the legal practice (meaning the work lawyers do) is inherently higher than automating back-office aspects.

The bottom line is that technology will continue to evolve. It is certainly in early stages in some areas, like contract review and data analytics, and in more mature stages in others like electronic discovery. But as technologies such as AI mature and cease to be buzzwords, it will bring a new age of computing that has the potential to replace legal judgment and analysis. No doubt that technology is augmenting legal judgment. There will be some areas where it may actually replace legal judgment to a large extent. Those will be the interesting areas to watch.

Technology will evolve further because it's still relatively new and changes quickly. Simply thinking about the amount of legal tech and conversations around it is forcing attorneys in-house to seriously consider automating. It is creating a pressure to think about how efficiencies can be brought into legal departments through automation.

BUSINESS STRATEGY AND PLANNING

The second quadrant of **Figure 3-1b**, **business strategy and planning,** entails a different type of skillset that is common among business-minded professionals. This set of capabilities is designed to enable the law department to act like a business in many ways, and to conform to expectations that apply to all departments of the business to which it belongs. Those who regularly engage with corporations or businesses understand that it is very common to have business strategies or sessions where plans are laid out, such as annual plans, and three- or five-year plans.

The same disciplined approach to running a corporate department is often sought in the legal department.

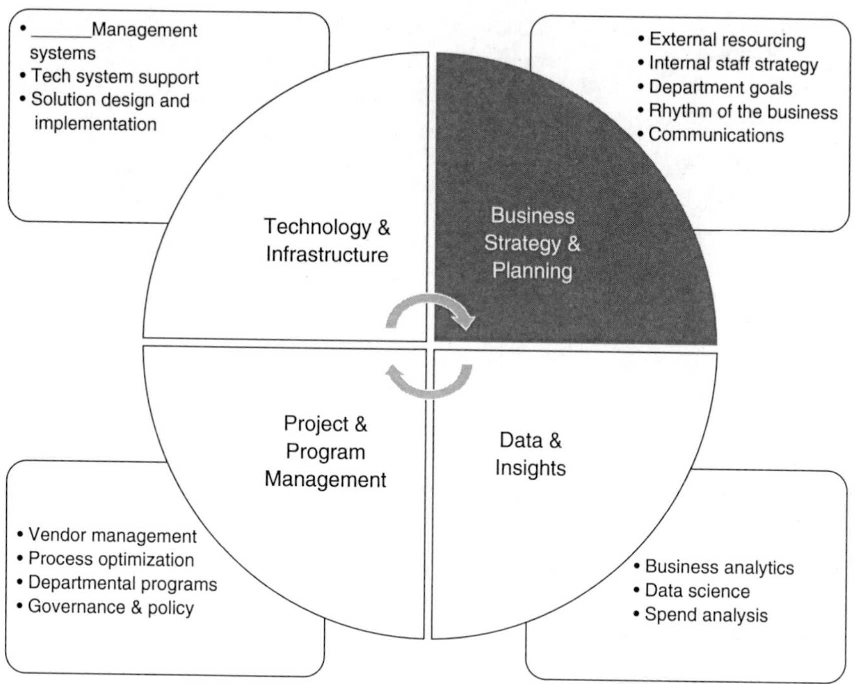

Figure 3-1b. *Legal Operations Functions*

Commonly, it is the CEO or CFO that asks the GC for these kinds of plans, but sometimes it is also coming from within the legal department as a need to be more organized, more strategic, or visionary and mindful about how they are allocating resources and time. Logically, a common set of skills found in this category is related to managing external resourcing.

> Corporate legal teams are asking: *How do we use external resources? Do we use only law firms? Or do we also use alternative providers? Who does what kind of work? What is the proportion of the firm's spend, and should we allocate to different types of resources? What are the right resources for the right work?*

There's also internal staffing strategy that can be overlooked as legal departments evolve organically and hire only lawyers. It is critical to ask questions of internal workload alignment similar to workload allocation questions we ask of our external resources. "Do we have the right people doing the right work internally? Do we have the ratio of attorneys to

Think about the rhythm of the meetings: Are all the department heads at the meeting? Are there quarterly meetings? Should there be a training and development program in place? Maybe they partner with a human resource professional for that.

It is really thinking clearly and objectively about how the business of the legal department is run and organized.

other professional staff? What are the departments' goals, and how do we best advance those with staffing and work assignments?"

Although those are specific areas of focus, namely resourcing, there is broader strategy work that happens in this quadrant. Setting out a vision, a mission for the department and specific goals—ideally measurable or actionable goals—are what usually come from a business strategy and planning team within the legal ops group or those professionals. This quadrant cares for the smooth management of the department, department-wide agendas, handling relationships with other departments, setting priorities; many of the functions are often referred to those tasks that "keep the train on the tracks."

Overseeing how the legal business is running and the rhythm of the business is often not top of mind for a GC (and rightfully so!), so the legal ops business planning function handles that for a legal department. A rhythm of the business model, or ROB, is so critical to the operation of a company that it is no wonder creative legal departments are realizing that a mirrored function like the one that exists at the corporate CEO level should exist inside the legal department. As legal departments move away from being the reactionary legal counsel who responds to needs raised by the business, these in-house legal partners to the business are better able to serve when they have a clear picture of the corporate ROB and can snap into it.

A legal department ROB model will ensure that legal department quarterly reviews are done just in advance of the corporate quarterly business review, so that the GC is prepared and applicable information is shared. Similarly, a good legal department ROB model will include a plan for the GC to debrief his/her deputies on what transpired at the corporate meetings.

A key component in all of this is communications. Communications within a legal department are as important as communications across any company or any of the other departments and often requires planning and some particular skills in communications, or in public relations, or potentially even internal marketing.

By the same token, big technology infrastructure changes often require a strong focus on communications. There is a lot of cross-enabling and overlapping that has to happen across these categories of skills to be successful. A great example is when the legal team realigns their support model and reassigns certain attorneys to different parts of the business. Rather than relying on scattered emails to clients, legal departments should have clear approaches of cascading group announcements and links to newly defined charts on an internal company website where business clients can go see who they should contact. Similar communications are critical as new process or systems, which impact the business, are launched. Coordinating communications in a way that is clear and concise is an absolute requirement in today's age of information overload and instant availability to content.

This combination of functions that fall within business strategy and planning span from forward-thinking high value strategy all the way to the very necessary, but often underappreciated, basics of managing a cadence of department meetings that ensure transparency and flow of information (which typically feed a culture and employee morale—very important aspects of any department!).

PROJECT AND PROGRAM MANAGEMENT[18]

Legal **project and program management** has been on the radar for some time, and properly so. The third quadrant of **Figure 3-1c** on the next page, project management as it applies to the law practice or to law department operations, is a natural. It applies general project management principles to the legal department and perhaps the legal work itself.

Project and program management are quite different, though both can benefit from a common set of core skills. Projects have a start and end; programs are ongoing, mini-businesses that require tracking, monitoring, reporting, and continuous improvement. A program can be made up of many projects that start and stop, and then impact the overall program. People are brought in to help manage various functions such as process optimization, departmental projects, and setting programs for governance and compliance, to name a few. Programs can be run by the legal ops group, or projects that conclude with the launch of a new program can be handed back to other parts of the legal department. Without getting into the nuances, a key capability of any legal ops organization is the ability to handle and run very complex projects, and similarly to oversee programs on an ongoing basis.

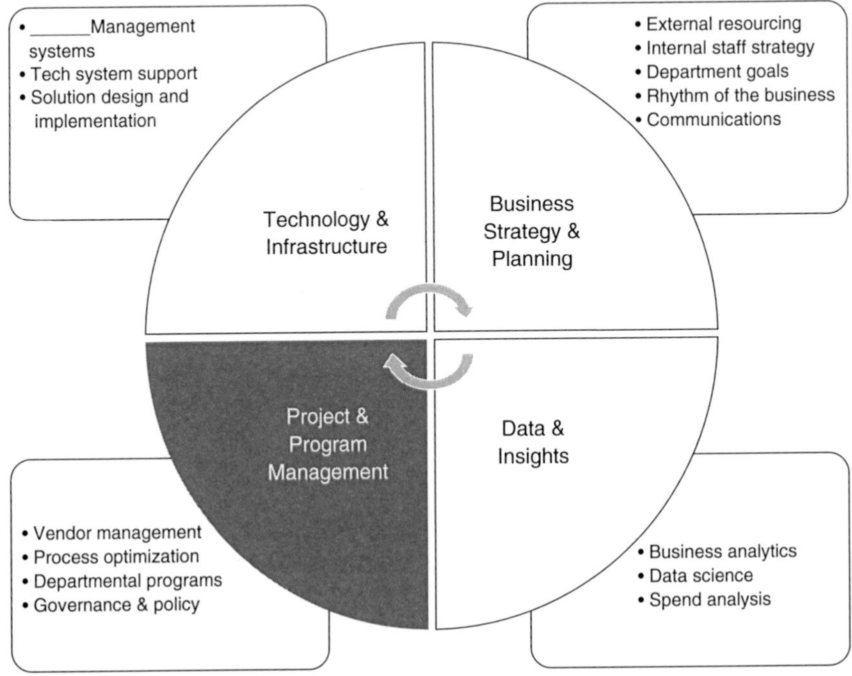

Figure 3-1c. *Legal Operations Functions*

> An overhaul of law firm engagement practices is a big, meaty project that requires the help of a skilled project manager. Once the overhaul is done, however, there is a program to run. The spend management program can sit in another part of the department—perhaps it is all about litigation spend, in which case it can be run by program managers in the litigation team—but more effectively it should be an ongoing program run by the legal ops team, with access to all parts of that department.

Often process optimization is something a good project manager can help do for any legal practice across the legal department. Although process optimization is a very specific area of expertise in concepts such as *Six Sigma* and *Lean,* many project managers have worked closely enough with such experts that they pick up some basic process improvement skills, which can be enough to satisfy the process improvement needs of a corporate legal function. Since project managers swoop into a messy situation and swoop out once they create a clear plan, they are excellent at bringing a fresh perspective to various parts of the department.

Often a really solid project manager from the legal ops team will help plan and streamline workflows across the department. So, for example, it could be a compliance program; and maybe legal ops doesn't own compliance, the strategy, and the outcome, but they can run the program by determining and implementing the key performance indicator metrics, helping to ensure things are on time and within budget, and making sure communications are tight.

> Somebody from, maybe a trademark team, can say, "Hey, you know what, we are a little overwhelmed; we are not sure that we are doing things the best way." An experienced project manager can map the current processes and identify improvements.

In addition to project management, there is a governance/policy aspect to program management that can go hand-in-hand with some of the business strategy and planning work. A legal ops function can help organize the law department policies it implements for the rest of the company. Or maybe these are internal policies that the law department uses to enable itself and assure it is aligned and complying with established best practices.

Another example of project management is in litigation. Often, paralegals end up performing the project management function in a large matter. Although they tend to have significant experience in managing litigation matters, they could be lacking the project management skills that would simplify their role. They can acquire those skills through training, or alternatively, paralegals could pair with project managers (PMs) so that they are each doing what they do best. Paralegals could get more involved with the legal aspects of the case, while the PMs manage all the moving parts and keep tight timelines. Though this is an additional resource for the litigation team, it is one that could be leveraged in multiple cases, and will free up time for the paralegals to do the same.

Ultimately, the goal is not to add costs, but to redistribute resources based on expertise and skills.

Project and program managers bring order and rigor to any project, by keeping people on task and on tight timelines. A complex contract negotiation that might take months to close requires coordination among many stakeholders, scheduling meetings, taking notes, and following up after meetings to summarize decisions and next steps. Checking in on people who are delayed in delivering their inputs or revisions is often time-consuming for the attorneys and the reason for delays in contract

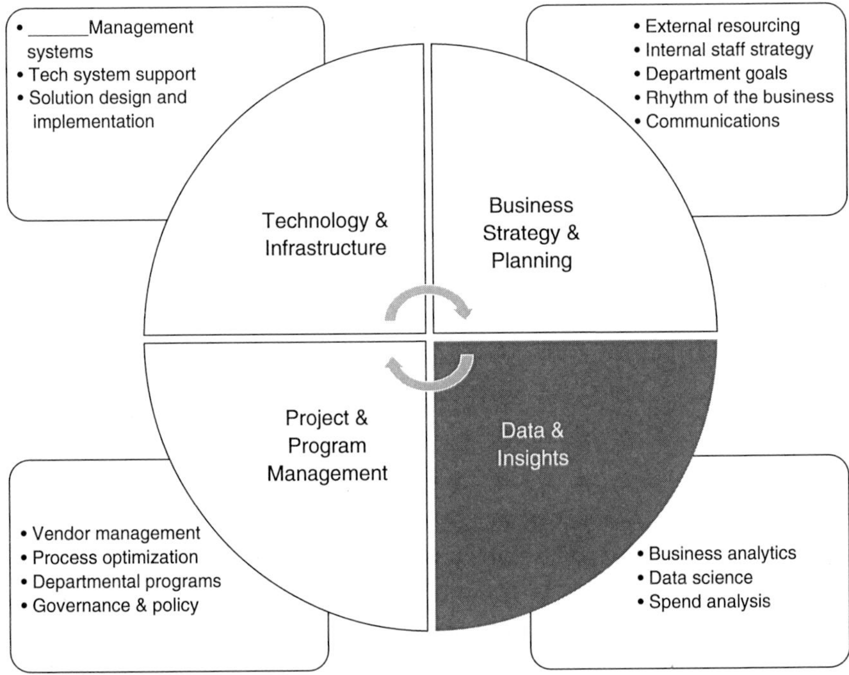

Figure 3-1d. *Legal Operations Functions*

negotiations. Simply keeping up with who has the latest draft and who owes the next round of revisions becomes a daunting process, and time easily slips by without progress. *Project managers hold everyone accountable. They are a neutral party that can keep everybody moving forward on the established timeline.*

DATA AND INSIGHTS

Data and insights is listed in its own quadrant in **Figure 3-1d**, but it is actually an enabler for the other three quadrants. It is an enabler of everything, or certainly a critical part of any good project management, technology solution, or business strategy. Simply put, if you don't know the data you are targeting, it is difficult to achieve your goals.

There are now skillsets that are becoming more nuanced and specific in this area. In developing legal ops teams, a good project and program manager was expected to be an expert on data to the extent that the data was available in systems that allowed for data gathering. Many project managers are becoming more impactful in the way they use data because they are also leveraging the skills of other data professionals such as data scientists and data analysts. Those are examples of roles becoming more common in legal departments and law firms that did not exist until recently in those settings, as this evolution occurs across the industry. I put spend analytics in this category as well, because while spend management or vendor management could be a program, it is so data-heavy that it is often a dedicated analytical role as well.

Information and data make the right-sourcing of work more targeted as time goes on. What happens is that the business gets maximum bang for its legal buck; the legal department as a whole is freed from the low-value flood of work that clouds its effectiveness every day; and business and legal are free to partner on high-value strategic work that takes the company to the next level.

None of this is possible without good data analytics. Similarly, all the benefits promised by AI and blockchain, and any of the other hyped game-changing tools, will not get off the ground without good data at the foundation. Without proper analytics, you can't prove you need those tools, you can't prove they work, and you can't identify areas where you'd use them.

Gathering and deploying data is what every other sensible business function does. If legal wants to be a business partner, then the time when we could get by without data is gone. Every outside counsel should be providing you with data on their costs, their timelines, the level of resources they're providing to you, the volume, and response times of communications. It is time to be clear to partner law firms that from now on, a defined set of data points are expected and should be delivered promptly and regularly. If they struggle with this, it's a great way to stoke competition between vendors because why should anyone pay for an inferior service at the level that competitors provide? Particularly with the arrival of business-savvy ALSPs, there's no excuse for a modern legal services provider to be data-illiterate.

Analyzing Spend

Regarding data analytics at in-house departments, measuring outside legal spend is the first thing to do. It sounds logical and simple, but in a corporate setting, where the number of service providers is high, it's easy for spend tracking to get out of control. Losing control might not mean a catastrophic collapse in operational capability, but the volume and complexity of spend can quickly require so many hours focused on mere management that the team doesn't have time to analyze, forecast, or budget properly, meaning that planning goes out the window, and the department becomes reactive.

Basic spend is black and white, and should be easy to measure; so many begin there. Once that basic data is gathered, they start adding more metrics: historical trends, payment cycles, vendor numbers; these will unearth insights. For example, if payment cycles are fast, can better rates be negotiated in exchange for a faster payment cycle? If the number of vendors has crept up, but without an increase in spend, can you consolidate work with fewer vendors to make billing easier? Basic insights can quite quickly become powerful when it comes to basic resource allocation. Legal departments shouldn't run before they can walk, and properly tracking the cost and allocation of work is walking. Even between those two critical data sets, spend management is more of a crawl. That is the first place to start.

Analyzing Transactional Data

Legal teams that are ready to do more are starting to track contract data in ways that add real value for the business. Every company deals with contracts—they're the foundation of business, after all—and an increase in the volume and complexity of contracts is often the decisive factor that compels a growing business to hire its first lawyer.

Capturing contract volume is fairly straightforward at the start. There is a finite, knowable number. Ask a sales team how many deals they have and they'll know immediately how many sales they've made. Similarly, HR will know straight away how many people they've hired. But ask legal how many contracts they've produced in a given quarter and you might well be disappointed with the answer. To avoid embarrassment, make sure nobody knows more about contracts than the legal department does. Whether employment contracts, sales agreements, or other type of contracts, the business is likely more in tune with volumes than the legal department that is supporting all those contracts.

Smart in-house teams will move beyond the headline figure to capture turnaround time, type of contract, involvement of outside counsel, cost, most and least negotiated clauses, and so on. These might seem like softer metrics but the lessons they bring will allow delivery of actionable insight to the business.

Data Visualization

EXAMPLE: A transactional lawyer might find a financial management class interesting; a more process-driven lawyer might prefer to learn *Six Sigma*. However it is addressed, make sure you're keeping up with the kind of role that "in-house lawyer" is becoming, not just now, but five or ten years from now.

Departments armed with data must make sure the right people see it and use it to make strategic decisions. There have never been more options when it comes to data visualization, and even the most basic pie or bar chart is a step up from a list of numbers. It's also guaranteed to land well with business-minded audiences: Nothing animates budget controllers more than pointing to a huge slice on a pie chart and advising that their money is going to one or two firms. That creates an immediate focal point for opportunity.

It is probably helpful to communicate spend each month, as financial data always has a keen audience. Workload and workflow-related data is better suited to a quarterly strategic meeting, where it can be presented to the relevant senior leadership. Key indicators like contract volume, headcount touched by legal matters, and turnaround times are the headline figures the GC needs to know. It's important to arm the GC with hard stats for the tough conversations she or he has to have at that level; it's likely the CFO is grilling them for information, and historically, legal hasn't always been able to provide it. In this era, this is no longer acceptable.

To become data-driven and data-enabled, in-house lawyers will have to overcome inertia and a skills gap in the profession. Although some progressive law schools are catching up, and the number of law schools that teach skills like forecasting and data manipulation is growing, progress is still needed. More worrying is the huge cohort of mid-career lawyers who were never taught any data skills as part of their training, and now face another twenty years of practice without them. To stay competitive in the job market, it's crucial for lawyers to try to address this, and in a way that holds their interest.

The need for data and metrics is becoming much more obvious as chief operating officers and CEOs pressure their GCs for data. Gone are the days when an attorney can say: "I don't know how much things will cost. It depends. I don't know what budget I need. We'll see."

Every part of the company is expected to provide data, and law departments are no longer the exceptions that they probably were in the past.

Conclusion

I have tried to show that the *practice of law* can no longer be in conflict with *operating the business of law.*

There are so many different functions that cover every part of being a lawyer, whether practicing law or running a legal department or law firm. What is the difference between the practice of law versus operating the business of law? Traditional lawyers practice law. That is what they have been trained to do for about two hundred years. They provide legal advice based on the facts presented. They can identify risks and potential issues that may arise in the eyes of the law. What they are not trained to do is run the business of practicing law. Lawyers are not taught how to manage their budgets, procure technology, operate processes, and a list of other activities involved in running any business. The deep professional expertise that lawyers have in their subject matters outshines the big gaps of experience needed to run a business (which every law firm is!) and that is where inefficiencies and wasted resources are so obvious.

Future lawyers, however, must understand how to operate the *business* of law, whether they work in legal ops or as a lawyer in an in-house department or a law firm. They are going to either have to operate a law firm or a legal department, or their own practice area. They aren't going to survive solely on the fact that they are excellent lawyers.

We see that there are all these other aspects of the practice of law, ***how*** we deliver that legal service, which is now forcing major changes. Attorneys must learn how to operate their own practice or they will have to engage the right professionals who can help them do it. The problem is that attorneys are not naturally trained for the operational aspects evolving around their legal practice.

We have to start thinking of the practice of law as the delivery of a service. That is how the alternative legal service providers think of it. They are often the ones who are teaching in-house clients and other players in the industry what it means to deliver a legal service, which is very different than how legal firms, for example, have long practiced or how a general attorney would provide a piece of legal advice or work product.

This failure to think about the actual *delivery* of legal services is exactly what needs to change. As the pressure continues to mount from in-house teams who don't want to pay by the billable hour, and who want to get more for less, that intrinsic value will alter the resource structures of the legal practice by forcing the addition of other professionals into the practice of law: those who are not actually practicing law, but doing many other necessary things more efficiently at lower costs. Delivery is the name of the game. That is operations.

CHAPTER 4

Legal Education Landscape

"Law schools and bar associations, including the ABA, should offer more continuing legal education and other opportunities for lawyers to study entrepreneurship, innovation, the business and economics of law practice, and other relevant disciplines."

—ABA's Report on the Future of Legal Services[19]

The legal ecosystem is highly complicated with many moving parts, as we've reviewed earlier. Note that I didn't spend much time on the law schools, because they deserve a deeper dive. Legal education in general deserves a closer look, with a concentrated focus on what sort of education exists for the practicing lawyers.

QUICK LOOK AT LAW SCHOOLS

We hear all the time that in-house departments don't hire straight from law schools. They want law firms to do the "training" of young associates before they become valuable to the practice of law in-house. Just what kind of training is expected from the firms, and what does that say about the law schools? Who is responsible for teaching young attorneys how to actually do their jobs? Reality is that most law schools teach curricula that has been fairly unchanged for decades.

Law schools continue to produce graduates that find work in law firms, meaning that law schools play the traditional role of supplier in the supply and demand mechanics of the legal market. The law schools supply what the hiring "customers"—the law firms—demand. Shouldn't law schools be held to a higher standard? They *should* be the educators that everyone looks

> Although tenured professors hold on to their tried-and-true curriculum, which is much like partners at law firms who resist change, incoming students are interested in different topics and modern educational practices. These students often have very different career goals than students of the past.

up to and learns from—in short, they should lead the way. But it's remarkable how many of them don't.

No one who goes to law school should feel they are part of a money-making sausage factory; however, the reality is that law schools *are* much like a business. They need to attract tuition-paying students, and they need to produce lawyers who will find jobs. In addition, the schools need to score high on the influential *US News and World Report* rankings of law schools.[20] So, law schools can't afford to be *pure* educators.

There is another customer for law schools—that is, the student body itself. It seems that millennial[21] lawyers are entering the workforce with different expectations than previous generations. Law students are studying law in a time of such rapidly changing technology that includes instant access to information; meanwhile, the pace of disruption is often beyond the capability of a law school faculty to accommodate. Millennials are interested in a flexible work-life experience and alternatives to the traditional definition of a "successful" law school graduate—one who lands a high-powered job and works like crazy to reach the coveted status of partnership. Forward-looking law school administrators should acknowledge these tensions and make changes.

Law schools are serving two very distinct communities of "customers," law students and law firms. They are demanding changes in unique ways. The market is a harsh indicator of the changes occurring in the legal industry. In general, law school admissions have declined,[22] but they have shown an uptick more recently.[23] Internal philosophical differences within law schools often leave them paralyzed to react to this trend.

Although some law schools are closing their doors because it is so hard to survive in the current market, others are seizing the air of innovation in legal services and choosing to lead the charge. The number of law schools offering modernized curriculum and creative study programs is growing across the country, and every year new players enter the game. These schools are making changes, all of which have their own spin or special flavor, but each reflects that school's culture, willingness, resources, and other factors that enable their program goals.

Some schools focus on technology, while others on teaching business-related skills. Some schools are expanding the hands-on practical application experience within their curriculum beyond the typical and familiar mock trial or moot court programs. Others are developing strategic partnerships with commercial legal services companies to create real-life hands-on work experiences for students.

> The "next generation" of law schools are challenging the traditions of a legal education while still laying the foundation for the core modern skills that lawyers need.

Law school students have more options than ever regarding what they can do with their legal education. It's an option to get a legal degree and not practice law, but there are limited opportunities to actually apply the skills acquired in law school. Often, graduates who end up in different fields simply see their legal education as some sort of foundation, with little practical benefit. That is changing. The demand for skills ***related*** to legal practice is on the rise at an accelerated pace, evidenced by the hiring of more business professionals into legal departments and law firms (such as project managers, business analysts, pricing specialists, and many others), all of which can enhance the practice of law.[24]

Law firms and corporate legal departments are hiring people with a combination of skillsets. At firms, newer positions like chief innovation officer, client services officer, or practice management officer provide professionals with legal education backgrounds, and business operations experience new opportunities. For recent graduates, roles in project management, operations, and technology are opening across a variety of legal industry employers. Beyond law firms and corporate legal departments, the legal aid community, ALSPs, and court systems also seek multifaceted skillsets. These new roles allow graduates to apply the traditional problem-solving skills they are taught with the related skills now offered at more law schools around the country for careers in the legal industry, though not necessarily as practicing lawyers.

As the number of law schools offering new skillsets continues to rise, some have become leaders at a time when tensions in the ecosystem are demanding creativity and innovation to compete. Schools such as Harvard and Stanford are well known for their differing programs. Although Stanford Law's Codex[25] focuses on technology and educating interested law students and legal professionals in hardcore coding skills, Harvard's Center on the Legal Profession[26] is dedicated to the evolving legal profession and what it means for practicing lawyers and the educational landscape. Suffolk Law School's Institute on Legal Innovation and Technology[27] has partnered with a legal services company to give law students practical experience in alternative legal services and legal technology.

Fortunately, there are many more,[28] including Northwestern,[29] Chicago Kent College of Law,[30] Duke,[31] and others that offer training or courses related to the business and technology side of legal services. Classes in project management, data analytics, process improvement, financial modeling, and change management are common at these law schools. Some professors are introducing innovative programs and curriculum at their law schools, in effect becoming an innovation brand name for their law schools.

Any effort to innovate the legal education system and curriculum is welcomed by the industry broadly and is slowly becoming the norm. Law schools that do not keep up will be left behind.

> *I figured out quickly that I had better figure out how to become a lawyer, and quickly.*
>
> —Miriam R. Albert upon graduation[32]

CONTINUING LEGAL EDUCATION: THE GAP FOR PRACTICING LAWYERS

What about people who graduated years ago? We're experienced, confident experts, right?

There is something chipping away at the confidence of many attorneys, particularly in law firms. The legal industry is transforming and any lawyer who doesn't adapt will certainly be left behind. It almost seems that in some circles innovation is now prized over experience and the status quo is scoffed at as stodgy, antiquated, and no longer a real option.

Most lawyers try to stay abreast of the changes in law, as well as the practice of law, but it is hard to stay on top of what is happening to the profession itself. Every lawyer needs to know practical information about various buzzwords such as "legal ops," "legal tech ancillary services," "artificial intelligence," "alternative service providers," "alternative fee arrangements," and the need to move from "legal practice" to "legal service delivery." Those terms are thrown around, but in daily practice these concepts are more peripheral hype than imminent reality.

This might not be the case much longer. So where can lawyers turn for legal education that will give them a handle on the macro changes happening in the legal ecosystem and ultimately modernize their client offerings? Actually everywhere . . . and nowhere.

> There has to be something out there that can help synthesize what the legal press is talking about. But what should it look like? What is really happening across the industry?
>
> What will help bridge this education gap for attorneys who are willing to adapt and want to try practicing out of their long-established comfort zones?

Searching about continuing legal education (CLE) possibilities yields a tsunami of choices. For a mere $59.99 or $500 or $1,500, anyone can become an expert in blockchain or learn how the General Data Protection Regulation (GDPR) is handled in multinational transactions. There are conferences devoted to legal tech and live webinars on how to get "tweets" admitted as evidence. Lawyers can even self-study from pre-recorded online videos about artificial intelligence (AI) or go back to tech basics with classes on creating "Powerful PowerPoints" or becoming a "Microsoft Word Wizard."

None of these hit the mark, not surprisingly. Nor do they explain the macro changes and opportunities across the legal ecosystem; they fail to offer solutions on how to become a leader in the changing practice of law. We need to fill this continuing education gap with practical information that can be applied in a real-world setting to deliver services. We need an easily digestible legal industry overview along with practical tips for lawyers looking to guide their corporate clients toward these new services and opportunities.

I envision a professional development program that would fulfill the need for a holistic skillset necessary to practice law in the modern age and fulfill CLE requirements in an engaging way.

But today that vision is still far away. A quick overview of the current CLE requirements and options available to attorneys gives perspective.

CLE Requirements

Lawyers in the nation's capital are off the hook with mandatory continuing legal education (MCLE). Years ago, DC regulators decided there was no proof that *requiring* CLE was making lawyers more competent.[33] Joining DC in shunning MCLE are Maryland, Massachusetts, Michigan, and South Dakota. Michigan had implemented MCLE for seven years before

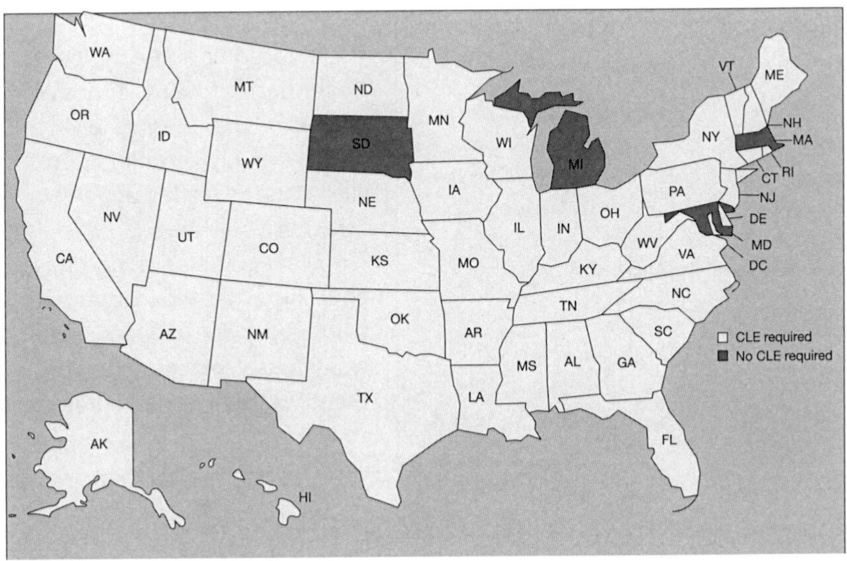

rescinding it in 1994; the state ultimately decided that MCLE was not effective in enhancing their attorneys' knowledge of substantive law.[34]

The remaining states recognize the potential of CLE to ensure their lawyers carve out time every year to brush up on the rules governing their practice areas or specific legal topics of interest to them. Since every state with MCLE requires an ethics or "professional responsibility" component, lawyers must take a moment to check their ethical obligations, take care of their mental health, and potentially acknowledge unhealthy lifestyle choices common to stressed-out practitioners.

On average, states require between 10 and 15 CLE credit hours per year, a small chunk of which must focus on ethics or professionalism. Reporting cycles typically range from one to three years with many states allowing attorneys to stockpile a certain amount of credits and roll them over to the following cycle.

In recent years, thanks to advances in technology, there has been a surge of methods available to complete CLE. Traditionally, credits were earned solely in a live, in-person classroom setting. Now, a key component of CLE are various self-study delivery methods. These can include live webinars; conference calls; video replays of live events; pre-recorded, on-demand video; and audio lessons.

States regulate the use of these online options to varying degrees. For example, many states favor the live, participatory webcasts and restrict the number of pre-recorded courses. However, I see a trend to loosen these restrictions. Recently, Rhode Island doubled its on-demand limit per cycle from three to six credits.[35] In 2016, the state of Washington ended its "live" requirement altogether.[36] At least twelve states place no limitations on either the quantity or style of online options. At this writing, only eight states still required at least some credits be earned via in-person traditional classroom settings.[37]

Another CLE trend is using what I call "extra-curricular lawyering" to chip away at a mandated CLE obligation. This can include any number of personally enriching activities that serve the community, future lawyers, or the legal profession as a whole, including:

- Teaching an approved CLE course
- Legal research, writing, and publishing
- Serving on the State Board of Bar Admission or Bar Examiners
- Serving on committees devoted to rules, professional responsibility, ethics, professionalism, or the unauthorized practice of law
- Enrolling in or auditing a course at an accredited law school
- Enrolling in an approved bar review course
- Serving as a member of the state legislature
- Acting as a judge in a mock trial or other law school activities

A state-by-state analysis of CLE requirements offers up these other interesting opportunities: At least ten states allow pro bono work to count for CLE credits. Florida gives credit for participation in the state's "Adults Civics Teaching Initiative" and "Justice Teaching Classroom Initiative." Ohio and Oregon encourage CLE study of Access to Justice topics. Indiana allows credit for "non-legal subject matter" courses (for example, accounting or medicine for attorneys) while Oregon allows up to six credits for attending courses on business development and marketing or participating in personal management assistance activities. The state of Washington's requirements might be the most flexible, allowing for more than one-half of the credits to be earned in areas like personal development, office management, improving the legal system, or any "nexus subject" related to the lawyer's professional role, but not directly related to the practice of law.

In addition, mentorship programs are available in at least seven states, where experienced attorneys are given credit for helping new lawyers transition into practice.

If taken advantage of, it is often these extracurricular methods that provide the greatest potential for attorney growth and opportunities for participants to go beyond mere check-the-box CLE. But as with most things, many options require personal initiative, or a significant investment of time, a rare commodity in the legal community. The reality is that practicing attorneys cannot take time to figure out which options make the most sense or are most appealing and it is simply easier to review the latest spam mail of CLE offerings from the state and sign up for some of those.

Technology Requirements

The epicenter of any legal ecosystem overhaul is the use of technology to improve efficiency and client service. At least thirty-one states have made it a lawyer's ethical duty to be competent in the risks and benefits of using technology.[38] Although the definition of "competence" is somewhat vague, it is widely considered to mean that attorneys should have a general awareness of the technological opportunities available to serve their clients.

The reasoning behind tech requirements competency is clear: Even the most old-fashioned lawyer is now forced to spend a significant amount of time online and or using technology every day. They email, draft documents electronically, manage a calendar synced to their phone, and video conference with clients. Many lawyers interface with e-billing, eSignatures, and automated workflows. Twenty years ago, this was not the case. Only within the past twenty-five years has the internet become the heart of legal service delivery.

Writing for Thomson Reuters, Tad Simons says, "Technological competence isn't a skill attorneys can simply add to their CLE checklist—it's something that needs to be woven into their DNA."[39] Changes are happening continuously and at hyperspeed, making it all the more critical for lawyers to get a baseline understanding of technology as soon as possible. This can be a scary thought for those nearing the end of their careers.

Following is a sampling of the ways Florida's technology CLE requirement can be met. They are from the Florida Bar CLE and Resource Center, and Lawline.com[40] and range in complexity from basic to advanced, with many practice-specific options:

- Basic Technology for Today's Law Practice
- Basic Law Firm Data Security, Privacy, and Cyber Liability
- How to Manage Your Email Using Technology—and Get Your Time and Sanity Back

- Using Technology to Make Judge-Friendly Briefs
- Running a Better Law Firm Through Project Management
- Productivity with an Emphasis on Cyber Security in Law Firms

I want to emphasize that dedicating a single hour a year to technology will not make someone an expert. But even if basic technology seems advanced to you, the Florida programs offer a small taste of what is happening in the legal community. An awareness of the opportunity is the first critical step.

CLE: A Sampling of Options

Where are the practical, well-rounded CLE options that help lawyers get up to speed on the macro changes happening in the legal ecosystem?

CLE course options are riddled with sponsored nonsense, deep dives into one practice area or ultra-specific details for the already experts. There is no shortage of offerings on legal practice or procedure, but a holistic overview of the essentials is missing. To be fair, on each CLE provider or conference I have come across in my research, I have usually found at least one course that tries to bridge this education gap, one small step at a time. For example:

- ***LexisNexis:*** Drinking from a Fire Hydrant: Basic Legal Research in the Age of Technology[41]
- ***Practicing Law Institute (PLI)*** one-hour briefings:
  - Process and Project Management for In-House Counsel
  - Evolving Your Metrics and Analytics Process
  - The Ethical Challenges of Incorporating New Technologies into your Legal Practice
  - Think Like a Lawyer, Talk Like a Geek 2018: Get Fluent in Technology.
- ***Florida Bar's Legal Fuel Resource Center***: How to Increase Profits and Stay Organized by Running a Lean Law Firm
- ***Association of Corporate Counsel (ACC):*** Legal Operations Maturity Model Series or Mini-MBA for In-House Counsel

There are also "just-in-time" video learning resources available online (for example, Hotshot Legal), and for those who learn best from formal peer discussions, there are roundtable legal forums from providers like Consero.[42]

This is a sampling of the dozens if not hundreds of similar choices, again creating an overwhelming selection, which are often sponsor-driven. It is important for attorneys to get an unbiased view on what is important for them to know about the legal industry. Who will help shed light on the fast-moving changes that the Big 4 are making? Where can lawyers look for a simple explanation of which legal tech is real and which is hype?

> *There is so much legal technology out there with AI and blockchain and other stuff. How do we know what is hype and what is real?*
>
> —Partner at law firm innovation event, February 2019

Conclusion (Read Chapter 7)

There's a conundrum for MCLE: For lawyers who take the responsibility seriously to stay current with case law and trends, they would seek out continuing education even if it was not required. Most lawyers have curious minds and look forward to new information that will improve job performance and client service.

CLE, just like the legal industry itself, has exploded with new opportunities, resulting in a multitude of pathways that could lead to modern-day success or further confusion.

There is a need and an opportunity to simplify and clarify for the hundreds of thousands of practicing lawyers who need a synopsis of those pathways to determine what is going on in their industry. That is entirely the purpose of this book, and specifically the purpose of chapter 7.

CHAPTER 5

Legal Technology

There's an app for that! Well . . . sort of . . .

CAUTION:

This chapter is not intended for a highly technical audience. In fact, it is intended for readers to simply acquire some basic information. There are a lot of explanations on what exactly constitutes "AI," what blockchain actually is, and how all of this technology will impact the practice of law. If you are seeking a thorough technical definition of these concepts, please seek a more appropriate (though sometimes incomprehensible) source.

Technology has always been an enabler of efficiency goals as a core component of the practice of law. Since the dawn of the fax machine, advancements in technology have slowly transformed the way law firms operate.

In general, while technology is advancing at an amazing rate, the legal sector is slow to adapt to change. Despite this, it seems like new legal technology solutions hit the market every day. Some technologies are "better mouse traps," such as more sophisticated versions of technologies that already have a place in the hands and hearts of law firms and legal departments across the world. Others are genuinely new solutions to existing problems, leveraging the exciting advancements in technology, including artificial intelligence (AI) and blockchain.

These days, one can find technologies that intersect with nearly every aspect of the legal profession—from legal education and research to document automation. To help frame the areas of impact, the Stanford TechIndex[43] is a growing directory of promising legal technology companies. The index has looked at each product and defined which function of the legal practice or profession they fall into. The TechIndex outlines nine categories:

1. Legal Marketplace
2. Document Automation
3. Practice Management
4. Legal Research
5. Legal Education
6. Online Dispute Resolution
7. E-Discovery
8. Analytics
9. Compliance

So, there are many categories or types of legal technologies out there. More mature solutions touch on eDiscovery, practice, case and document management, and legal research. Newer markets are taking on legal analytics—facilitating the rise of the data-driven lawyer—and using AI and expert systems for document automation. Of special interest is a more consumer-facing technology market that has significant potential to disrupt the status quo.

For the most part, legacy technology applications have made back-office operations more efficient. That is, most technologies entering law firms before the more recent legal technology advances have focused on driving efficiencies in the operational or infrastructure aspects of law firms and law departments. For example, word processing tools have long taken the place of handwriting or a typewriter. Here's a quick quiz: Does your firm or department have a typewriter somewhere, in a closet or on a shelf? (Actually, it might be wise to keep a couple of well-oiled typewriters around as safeguards for when the power grid and the internet go down, or more likely as an attraction for the firm's historical museum.)

> The rise of legal technology hinges on the fact that consumers of legal services demand more—and they want it better, faster, and cheaper. Legal technology is not only shifting the way law firms and departments undertake the business and practice of law, but it's transforming the delivery of legal services and the profession in a fundamental way.

From a more modern perspective, rather than manually filling out timesheets and billables in six-minute increments at the end of each day (or pay period), attorneys have benefitted from more streamlined timekeeping methods for some time. Administrative tasks like billing and scheduling meetings are also now comfortably done electronically. Even more recently, electronic signature tools have paved the way for faster approvals, which reduces a lot of friction. History suggests that attorneys have no qualms with improving efficiencies and outcomes for these types of tasks and have embraced new technologies in the "back office."

> Although the jury is still out on a formal definition, "artificial intelligence" is widely accepted as the development of computer systems or programs that can perform tasks that require human intelligence. These include tasks like image and speech recognition and applying logic for decision making. Of course, decision making is a core component of practicing law, so the industry is rife with opportunities to leverage those technological advancements.

As time goes on, however, more routine "front office" tasks—i.e., tasks traditionally considered "legal work"—are being made more efficient through technology. Game-changing young legal tech companies are tackling tasks like drafting research memos, reviewing contracts and documents, and responding to discovery. More tools are on the horizon.

AI, BLOCKCHAIN, AND OTHER BUZZWORDS

Artificial Intelligence[44]

Many newer legal technology breakthroughs are thanks to advancements in AI. Before diving too deep into what legal AI applications are out there, it's important to first get an idea of what AI is, and what it is (and is not) capable of doing.

There are essentially three simplified concepts a lawyer should know about this technology—AI, machine learning, and deep learning.

First, AI, generally, is an umbrella term that encapsulates varying degrees of a software program's abilities. The term nonetheless represents the ability for a machine to do a task in a smart way, even if it is performing that task at the direction of a human who has coded or programmed it (or taught it) to do that task. In essence, a human must create the program and create a set of instructions for the computer to execute a task. Another variation on this sort of technology is called "expert systems," which requires supervised learning by the machine where a human is setting up the rules for the system. A common example of an expert system is TurboTax.

To illustrate, consider the following scenario:

Imagine that you want to extract dates from all of your contracts. A software engineer could easily write a program that could accommodate the known combinations and formats of dates. Some dates are just numbers, slashes, and dashes (8/10/19; 2019-08-10); some are full words (the 10th of August, 2019), while others are shorthand (Aug 10, 19). Taking each possible combination into consideration, the programmer could build rules that extract those dates and store them in a standardized format. But what happens if one country adopts a new format? Unfortunately, the moment the date deviates from the pattern, the program will not be able to fulfil its duties without being reprogrammed. What about relational data that is conditioned on other text?

As seen from the example, the level of human involvement in the basic types of AI is actually quite high.

Some advanced types of AI tools include those categorized as "machine learning." Machine learning is really the ability for computers to "learn" how to perform certain tasks by being exposed to structured or labeled data; they "learn" how to perform tasks by following patterns and making predictions. Considering the previous example, a machine learning program would be far more adaptable to new formatting methods. Rather than having to recode a program (as would be necessary with a very narrow AI program), the system could instead be exposed to new labeled data and "learn" that a new date format is the functional equivalent to others in its memory.

The final and most advanced subclass of AI (thus far) is "deep learning." This concept is also referred to as "neural networks." Deep learning is a complex topic and, though not new, its true reach is still being explored. It is enough to know that deep learning is the consumption of extraordinary amounts of data, from which a computer can identify simple patterns and combine them into highly complex patterns, to learn and perform expected outcomes without being specifically programmed. (Note that many of the recent advancements in image and speech recognition, and technology for self-driving cars, has come from deep learning/artificial neural network algorithms.)

With this baseline understanding of AI, we can dive into a few legal AI applications making waves in the market.

At the broadest AI level, automated branching logic decision trees (also known more colloquially as "chatbots") are taking the legal space by storm. As an aside, because of the up-front investment of human knowledge to build these decision trees, many don't think chatbots should be classified as AI. Nonetheless, because it uses a software system to perform a human task, leading to an ultimate outcome, it is still considered a very basic form of AI. Law firms and legal departments are leveraging this type of AI for things such as marketing and lead generation, client intake, and addressing frequently asked questions.

Legal research is a hotbed for more advanced AI solutions. Online research giants like LexisNexis and Westlaw are, of course, significant advancements in legal research in their own right. But their structure means they are a fountain of well-formatted data—a gold mine for machine learning. In fact, Thomson Reuters has unveiled its new and improved take on legal research—Westlaw Edge.[45] Other startup companies are also tackling legal research, providing a wealth of data in a matter of seconds.

Contract and document review are also heavily impacted by AI applications. For example, contract review automation company, LawGeex,[46] uses AI to review contracts and highlight any discrepancies a contract may have, compared to a company's policies. Thereafter, it serves up the company's default language and fallback positions for each clause, speeding up negotiations and approvals, and in turn, increasing deal capacity. In the ultimate test, this company put its software head to head with twenty highly experienced U.S. lawyers. The AI algorithm took a mere twenty-six seconds to review five non-disclosure agreements (NDAs). On the other side of the ring, the attorneys took an average of ninety-two minutes to review the same agreements. Surprisingly (but perhaps unsurprisingly to the software engineers), the lawyers' review resulted in only 85 percent accuracy, compared with the AI system's 94 percent accuracy.

The Tel Aviv, Israel-based company raised $12 million in new investment in 2018 for its automated contract review technology to help companies sift through things like NDAs, supply agreements, purchase orders, and software as a service licenses, to ensure "there aren't any unsanctioned legal gotchas buried deep in legalese."[47]

Blockchain

Many people know about blockchain as it pertains to the rise of Bitcoin and other cryptocurrencies. In 2017 there was a worldwide blockchain awakening. Blockchain technology is a fairly difficult concept to understand without a computer science background. However, the best

With blockchain, the ability to increase transparency and trust among users means that the legal profession has taken notice. Efforts have heavily focused on the contracting space through the use of smart contracts. Smart contracts gave rise to the idea of "code as law" by combining simple computer programs with events that trigger legal ramifications.

A successful smart contract begins by clearly identifying the ultimate outcome—for example, the transfer of funds—and the agreed upon conditions to transfer interest. From there, a developer can create a computer program outlining the conditions and the triggering circumstances that lead to the ultimate outcome. When the smart contract receives confirmation that the requisite conditions have been met, interest can be transferred automatically as previously agreed upon.

shorthand way to explain this technology is that it is an unalterable, distributed database. The moment information is shared to a "block" in the blockchain, it is instantly distributed and visible to all people that have permission to be a part of that specific blockchain. Each individual block is assigned a cryptographic, alphanumerical identifier (called a hash or key) that is specially calculated based on the previous block and the information contained within the new block. This means that if someone were to attempt to modify information in a specific block, it would alter the hash. An altered hash sends a message to the other participants of the blockchain that the data has been altered, and the verification of that new entry would fail. Mechanics aside, blockchain's major benefits are its inalterability and its transparency—and thus its ability to create trust and keep an excellent audit trail.

Despite the hype, blockchain has yet to gain much traction in the legal industry. Nonetheless, the logistics and supply chain industries, as well as food safety and banking, are finding more immediate utility in blockchain technology and will pave the way for more adoption in other industries, including legal, hopefully.

Task Automation

Technology is also enabling a significant shift in how attorneys can perform certain routine tasks. The multitude of practice-side technology entering the market means more competition; more competition means lower prices; and lower prices mean more industry-wide adoption. But many attorneys may be surprised to know that this innovation is influencing the way commercial clients and individual consumers access legal services and the justice system.

A look at new service offerings and new decision-making frameworks illustrates the efforts underway.

For example, "expert systems" are an increasingly popular law firm offering. Like chatbots, expert systems are a curated series of questions that collect information from their user, the client. The end of the questionnaire reveals relevant legal advice applicable to the client's situation—without going directly through their attorney.

For example, McCann FitzGerald created its "Credit Reporting Compliance Bot,"[48] to collect client information to give a comprehensive assessment of whether the Credit Reporting Act applies to their business or particular transaction. Even better, it goes further by working to identify where there may be gaps in the client's compliance. Norton Rose Fulbright has so far deployed two expert systems—"Parker,"[49] a system that lets clients ascertain whether they are in compliance with GDPR, and "Contractor Check,"[50] which helps clients accurately characterize their human resource engagement as either employees or independent contractors.

Ordinarily, clients would need to command their attorney's time and attention for these matters, incurring charges along the way. With these tools, clients instead pay a lower cost, one-time fee, saving their attorney's time for higher value work. A lot of this change is due to easier access to customizable software. But it is also triggered by the fact that clients are increasingly willing to pay law firms for lower value, routine work. This client-driven shift has caused many in the industry to consider whether generating fees on an hourly basis is the best path forward.

Another interesting and welcome advancement is the commoditization of the data-driven lawyer. Companies like Lex Machina[51] and Premonition—which brands itself as an "unfair advantage in litigation"[52]—give attorneys more insights into the viability of their clients' cases. These legal analytics platforms leverage huge amounts of public court data and give lawyers the ability to predict whether a certain type of case before a certain judge has a reasonable chance of succeeding. From there, attorneys work with the clients to help them understand the validity of their claims, and their best and most cost-effective path forward. This necessitates a long overdue partnership between clients and attorneys.

Legal technology's disruption factor also takes aim at the individual consumer.

In the so-called "small law" world, the rise of legal marketplaces like Avvo[53] and LegalZoom[54] have had extensive impact on how individuals obtain legal services. Routine procedures like divorces, business formations, and simple real estate transactions can now be done by simply filling out a form and following a few steps, with little to no assistance from an attorney. Likewise, the chatbots discussed previously are looking to take a slice of the pie by helping consumers do things like appeal parking tickets and complete simple court forms. Some firms are even leveraging client-facing chatbots by allowing website visitors to answer a series of questions that help them determine their true legal issue. In turn, this helps them decide if they want to seek advice and counsel or attack the issues on their own.

It is becoming increasingly clear that for common legal processes, technology has become the great equalizer, democratizing access to information so that anyone can make reasoned decisions about their situation. That level of access to information also has altered what services clients seek when shopping for an attorney.

ACCESS TO JUSTICE AND TECHNOLOGY

Unbundled legal services are both a surprising and unsurprising response to this phenomenon. More access to information and consumer-facing technologies restores power to those who need legal assistance. As a consequence, attorneys are leaning on discrete, limited scope representation to expand their market reach. Rather than engaging the client for the full spectrum of services, a client may only wish for assistance to review the documents they have drafted or provide limited legal advice.

Technology is shaping the way marginalized communities access legal help when they need it most. In 2017, the Legal Services Corporation conducted the Justice Gap study,[55] which brought to light some horrifying statistics; with one finding indicating that 86 percent of civil legal needs in the United States are going unmet or are inadequately served. If it wasn't clear already, that statistic put a spotlight on U.S. access to justice crisis, spawning an outpouring of support and creativity from the legal technology community.

The Legal Services Corporation has invested millions of dollars in technologies to expand legal services since 2000, making it a leader in access to justice-focused legal technology initiatives. But it really does take a village to make an impact on the accessibility crisis, and there are efforts to use technology to close the gap. Many legal technology companies are giving Legal Services Corporation grantees free or reduced cost access to their software. Others are focusing on using technology to build up a community of pro bono attorneys. All of this allows more people to be served with less time and resources, allowing legal service organizations to prioritize the most impactful work.

Overall, legal technologies are having a significant impact on all facets of the legal market. Commercial clients want more from their attorneys, and are showing resistance to paying for lower value copy-and-paste services. Individual consumers want to feel like they have the power to perform legal tasks that are simply mechanisms for existing in society. The status quo will no longer suffice, and each advancement carves out a new delivery model.

But be wary that some new models can lead to the unauthorized practice of law. Most attorneys agree there is a fine line between giving legal information and giving legal advice. Legal technologists grapple with this question every day.

COMPETENCY IN TECHNOLOGY

Relevant to our discussion on legal education, in 2012, the American Bar Association formally recognized the need for lawyers to have not just competence in the law, but technological competence. Rule 1.1, Comment 8 of the ABA's Model Rules of Professional Conduct states:

> To maintain the requisite knowledge and skill, a lawyer should keep abreast of changes in the law and its practice, *including the benefits and risks associated with relevant technology*, engage in continuing study and education and comply with all continuing legal education requirements to which the lawyer is subject.[56]

Anecdotes such as that of the Delaware attorney who botched his client's case thanks to numerous discovery errors, who proclaims, "I have to confess to this Court, I am not computer literate. I have not found presence in the cybernetic revolution. I need a secretary to help me turn on the computer," make it easy to understand why this amendment was necessary.

> As the legal tech movement enters the mainstream, attorneys must take the initiative to learn how technologies work and what tools are available to their specific practice area.
>
> In the future, failure to use commonplace technologies may affect their livelihood and ultimately push them out of the market.

As the court noted, "Professed technological incompetence is not an excuse for discovery misconduct."[57]

Most states have now adopted this amendment for their rules of professional conduct, with Florida taking a step further, adding three hours of required technology training as part of their annual CLE requirements. (See chapter 2.)

The easiest way to gain competence in this area is, of course, through CLE offerings from state or other bar associations. Other creative ways include working with a legal technology consultant who can help identify practice-specific technologies, or even self-study through online research or requesting demos of new or relevant products. Ultimately, if you feel that you reasonably do not have the skill to take on an engagement that requires extensive use of a technology or knowledge about how a certain technology works, the proper course of action is to engage with an advisor, or in some cases, decline the representation.

JOBS IN THE LEGAL MARKET

A common fear expressed by attorneys is that as more technology enters the market and replaces tasks, the relevance of and need for lawyers decreases. This is a somewhat rational fear for a subset of attorneys who find their day job comprised of repeatable tasks or form-filling exercises. Every day, there are new products and algorithms taking over tasks in nearly every aspect of the legal profession. Legal research and contract review can now be done in seconds or hours versus the days it traditionally took. On the other hand, as the market progresses and evolves, this fear is far from reality for most lawyers. The role of the "traditional" lawyer may shrink, but that can open the door to a flurry of other exciting and dynamic opportunities.

The onset of widespread technology acceptance and integration has naturally spawned a need for more tech-savvy folks inside the walls of law firms and legal departments. The growth of new professional niches for the tech-savvy twenty-first century lawyer is off to a running start. One emerging career track is that of the "legal solutions architect" or some variation of that title. In a law firm setting, these individuals are typically housed as their own team. In in-house legal departments, these individuals are likely embedded within the broader legal team, and work closely with attorneys, legal ops, and business owners who interact with the legal side of the business every day. These professionals live at the intersection of law practice and technology. They understand enough about the practice of law to know when technology can be helpful and can serve as a translator between the tech developer or provider and the attorney end user.

As legal services become a commodity, beyond the need for those who understand how the technology works, there's also a need for people who understand the *business* of law, and how and where technology can be leveraged as a true asset. And because technology and data go hand in hand, equally as important are those who understand the value of the data within a firm and how to best organize it. Legal ops and knowledge management professionals are skilled in just that.

MODEL OF COMPETENCY

Bringing visibility to the requisite skills of the twenty-first century lawyer is a cooperative comprised of the Legal RnD Program at Michigan State University College of Law, Northwestern Pritzker School of Law, and Thomson Reuters. Coined the "delta model of lawyer competency," the model outlines three types of skills every lawyer needs to succeed as the industry continues its fundamental transformation.[58]

The foundation of this model is, naturally, substantive legal knowledge and skills. Obviously, basic legal skills such as research and writing are essential to remaining competitive in the legal market. One side of the model, however, places emphasis on what the creators call "personal effectiveness skills." These are skills like communication, having a penchant for entrepreneurship, and emotional intelligence. Rounding out the delta framework are process, data, and technology skills. It is critical that attorneys remain curious about new technologies, understand data analytics and how to make data-driven decisions, and view their work through the lens of project management to be efficient and effective, and deliver more value to their clients.

It may seem overwhelming, but these skills can be learned with enough commitment to self-improvement. It is impossible for technology to solve every problem in the legal profession. It may even have some unintended negative consequences. However, with enough creativity and awareness, the profession dedicated to solving others people's problems can solve its own problems as well.

People, Process, Technology

Reviewing the conversations in the legal technology space reveals a heavy emphasis on the niche's unofficially official mantra: People, Process, and Technology. Each of these things are important in their own way in the practice of law and legal technology. But the order of this mantra has been proven time and time again as the most valuable feature.

As previously discussed, it's going to take a special type of person to succeed as a player in the twenty-first century legal field. Law firms and legal departments will best serve themselves by focusing efforts on training their own attorneys, as well as recruiting and retaining new employees with a proven track record of leveraging technology and process improvement in creative ways to push back against the status quo.

Beyond attracting top talent (who doesn't want that?), taking an inward look at pre-existing processes is the next critical step toward refocusing a law firm. Layering technology on top of inefficient processes only results in more headaches for the affected attorneys. This has shown to result in failure to adopt otherwise useful technology, as now it has only become an additional step, consuming valuable time and resources, and wasting all of the time and effort the firm invested into purchasing new technology and training employees on its use.

Only after (1) securing the right people, (2) critically assessing processes, and (3) removing or combining unnecessary steps is a legal team ready to deploy technology.

TECHNOLOGY IMPLEMENTATION

After a healthy battle to convince others that automation is necessary, a major challenge facing legal teams is technology implementation and adoption. Shifting the way people have done certain tasks for years or decades is not easy. Firms can spend thousands of dollars on evaluating internal processes, taking on new technologies, and training employees on their use. Nonetheless, without proper incentives and investment in change management, these efforts can fall flat, leading to frustration.

The dawn of this revolution had many firms and departments scrambling to flex their "innovation" muscles through the establishment of legal innovation hubs within their own firms. These innovation hubs are often separate groups within the firm that are in charge of innovation at that firm.

Some law firms have found success in this model. Those who used these teams as in-house process improvement specialists and project managers have thrived—and so have their bottom lines. What is interesting about their approach is that although these new types of roles are housed in a separate group, their work necessitates that each person dig deep and embed themselves with a practice team.

On the flip side, there are firms and departments that haven't been as effective at integrating new resources into their teams. Attorneys in these firms tend to view their new colleagues as a completely separate function: the people "responsible" for innovation within their firms. Ultimately, there is a failure for established attorneys to make a meaningful change in how they do their work.

One of the best ways that management can encourage change is by walking the walk, so to speak. Aligning attorney incentives with strategic goals is absolutely crucial to the success of these efforts. Some firms, while still operating within their traditional constraints, are experimenting with giving billable "credit" to attorneys who take the initiative to innovate and learn new technologies.

The early days of the legal technology revolution were filled with visions of a legal apocalypse—the end of lawyers and lawyering as we know it! Ironically, legal technology has come to mean that people—not technology—are a firm or department's biggest asset. The real value clients receive are intangibles like compassion, understanding, and strategy. Computers may never perform those functions, so it's crucial for attorneys to take stock in themselves and grow with the profession and its emerging resources.

Legal technology is certainly not about replacing lawyers; rather, it's about enabling them to do more, help more, and give more in the name of justice and the rule of law. The added bonus is that while doing more, technology enables attorneys to do less from a technical standpoint. Hopefully this will replace the drudgery and restore the joy of helping clients solve their problems, big and small.

In the end, take comfort in knowing that a robot lawyer is not coming for your job unless you let it.

CHAPTER 6

Women and Innovation: The Secret Weapon for Women to *Finally* Advance

***Note to reader**: This chapter contains some generalizations and broad statements, based on unscientific research I've gathered over the years. Although some points have specific citations, others are a summary of learnings, and some may be anecdotal from conversations with peers throughout my career.*

The year 2018 was a momentous year for women. From the boardroom to U.S. Congress, women in the United States lifted their voices in a historic year of victory and progress. But a different story occurred in the back halls of the legal profession.

Before diving into this chapter, take a mental stroll through your own law firm or the law firms you know. How many associate women colleagues do you have? Now, how about partner-level women? The numbers are bleak.[59]

More often than not, people performing this exercise will find that they are at least somewhat adequately surrounded by early-career women colleagues. The unfortunate reality is that according to the 2017 Report on Diversity in U.S. Law Firms,[60] women make up 45 percent of the associate population, but they only reach 20 percent of private-practice partnership positions across the United States. Women do have marginally more opportunity to lead in-house legal departments, where they hold approximately only about one-quarter of the coveted general counsel (GC) spots for Fortune 1000 companies.[61] Uninspiring, to say the least.

By now, I hope I have convinced you that the practice of law is drastically changing. Gone are the days where attorneys dictate all levels of their clients' outcomes. Technology and content marketing mean legal consumers are more informed than ever. The more educated clients become, the less willing they are to pay a premium for work that can be delegated to lower cost service providers and readily available technology solutions. This leaves them hungry for a strategic partner willing to go the extra mile to try new things.

As a new wave of empowerment meets a new wave of legal exploration and innovation, women are poised to lead the charge in changing the practice of law.

WHY WOMEN MAKE GREAT INNOVATORS*

Illustrating why women make excellent innovators begins by determining the answer to an obvious question: "What makes a great innovator?"

Defining "innovation" means identifying the qualities and characteristics that distinguish innovators from those who are comfortable grabbing the coattails of the bell curve. The simple definition is "making changes in something established, especially by introducing new methods, ideas, or products."[62] That's not extraordinarily helpful, but does shed light on a few qualities like comfort with ambiguity and the ability to be a visionary and strategist. In chapter 7, I dive deeper into innovation with practical examples. But basically—if you do something different in your practice—different than how most other lawyers do it—which results in real value to the business, that's innovation. So yes, the bar is still pretty low in our profession.

For the sake of conversation, design thinking is a widely accepted framework for innovation that can help us pin down more specific

> ***WARNING**
>
> *Although some parts of this chapter draw on research about the skills or characteristics common to women, please know that any lawyer can be innovative. The purpose of this chapter is to draw the attention of women lawyers who maybe have not considered this as a way to differentiate themselves. It can be a differentiator for any lawyer, but, hey, if it helps women get ahead, fantastic!*
>
> *Maybe this will actually work, after decades of trying other ways to advance us. Newsflash: being the "best litigator {or fill in the blank of your specialty}" simply won't cut it in the future.*

"innovative" human characteristics. The concept sets the stage for a six-phase (but iterative) process—Empathize; Define; Ideate; Prototype; Test; and Implement.

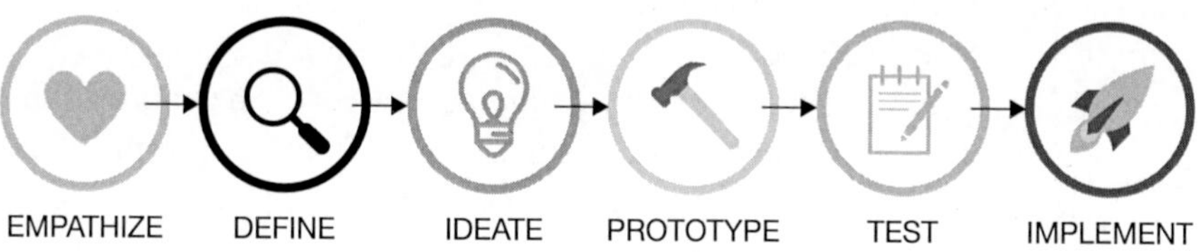

Shining a spotlight on each phase of the process illuminates the skills needed to become a transformative figure for an organization. A look at those skills shows that women really do have the secret weapon for making a change.

Empathize

In the "empathize" stage, innovators seek to understand—without preconceived notions. Through interviews, participation, and observation, innovators can get a grasp on the current state. This is a critical part of the process and serves as the foundation for any effective innovation. As you might imagine, this stage takes, well, a great deal of empathy. It also takes the willingness to experience some of the challenges and discomfort a team is facing firsthand.

Culturally, it's long been assumed that women were more "in tune" with others' emotions—more empathetic to what shapes people's behaviors. But beyond cultural expectations and anecdotes, the notion that women are more empathetic than men is scientifically proven. A 2018 study of 47,000 people found that women scored, on average, 10 points higher on an Emotional Quotient (EQ) test than their male counterparts.[63] This gives women an edge at the outset and can help set up an innovative project for success.

Define

Defining the problem that needs solving sounds innocuous but it's truly an art. It might be tempting to seek out the team member who complains about everything to help you identify your organization's problems.

Don't make that mistake, mostly because these people can be very convincing, and send people down expensive and ineffective rabbit holes. In contrast, in the define phase, true innovators seek to define the *real* problem by digging deep and looking for the root cause. They understand that often the "problems" they encounter daily are a symptom of something more significant.

For example, let's say your team struggles to meet turnaround times on a specific project or workflow. A surface-level view of the problem might lead to a surface-level solution: perhaps adding more human resources or even a technology solution. But a more intentional investigation into the root cause might reveal that the slowdown originates upstream. In that case, the more appropriate action might be to revise the processes already in place to address the issue—a much simpler and more cost-effective solution.

It's obvious that a failure to accurately define the problem has a cascading effect on the rest of the innovation process. Without a good grasp of the issues, the solutions that emerge from the ideation stage may be way off base. This will lead to a lot of wasted energy in prototyping and testing, and likely a failure of adoption once it's time to implement.

Because this stage requires a fundamental commitment to understanding *why* a pain point exists, an innovator needs a combination of empathy, curiosity, and a willingness to look beyond the first challenge that presents itself. As already mentioned, women lead the way in empathy. Their intuition and innate desire to ask "why" means they have the tools to develop a firm understanding of what really needs to change to improve outcomes. Even better, as excellent communicators, women can translate these frustrations into opportunities—a great skill for the next phase.

Ideate

Ideation is where much of the magic happens. Creativity is unleashed. Everything is worth considering. The notion of "no" is suspended, even if for a short period of time. It's the part of innovation that brings energy, hope, and excitement. It's also the part of innovation that can fall flat quickly without diversity of thought and experience.

Despite no credible scientific data or evidence, men are often perceived as more creative[64] than women—even by other women![65] The reality is that many studies are inconclusive or determine that neither sex has an edge over the other individually.

But women take the lead when facilitating diverse and productive conversations. Largely stemming from their own not-so-positive experiences in the workplace, women tend to have the aptitude to bring the right people together. And once they're there, women work diligently to make sure those people are heard in equal measure.

Time and again studies[66] show that companies that employ and play to the strengths of a diverse workforce solve problems better than their more homogenous counterparts. Enabling women to lead innovative efforts allows them to call upon their intimate experiences with systemic discrimination as a source of strength and creativity. It perpetuates a virtuous cycle of empowerment that leads to better team engagement and, ultimately, better solutions in the next phase.

Diversity by the Numbers

Diverse and inclusive companies are **180 percent** more likely to be **change ready** and **170 percent** more likely to be **innovation leaders** in their market.

Companies with above average diversity in their leadership teams report innovation revenues that are **73 percent higher** than those with below average diversity, and a nearly **10 percentage point increase** in earnings before interest and taxes margins.

Sources:

Sentence #1 source: https://joshbersin.com/2015/12/why-diversity-and-inclusion-will-be-a-top-priority-for-2016/

Sentence #2 source: https://www.bcg.com/publications/2018/how-diverse-leadership-teams-boost-innovation.aspx

Prototype and Test

Prototyping and testing often collapse into one stage of innovation. That's largely because the best prototypes are simple proofs of a concept or principle that are released into the wild and evaluated in real time. The goal is to quickly develop the solution(s) you've prioritized in the ideation phase and receive feedback from the community. What worked? What absolutely didn't work? Where are the gaps in the new process or tool?

This stage takes grit and the humility to accept failures, learn from them, and move forward with the next iteration. Some might feel that this part of the process is difficult for a lot of women to tackle. I say that only because for centuries, women have felt the pressure to reserve action until they are 100 percent confident in their likelihood of success. Accepting and learning from failures is not, generally speaking,

Beyond the Design Thinking Phases

Although it is convincing to review the phases and the skill sets women seem to possess that make them particularly qualified to be innovators, I like to look at what I see every day and what I've experienced. Women are multitaskers and efficiency seekers. We have to be. Many who balance work and life are expert innovators already. They have to get millions of things done, and they are pressured to get more done than their male counterparts who may carry a very light load of the family or household responsibilities, in addition to their careers.

Those who seek efficiencies are natural innovators. You need to be creative when there are not enough hours in the day, and not enough people to get all the work done. It is simple—those who pride themselves on getting sh#! done at work and at home (even if not perfect) are the ones we need to look to as future innovators. Being resourceful, leveraging others' skills, implementing multipurpose toolsets, and working in a community are natural to most working moms. So why not use those natural tendencies and skills to innovate at work?

the issue. It's pressing forward in the aftermath with the same confidence as before that brings on struggles for some. Unfortunately, these negative feelings have been engrained in women for so long that failure in this stage can be demoralizing.

So, perhaps there is an unwarranted, deep-seated toll that accompanies failure. The good news is that in innovation, failure is reasonably encouraged and certainly necessary. Especially in recent years, concepts like growth mindset made famous by Professor Carol Dweck from Stanford University, and embraced by Microsoft's CEO Satya Nadella,[67] encourage learning through failure rather than fearing failure. Women *do* have the extraordinary skill of adaptability[68] as evidenced throughout history and the changing roles that have been adopted by women, either by virtue of political climate, war, economic, and so on, often not by their own choice. Given the opportunity, women will rise to the occasion and prosper even in the face of challenges, or failures that come as part of the innovation process.

Implement

Getting it done. Without implementation, all that great ideation is of little value to business clients. Many hours of evaluation, planning, decision making, testing, and iteration must happen to get the right result.

The subsequent challenge of adoption and change management really puts things into perspective.

All the best-intentioned, creative solutioning, prototyping, and testing means nothing without adoption at scale. Doing this requires persistence, charisma, and a (sometimes hopelessly) optimistic outlook on people's willingness to modify their own behaviors. The ability to engage employees on a personal level and influence the way they tackle their work is a critical factor in a project's success.[69] Without that critical component, failure to adopt typically follows.

With another point on the scoreboard for women everywhere, Gallup research in 2015[70] found that women managers are better at engaging employees than their male colleagues. They're more likely to provide regular feedback, consider their teammates' opinions, and build a culture of transparency and inclusivity. They are teachers, facilitators, and champions. Perhaps most importantly, these simple qualities build trust between managers and their teams, providing unmatched influence.

For organizations looking to make strides in innovating the way they do business, this influence is a powerful tool.

SUPPORTING WOMEN AS INNOVATORS—OPPORTUNITY AND CULTURE

I hope you're sold on the idea that women can make innovation dreams a reality. There are two fundamental ways to enrich your department or practice by supporting women as innovators. The first—providing the direct opportunity—is the obvious approach. Beyond that, you should strive to build a culture that encourages innovative thinking, inclusivity, and experimentation.

Direct opportunities really are a great way to test the waters. However, as alluded to earlier, building a culture around innovation is a more effective long-term strategy. It's a strategy that allows the talent to self-select and rise to the occasion.

Culture-building is a significant undertaking that is not without challenges. It can make or break a company. Get it right and your team will thrive. Magical things can happen. Get it wrong, and resentment builds, productivity dives, and loyalty wanes. Innovative culture, specifically, is built on a foundation of respect, trust, and demonstrated confidence in your team. Layered on top of that foundation is an environment that values creativity, inclusivity, and smart risk-taking over the status quo.

Build this environment, and I guarantee that the women innovators on your team will naturally emerge. Part of it is driven by the security that such an environment provides. Since failure is virtually always an integral part of successful innovation, a culture of openness and trust is the greatest gift you can give a team because it encourages engagement with the process. Unfortunately, society has largely told women they need permission to do certain things, and the workplace is no exception. Build the culture that disregards that notion and instead emphasizes the freedom to experiment, have opinions, and lead change.

A statement stuck with me during a casual dinner with a peer in the legal industry. She casually said it when we talked about her role morphing into legal ops from a more traditional typical attorney role, over time. She said very simply, "I have the license to not be super cautious." Having a culture that encourages such a sentiment creates the platform for women to be more experimental and take chances.

An interesting observation I have made is that there is a significant number of women in legal operation roles, and serving as leaders in the legal ops industry groups. Prominent women leaders across various areas of legal ops have created and seized opportunity.

CONCLUSION (A.K.A. THE FINAL PITCH)

Attempting to breathe innovation into your team or department can at first be a bit overwhelming. There is so much "information" on innovation. Daily, you'll find articles on the amazing promise of AI, blockchain, process improvement, and so on. It is often difficult to see the true signal through the noise and focus on what actually gets you where you want to go. It's important to remember that those articles, newsletters, and webinars offer *solutions* and tell a good story, but they don't address your specific problems. It's reckless to buy into the hype and take on a project if there is uncertainty about the problem and the solution. Instead of working backwards, meet problems where they exist by finding someone on the team possessing the qualities that make them a catalyst for real change.

Reflecting on the innovation process and the skills required to succeed reveals a few key themes. Find someone on the team who embodies these characteristics, and you're on your way to make magic happen.

Innovators—Including Women— Are Curious and Thrive in Ambiguity

There's often anxiety around tackling a new and innovative project. Will this project strain the team for precious resources? Will all of this effort be worth it in the long-run? What if we fail? Do we really need to do this? Most of the time, that anxiety is a necessary byproduct of charting inherently unfamiliar territory. To that end, successful innovators handle ambiguity with confidence and grace. They face each challenge head on with confidence, optimism, and decisiveness.

That's not to say they should have the answer to everything. Rather, they're intensely curious, and aggressively pursue the valuable information needed to make sound decisions—to thrive in ambiguity. They leverage their team and network to better understand not just the problem, but what those affected by the problem might like to see in a solution. This curiosity, of course, gives them an edge over others who may simply offer solutions at face value. Even more than that, it helps create buy-in at the early stages, making people feel that they are heard and that their personal experiences are part of the equation.

Innovators—Including Women— Can Multitask, Prioritize, and See the Bigger Picture

Pushing a new initiative forward can be a little tricky. It's not always easy to keep the eye on the prize, especially when other day-to-day work functions take precedence. For some, finding the mental space for innovation can just become another "fire" to put out—a chore even. When everything in this person's world is on fire, it's unlikely that there's time to reflect on *why* things are the way they are and divert effort into fixing those issues. And directives to take on new projects can lead to half-baked or off-base results.

For others, innovative projects kindle their personal evolution. These efforts give them the energy and excitement they need to balance their current workload while developing and implementing new skills and tools that will eventually become mainstream. They are innately motivated by the future. Importantly, they don't let this motivation interfere with the work that needs to be done. It takes great attention to detail and the ability to see the forest for the trees.

This tension between the present and future means innovative team members are amazing multitaskers that can visualize the future, fill in the gaps, and act. This leads to my next point. . . .

Innovators—Including Women—Have a Bias for Experimentation

Many people are familiar with the concept of "bias for action." You know who those people are on your team, and often rely on them when the going gets tough. Certainly, for innovative projects to take flight, someone is needed at the helm who has a bias for action. But for real change to take hold, you need to find someone who has a bias for *experimentation.* It's easy to justify the status quo when there's nothing inherently "wrong" with the way you're doing things—it is even comforting. The wrong leader might find the reason a project shouldn't go forward. But the right one will find 1,000 reasons it *should.*

Someone with the bias for experimentation is a great team member, and brings an extra bonus to the regular, everyday rock star. Naturally, they have that bias for action. The difference is that it's also paired with a fearlessness to try new things in the face of failure.

Not every project or effort undertaken is destined for resounding success. Some people are more comfortable acting on obvious or logical extensions of the current state. It's easy, comfortable, and a necessary part of any job. There's not much risk involved. As we discussed at length earlier in this chapter, however, failure is simply part of the innovation process. The right leader will be OK with calculating that risk and experimenting when it makes sense. They have a mental toughness to keep trying without taking every loss personally. Every failure is simply a new bit of information that does indeed get you closer to the ultimate goal.

In Sum

The best advice I can give is to *take action.* Volumes of literature lead to the same conclusion—nothing new ever gets done unless you go for it. Innovation is not a single thing, but rather a collection of thoughtful experimentations that move the needle forward. Creating a welcoming culture where experimenting is truly welcomed and rewarded will enable the kind of foundation that true innovators need to flourish.

The human element of innovation is what really counts. *Successful* innovation is dependent on how well it is cultivated and executed. Execution is closely tied to the qualities of the person leading that work. And so it follows that you should be sure you have the right people in place to make good things happen.

The good news is that you likely already have access to capable women ready to lead you into the future.

PART III

Just Enough on the Key Topics That Every Lawyer Needs to Know

CHAPTER 7

Talking Points on Each Topic

The purpose of this book is to provide practicing attorneys with a simple view of what they need to know about what's happening to the practice of law. The prior chapters provided some background and deeper insights into the legal industry, while this part of the book really focuses on the key points. What should every lawyer know today to provide the greatest value to their clients, regardless of what type of law they practice or for which clients they work? My goal is to empower every reader to be able to speak on these topics at a high level and inspire their clients and peers to think about new ways of delivering legal services.

I picked a list of the key concepts[71] that every lawyer should be familiar with. I have devoted a subchapter to each one. If you read no further, or have not read much until this point, then you're in luck. This introduction is the summary of what you need to know. I envisioned this short reading before all the other content grew around it to make a whole book. Lawyers have limited time to read outside of their required reading for their subject matter expertise, so I hope this summary gives enough to whet the appetite and inspire further exploration.

1. Definition of Innovation

There is no one definition. Doing something different today than what has been done before in a way that brings greater value for the client is innovation. The bar for this definition is quite low in the legal profession. Using technology does mean it is innovative, if the technology has been around for decades and you are only now getting around to it. Basic tech (like eBilling and word processing) is table stakes these days.

2. Project Management

Much of what lawyers do every day is project management. Many don't realize that they are managing projects, but in fact, tracking tasks and deadlines with multiple documents and stakeholders, where there is a clear end goal in sight, is project management. There are better ways of doing that than many lawyers realize. Some simple tactics and templates can make a notable impact and improvement.

3. Process and Efficiencies

Thinking about the legal practice as a series of takes inside a process is still a difficult perspective to accept for most lawyers. Granted, not all legal practice can be reduced to process steps, but many areas of legal practice can be mapped and improved. A process map demonstrates "how" work is done in a visually consumable way, making it obvious where improvements can be made. Everyone has too much work with not enough time. As in-house teams strive to become more efficient, law firms must keep up to deliver legal services more efficiently.

4. Automation

Legal technology is exploding and creates so much opportunity to be more efficient, but it is not the cure-all. In fact, it can create more problems if not implemented properly after optimizing processes. There are many options in the market and selection must be made very carefully only after processes have been optimized and resources have been properly aligned. Perhaps the greatest impact on the legal ecosystem is the conversation that the legal tech explosion has started. And if implemented successfully, can be a real game-changer.

5. Value and the Law Firm Managed Service Model

Driving down the price of legal services is old news. It is not about getting discounts off of law firm rack rates or preventing annual hourly increases. Real value comes when law firms deliver related services and data insights about the legal work. Quality legal advice and deliverables are table stakes, but workflow, metrics, and some basic automation can take the law firm engagement with its corporate clients to an entirely different level—the level that solves the ultimate corporate/business problems (rather than just addressing legal issues).

6. Alternative Legal Service Providers

Delivery of legal services by providers other than law firms is becoming more common across most legal departments. As they continue to climb up the value chain and challenge the definition of the practice of law, they provide great value for certain types of legal work. They have now firmly established their place as a key player in the legal ecosystem and a necessary part of the corporate legal department resource model. Regardless of what they are called, they are definitely no longer "alternative" legal service providers (LSPs).

7. Data

It's all about data. Every law firm is sitting on tons of it. Every legal department is craving more of it. To benefit from automation and the potential that artificial intelligence (AI) has to offer, data must be available and consumable. It already exists in unstructured forms in many systems, and investments must be made to extract the valuable insights that are hidden within. Data can be used to optimize processes, to support additional resources, to increase efficiencies, and most importantly to justify change.

8. Modern Legal Workforce

The legal workforce is changing for a number of reasons. Tech-savvy millennials are joining traditional law firms with expectations of purpose and flexibility in how they work. Future legal leaders within law firms are recognizing the need to enhance the legal services their firms are providing. Business professionals are being embraced by the law firms and their skills are being sought out by corporate business clients. The modern legal workforce is made up of legal and business professionals coming together to deliver more holistic services.

9. Outsourcing Legal

Sending work to law firms by playing ping pong with documents is not optimal and there are lessons we can learn from the outsourcing of other business functions. Let's leverage what we know about outsourcing IT or finance, and apply those principles to legal services, and, yes, to law firms. Transitioning from a traditional engagement model to an optimized managed service mode of outsourcing takes planning and time, but it is well worth it if done properly for the right kind of legal work.

10. Corporate Legal Spend Management

Most law firm associates have minimal knowledge on the financial mechanics of a law firm. As they become partners they must learn certain aspects, even those partners who have minimal insights into how legal departments manage their outside counsel spend. It is all a connected loop of financial dependencies (inputs and outputs) and if law firms could understand more about corporate legal departments' budgeting processes (to the extent they exist) and philosophies on legal spend, they could be that much more effective in how they pitch work and manage engagements.

NEED TO KNOW #1: DEFINITION OF INNOVATIONS[72]

> "I have no idea what this innovation stuff is about. We have a group dedicated to it, but I don't know what to do with them. My clients keep asking for change, but I don't know where to start." —***Partner at Global AmLaw 50 Firm***

I realized that something was terribly wrong when some of the brightest lawyers I know, partners at very prestigious law firms, would make comments that demonstrated a complete lack of understanding about what innovative practice is or can be. It is not a lack of interest necessarily, but definitely a lack of general awareness.

It is overwhelming to take in all that is happening across the legal industry. The amount of change is unprecedented, and the pace is faster than ever, as it should be. The explosion of legal tech alone is impossible to keep up with. So, how is a law firm lawyer, buried under the billable hour demands, supposed to engage in creative conversations with clients if they are not quite sure what to say about "innovation?" What does it really mean to be innovative? As I explained earlier in the book, the simple definition of innovation is "making changes in something established, especially by introducing new methods, ideas, or products."[73]

I suggest that anything a lawyer does that deviates from "We've always done it this way" frame of mind is defined as innovative. That leaves a world of opportunity for lawyers to innovate their practice. Much of what lawyers do is the way they've always done it and the way they were taught to do it by other lawyers who've always "done it that way," too.

So, let's keep things simple. If a lawyer decides to deliver service in a different way, let's call that lawyer innovative. The reality is that we have a shortage of innovative lawyers, regardless of how broadly the term is defined. Lawyers with some basic ancillary skills that they leverage to enhance their clients' experience are exactly the types of lawyers the legal industry needs. These lawyers represent the needs of today's market. In fact, to be spicier, I have a name for them: unicorn lawyers. Why unicorn? It is a mystical and mythical creature that always leaves a lasting impression.

Areas Ripe for Innovation

Whether practicing in-house or at a law firm, certain aspects of the work in the legal ecosystem are so ripe for innovation that it is becoming unacceptable to keep doing things the same old way.

1. *Responding to client questions*

Every in-house lawyer handles a deluge of questions. In fact, one of the biggest distractions from getting "regular lawyer work" done (such as the many contracts that cross their desks or the research that needs to be analyzed) is responding to questions from business "clients." In-house attorneys easily bond over the shared frustration of repeat questions coming from their clients—often the same questions from the same clients! The time it takes for attorneys to stop what they are doing to answer a question, and then refocus on the task at hand, can easily be reduced with a few simple changes. Similarly, the time it takes to get the insights needed from the client to start work on the client's request is often just cycles of emails and waiting for responses. It can be frustrating and lawyers often want to scream, "Help me help you!" to their clients.

One way to reduce this kind of friction is to create an *intake form*, such as the form on the next page. In the lowest tech sense, it can be a document that is sent to the client in response to an initial email. If the email shows patterns of similar questions you've answered before, but the answers need to be customized, a simple intake form with a few questions that will help inform a more accurate answer is an easy first step. This way, with one exchange of emails, there will be a more organized and holistic set of initial information to enable more effective responses.

Further steps are to create a *list of frequently asked questions* (FAQs). The FAQs should be easily accessible to the clients, or easily retrievable by the attorney to send in response to recurring questions. If there is an opportunity to innovate, certainly in an era of AI, there are some fairly simple tools available that can build a basic bot-like experience by feeding it a robust list of FAQs. That still may be a little far-fetched for many in-house IT resources, but an easily accessible set of FAQs can be created. If you can find a place where clients naturally go for information on the company intranet (or law firm extranet ideally), then you can post questions there. A law firm can be a great enabler for their in-house clients by identifying FAQs based on the work they are seeing and providing it to their client (free, of course)

FAQs

1. Where can I find a template contract?
2. Am I allowed to sign a personal NDA?
3. Who reviews my marketing materials?
4. Can I attend a conference and give out swag?

Contracting Help
New Request Intake Form

General Information

Request Title* [Ex: SOW Template Help]

Requester's Location: [ ]

Requester's Name: [ ]

Company Code: [ ]

Department Contact: [ ]

Is this related to an existing request? ○ Yes ○ No

Is this related to a strategic contract? ○ Yes ○ No

I need to*:

- ☐ Approve, sign, & store
- ☐ Find a contract
- ☐ Store a contract
- ☐ Get a contract signed and stored
- ☐ Get a contract reviewed
- ☐ Get a contract template
- ☐ Ask a contracting question
- ☐ Update a contract record
- ☐ Other (please describe):

as a bonus piece of collateral. This is a great way to be an extension of the internal legal team and really create that continuum between in-house counsel and an outside law firm. Another option is to *insert an intermediary as a triage center* into the questions coming in. By creating a simple email alias managed by either a group of paralegals or other business professionals, certain questions are answerable before they get to the attorneys, or without sending them to attorneys at all. This will require some training and documentation of those same FAQs, but can be more effective since often there is a resistance by clients to reading even the best crafted FAQs, unfortunately. So, if creating an intermediary saves attorney time and gets answers to the business, then that is a win for everyone.

A final example of innovation in the front office is the use of *legal project management*. Legal project management is no different from basic project management (PM), but it is the application of PM basics to the practice of law that makes it interesting. Basically, if attorneys accepted that many of the functions they do are actually projects, then the application of PM principles is much more obvious and the legal profession would seek the help of PMs with more urgency. Once an attorney experiences working with a professional project manager, it is hard to go back to working without a PM's help.

Those are examples that may not seem like rocket science, because none of this *is* rocket science. (Although perhaps a really capable bot is!) Most of these examples are about reviewing the steps in a lawyer's day job and then thinking about how to have someone else do them, ideally at a lower cost. Even if cost savings are not attainable, undoubtedly, time savings are just as valuable for most attorneys.

2. *Contracting*

This topic gets extra attention because *every* company has contracts and *every* legal department struggles to keep up with contract volume.

Contracting is an area that attracts attention in the legal ops and technology evolution that is occurring. Every company and every law firm must deal with contracts. Any general practice legal firm will engage in some aspect of commercial transactions. Every company, to make money and engage with its customers, has to have contracts. So, contracting is basically a sleeping giant that is legal in nature

> Contracting is a great example where operational efficiencies and an operations mindset are starting to take over in the practice of law. Contracting is where attorneys spend much of their time providing legal advice in the context of contract negotiations, editing, redlining terms, and risk analysis.

with a big operational aspect that crosses into the back office of legal service delivery.

It is also in a unique place because contracting crosses into the back office of legal service delivery, which is related to infrastructure and foundational areas where technology is used, for instance, in managing documents, information, and billing processes. As discussed in chapter 2, those are the behind-the-scenes processes of the practicing lawyer.

Legal technologists can and should focus on contracting. In litigation, for example, legal technologists went through a similar evolution with electronic discovery. It's an area that has bridged the gap of operation and efficiency in the back office by showing how litigation was managed and processes were handled by shifting the work done by junior attorneys, for example, in reviewing documents and preparing for discovery. First, that work was outsourced to less expensive resources. Then automation became an option and that sort of work is automated to a very large extent these days. Contracting is undergoing a similar evolution and is a great example of many different capabilities of the legal ops function.

The desire to innovate is different for attorneys in law firms that have built up a financially rewarding practice through large volumes of contracts. In-house, the perspective is very different. Corporate legal departments have something in common because they all deal with contracts. They share the same feeling that there are too many contracts and not enough time to deal with them. Sometimes contract volume is so high that even a combination of internal lawyers and law firm support is not enough to meet the needs of the business. That situation, where the business feels lawyers are taking too long, and where the legal department already thinks it is spending too much money on external law firms to help support the volume of contracts, is the right scenario to take immediate action and try a drastic change.

A non-disclosure agreement (NDA) is the most common type of contract to start the innovation journey. Often, NDAs are basic templates and repeatable. NDAs are often the first step in any business-to-business relationship, and a necessary part of the engagement. The good news is that both sides are usually equally interested in getting the NDA completed, making it slightly easier to try something new. Experimentation with NDAs can come in many forms—automation, outsourcing, and business self-help, to name a few.

A simple first step is to create templates for NDAs and applicable playbooks (guides on negotiation and fallback provisions), working through the acceptable negotiated positions. That playbook can be used to empower business leaders to handle certain negotiations on their own. If that is not a viable solution, replacing in-house lawyers with lower cost resources should be. Consider handing off NDA negotiations to people who have other transferrable skills that can be leveraged.

Or consider establishing a relationship with an outsourced group of lower cost resources, whether attorneys in international locations, or onshore resources who are not practicing attorneys. The first step in this process is to accept the risk that negotiations will not always go exactly as in-house attorneys may plan, but by setting the right parameters with a good set of templates, there is little risk to assume. The benefits of time or cost savings significantly outweigh any perceived risks.

To be clear, I am not only suggesting, but actually encouraging, lawyers to allow work to be performed in a less than perfect way. A colleague of mine has taught me to ask "is the juice worth the squeeze?" Meaning, is it really worth it to burden high-cost resources with low-risk work? The work is by definition low-risk, so what if a few of those transactions are suboptimal? What is the real risk?

In short, the front office is ripe for innovation, and it can learn a lot from the back office. Doing things faster is key for everyone in-house. Although automation is a top-of-mind issue, innovation can happen in many other ways that do not necessarily require technology. The real key is to accept some risk and want to do things differently.

All good ideas, *but* . . .

Who Is Responsible for Innovating?

Innovation is getting a bad reputation because it has become such a buzzword in the legal industry. That is not fair, because it really is the right word for what the legal industry needs. Every practicing lawyer should be re-envisioning their practice and modifying it to be more modern and responsive to client needs.

The word, however, has taken on a life of its own—especially in the law firm environment. Now, people have "innovation" in their titles. There are strategies and mission statements focusing on innovation.

There are events and activities with innovation as the theme. It is not clear when innovation became a stand-alone concept, and no longer part of continuous improvement of our craft. It has taken on a mysterious meaning, something overwhelming for the regular practicing lawyers to grasp.

On one hand, it is exciting to see that there are positions created with a specific focus on innovating the practice. It seems like things are moving in the right direction. On the other hand, the reality is that law firm practitioners now have someone they can point to who is responsible for innovation, and that means they are excused from worrying about "that stuff." After all, it is in the title for that other person. So, at client pitches, there is someone to bring along who can talk about what the firm is doing to innovate, and someone to tap when responding to RFPs. It can't and shouldn't be that way, but somehow it feels that way. Lawyers are often confused about their own firms' innovation projects and resources, even as those resources continue to grow and expand, arguably increasing the capabilities of the firms' lawyers.

Sadly, very few firms have tangible rewards or measurable standards for innovation. Attorneys have few accountability measures besides the billable hour and a few other metrics related to tracking time (pro bono, committee service, client development). With the clarity and ease of tracking hours toward goals and hefty rewards, why would an attorney try to change how he or she works? Particularly when that way of working has been so successful for so long. The answer is simple, but not obvious. Client needs are changing and to retain clients or get new ones, practices must evolve. That's why law firms are hiring people whose job is to focus on innovation.

With experienced people in place at well-resourced firms, it is logical that innovation will follow. Unfortunately, that is not necessarily the case. The reality is that even where there are specified champions for the cause, progress is slow. Progress is hindered by the practicing lawyers, the day-to-day billing attorneys who are deeply wedded to their current ways of working and delivering services. They have not been educated on how to engage new innovation champions or how their contributions can benefit the clients. There is still a disconnect. Even with these tremendous (and expensive) resources at law firms, most of the relationship lawyers are still underusing these new skillsets. The innovation leaders often feel frustrated and find the firm's goals to be unachievable without the engagement of the practitioners.

There is a lot of excitement about these innovation leaders, which is great for forcing the right conversations. The reality though is that their ability to make an impact is still very much dependent on the culture of the law firm. Unlike the role of a managing partner, which is fairly predictable (though personal styles vary wildly!) and common across law firms, the innovation role's success is completely driven by the collective culture of the practice leaders of the firms. Those rainmakers still hold significant control over how the firms' resources are allocated, and guess what—innovation takes resources.

If the practicing lawyers don't focus on change, and those tasked with enabling change have trouble convincing the practicing lawyers, who is left? Sadly, at law firms, that leaves few people who can really encourage the changes needed to delight their clients. Perhaps it is up to the clients to drive the innovation? Yes and no. Corporate legal departments who hold the purse strings arguably have the greatest power to encourage changes at their law firms, but it is not right to excuse the firms from innovating and rely on the corporate legal departments.

Law firms can play a unique and pivotal role in revolutionizing legal service delivery. They should already be thinking about changing how they practice and deliver services, as they move to become more profitable while keeping their clients' bills flat. Firms have been feeling billing pressure for years from their clients and from the increasing number of alternative legal service providers (ALSPs). By responding to that pressure, those firms that are already on the cutting edge of innovation have another role to play in this evolution. They can be leaders in the eyes of their clients, rather than responders. Innovative firms can pull their clients along, because firms won't change unless their clients demand change.

Although that is generally true, there is an alternate perspective: firms that independently lead the way can become a catalyst for change in their clients' organizations.

Reversing the premise, let's say that legal departments won't make changes until their law firms start to deliver services differently. I've heard from some very creative law firms that their clients are not ready for change. The firms are willing, eager, and able (a critical element) to deliver differently, but the clients are not biting. I was surprised at this because

I assumed all in-house legal teams are ready for an evolution in legal services, but it turns out not everyone is. So, in those instances where clients are not pushing law firms to change, law firms can push, or encourage, clients to change.

So why is that? How can it be that in-house legal departments are not ready for this new world? After all, every in-house attorney is buried with work that never lets up. So how come some in-house teams are not open to trying new forms of engagements? Well, it is as simple as not knowing any differently or not having the time to step back and think through the possibilities; that is easy to fix: They should *ask* for help.[74]

Most in-house attorneys come from the very same law firms that we now expect to drastically change their delivery of services. The move in-house does not magically transform the thinking or approach that the former law firm lawyers have. If the need to be more efficient does not prompt the desire to innovate, then a nudge from a trusted advisor at a trusted firm may be exactly what is needed to get the ball rolling.

Law firms are in a position to become leaders by counseling their in-house clients through the evolution of the legal industry. The people at the firms who are doing critical legal work for their corporate clients hold valuable information about the work they do for their clients, but they don't yet realize the power that data has. Yes, in-house teams hire firms to perform a service, but sometimes the in-house teams don't even know what to ask for beyond the specific legal advice or transaction. Law firms can and should offer ideas on how to do things better, more efficiently, and more effectively. It's true that some in-house clients are not ready for change, and some firms are also not ready. For the firms that are ready, they should find in-house clients that are ready and do innovation magic together. Jointly discuss opportunities not just for more work for outside counsel, but opportunities to really change *how* services are delivered and *which* services are being delivered. The evolution does not have to be systematic; people can drive small changes every day. It takes curiosity and courage, but every person involved in the legal ecosystem can impact change.

Despite the challenges within the firms, firms are obligated to offer their clients new and creative solutions, especially to old, well-defined problems. If the firms are waiting for the clients to push them, and the corporate clients are waiting for their firms to come up with creative suggestions, nothing much will happen.

Special Note on Legal Tech and Innovation

Luckily other players in the ecosystem are creating great incentives for innovation. Meanwhile, legal tech is forcing a broader discussion about innovation in legal services. Tech gets lots of credit for bringing the innovation, but it is doing more than that. It is sparking curiosity. As pressure mounts on law firms from the law tech startups and cloud solution providers that are turning their attention to the legal industry, the desire to innovate—specifically to automate—is growing. Legal technology is proving to be a great catalyst for change in the legal industry. The pace of legal tech advancements is certainly unprecedented, and the areas of legal work being automated are expanding daily. Even if the technology is not quite ready for prime time, it is doing a great job of forcing conversations between law firms and their clients. It is raising curiosity and interest in the possibilities of automation.

Legal tech advancements are making lawyers begin to wonder which parts of their work can be automated. Some may be fearful that automation will take over their work, and there is plenty of sensational press on that topic. Others realize there is better use of their time if some of the more predictable work can be offloaded to technology.

There is a big chasm between being curious and actually embracing technology. Still, even with that gap, legal tech is inspiring the right conversations. Even if lawyers aren't considering how to automate their own work, they may consider how to be more effective in some of the more administrative aspects of their work.

Firms Can Innovate NOW

Innovation takes many shapes. Given that legal is so traditional and slow to change, when a law firm does something different from what it has done in the past, by bringing in some aspect of technology or automation, consider that innovation. For example, using an online system for time-keeping instead of paper time sheets was a step in the right direction. Automating invoicing, using word processing technology, and document management systems are all advances that by now are common, but at one point were innovative. Now innovation is moving into the front office, and more directly impacting the lawyers' work.

If not directly impacting the lawyering work, law firms should be using legal tech to engage with clients more effectively. Law firms are responsible for making sure that the engagement is proceeding most efficiently and effectively.

There are a few easy steps that every law firm lawyer can do to demonstrate their willingness to innovate:

- **Use the Data You Already Have.** Law firms hold an incredible amount of valuable data about the work they do for their corporate clients. It is amazing how much value a client will derive from some basic data points. How many memos/contracts/pleadings/and so on did Firm X create for Client Y in any given period? How many times did the same contract provision get negotiated in the contracts that Firm X handled for Client Y? Deliver this information in a nice, consumable format, with some easy-to-read visuals, and clients will be delighted, asking for more.
- **Pre-empt Recurring Engagement Problems.** When law firms deal with clients over and over, they not only get to know the in-house lawyers who request the work, but also get to know lots of the business people who engage with the in-house lawyers. In fact, the law firms become quite familiar with the repeat "customers"—the business people who repeatedly seek advice at the last minute, or repeatedly start with the wrong contract template. If there are repeat engagement issues that the law firm identifies, then the in-house team should know about it. Firms can bring business client issues to the in-house team's attention along with a proposal on how those problems can be solved. Firms can suggest training the business or creating materials for the in-house team to use to train the business. Creating self-help guidance that encourages self-sufficiency in the business will be very much appreciated by the in-house legal team. Yes, it is potentially lost revenue for the firms, but the value created will surely be rewarded with more work in the future and deeper engagement.
- **Suggest Even the Slightest Process Improvements.** Never mind Six Sigma belt colors. Don't worry about Post-it notes and process maps. I am talking about the basics. The way the engagement flows between Firm X and Client Y is usually organic and follows general communication patterns: inquiry via email or call, response in the same medium, back and forth until the final deliverable results in an invoice to the client.

  A few small tweaks in the engagement process can make each side much more effective. For example, if the firm seems to always ask the same sort of questions at the start of certain engagements, why not provide those questions in advance to the client? If the client becomes accustomed to providing these "intake" details at the start, the firm will get to work faster and with less back and forth. As for delivering the work product, why not put it on a shared online platform, so that the client has easy access to it and it can be refreshed as needed? Even if the client only accesses it once, the fact that the firm offered delivery via an online collaboration site demonstrates a genuine interest to innovate.

These suggestions are focused on improving the engagement experience. But even these suggestions require the practicing lawyers to embrace new concepts to discuss them with clients. Right now, most lawyers, busy with billing hours, are overwhelmed by the amount of legal industry news coming to their inbox. It is hard to sift through what is real and what is hype. The previous examples are pragmatic and easy to try. Most lawyers, however, are not comfortable talking about data or process because they have not been trained on how it applies to their work, nor have most of them worked with these capabilities in practice. Lawyers don't need to be experts in these skill sets, but they *must* be familiar with them.

Creating the Opportunity to Innovate

Providing the direct opportunity to innovate is a great way to make an immediate impact. Every manager has a list of new ideas or initiatives they'd like to try "when the time is right." We all know the right time never comes. So instead of pushing it off a few more days, weeks, months, or years, give someone on your team the opportunity to create the future for you. Allow a stretch goal. Make sure the reward for such experimentation is clearly articulated and understood.

To get what you want, start by defining goals. What outcome do you want: a shorter turnaround time on contract review? An increase in deal volume month over month? Decreased spending for a specific workflow? Faster answers for clients? More visibility into workload? Whatever it is, make sure the goal is clear so you can empirically evaluate the project's effectiveness.

Present this challenging project to those in your organization who have shared an interest in innovation, or who need a new opportunity to shine. Selecting a project leader comes with its own challenges. Selecting an "innovative" one, even more so. Refer to the discussion about the design thinking process in chapter 5. By creating such opportunities for those within your organization who possess the qualities required to bring an innovative vision to life, culture will naturally evolve in the right direction.

NEED TO KNOW #2: PROJECT MANAGEMENT

We know legal ops is a combination of many different functions. One of the most important functions is legal project management. The use of project management is on the rise and has been for years. It's been around probably the longest of all the functions, so there is a vast amount of information about project management. There are legal project management certifications, programs, specializations, and universities. Entire study programs and educational products are available.[75]

So, it is a well-established topic, but it's still interesting how rarely it is implemented regularly. Some places and certain firms specialize in it, but it is more likely found in corporate in-house departments as one of the underlying functions of the legal department. It is still not common. Project management is not a part of the DNA of legal services—at least as of yet.

Legal project management can be applied to almost any law practice. Much of what lawyers do day to day is not actual practice of law, but some form of project management. Tasks like gathering documents, planning meetings, organizing research, updating clients, and tracking their time (yes, time tracking!) are all aspects of project management. The real challenge is that most lawyers don't identify it as such and continue to think of it as part of their legal work. Well, it isn't actually core legal work at all. More importantly, it is work that can be performed by other people that are more skilled at project management. This gives attorneys more space to focus on core legal work.

Defining Project Management for Lawyers

You may be asking, "what does project management have to do with the practice of law?" Or secretly wondering "what is legal project management?" To answer, we've got to look at the more important question—what is a project? A project is something that has a beginning, a middle, and an end. It produces an agreed upon, deliverable set of outcomes. It is really quite basic. Why is that definition important?

For those who are familiar with project management and program management and the differences between the two, it is important to understand that not everything is a project.

Down to the basics, just about any part of your day job can fall into the definition of a project. This is an easy way to view it when you start thinking about segmenting work or segmenting the different parts of the day that one wants to focus on or drive efficiencies in.

Remember, if it has a beginning and an end then it is likely some sort of a project.

Now what makes it legal project management? Answering that question is also quite simple. Legal project management applies generic concepts in a legal setting. Otherwise, it is just basic project management. It requires a bit of modification of the terminology that you use and slight tweaks in engagement. Stakeholders are included who are possibly slightly different than those outside of the legal community, but the core concepts are the same. Make sure not to get overwhelmed by the concept. It really is just project management applied in a legal setting. That is the best part. And that is what every lawyer gets hooked on once they get a taste of it, and a great project manager provides project certainty and stability.

The Power of Project Management and Pitfalls to Avoid

Good management provides clarity around these key attributes of every project: *scope, cost, time,* and the *general plan.*

There is nothing more frustrating than not knowing what you are getting into—that means there is no project management. Once there is project management, it is the complete opposite experience and feeling. You suddenly feel empowered because you have an abundance of information that allows you to go into the project with eyes wide open, knowing the scope, the estimated costs, the timeline, and a general plan.

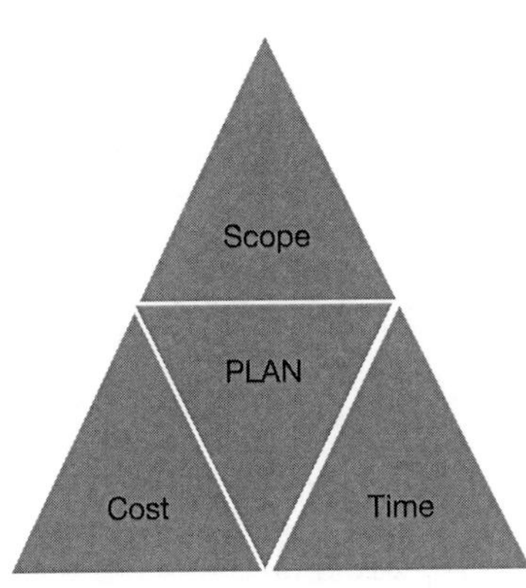

Now, some things should set off some alarm bells. One of them is *scope creep.*[76] I heard this term years ago when I first started engaging with project managers. This is a project manager's worst nightmare. Savvy business owners and stakeholders who know about scope creep know how to prepare for and prevent it. So the best way to avoid it is to know very, very clearly what is "out of scope" and stick firmly to that.

It is always tempting to expand the scope. I'll use remodeling the house as a project as an example of scope creep. In the beginning, the project is just to remodel the bathroom. Once this project starts you realize where the bathroom floor connects with the hallway, and you think, "gosh, it would really look nicer if we also did the floor in the hallway." Is it necessary? No. Can your contractor do it in a way that is appealing and aesthetically pleasant to look at? Absolutely. But since they are already here maybe the floor guy will give you a deal and the next thing you know you are redoing the flooring in the hallway. Then of course the wall colors in the hallway don't look right because you weren't planning to change the flooring and so on, and so on. That is precisely the definition of scope creep. This happens all of the time in our personal lives, and our work lives are also susceptible. So, the lesson here is to go in with a hard line of what is absolutely out of scope and stick to it.

The best way to avoid scope creep is to have a clearly defined *goal*. Remember *why* the project was launched, and don't move the goal post! Unfortunately that is a common experience. But goals can change as events and business happen, and you can't always control the actions of your counterparty, so some degree of flexibility around goals is good. For example, expect unexpected expenses. That sounds a little crazy, but you should expect unexpected expenses because they happen. A good project manager will keep tight control of expenses so there won't be any surprises when the invoice comes. Project managers are skilled at finding ways to balance and mitigate expenses in other places to try to get savings.

But sometimes unseen costs are unavoidable; there is potential for an unexpected expense to creep up on a manager. Try to be psychologically prepared for the fact that it might happen and what can be done to mitigate—it is not an option to go above and beyond the budget.

Good project management ensures that you don't go beyond budget. So, expenses are within the project; sometimes there won't be enough on one part of the project, so start thinking about how to recover savings somewhere else.

As for time management, there also might have to be adjustments during the course of the project. Think about the home remodel example. Everyone knows that contractors almost never end on time and that they are in the house forever. Good and informed project management should prevent and mitigate that inevitability. Prepare for time to slip a bit, and have some contingency planning for what that might mean. Hopefully

Plan B will not have to be implemented, but good project management means always having a contingency.

So invest time to define project scope, to map out the budget as carefully as possible, and to plan the timeline of the deliverables so that surprises are avoided beyond the ones that may happen anyway.

Project Management Is Only the Beginning

With all that in mind, you are ready to actually *plan*. You are ready to define project scope and purpose. Now you know: Planning the project is key, and it takes time. Without good planning, the project just can't be successful. Put in the investment to define the timelines, activities, and stakeholders. But it doesn't end there.

Change management is its own discipline entirely and should be contemplated in almost every part of legal project management because, well, there is a lot of change that needs to happen in the legal industry. That is what is happening: change. And how you manage that change often helps define at least the perception of whether the project was successful. That's because, even if by all accounts and measures your project might have been successful on paper, if there are a lot of dissatisfied people, in the end it will not be perceived as successful.

One final concept to emphasize is the post-mortem. This comes after the project has ended. Truthfully, as lawyers, we don't regularly stop and look back on how something went. It is very enlightening to check back on how something transpired. In every good project there should be a post-mortem. There is always a lesson or lessons to be learned. One of the most valuable parts of doing a post-mortem is what comes out of the lessons learned because you know not to repeat those same mistakes again.

> So, you have preplanned, you have started your project, and now you are executing. With execution, you are constantly monitoring and measuring. Are you on time? Are you on budget? Are you going to be successful based on the goals you set out at the beginning?
>
> Constant assessment needs to happen. And if you need to make some changes in the course, better to do it in live time with all of the stakeholders clearly articulating and communicating why the changes need to be made. Then reset expectations and manage that change. Be on top of that change.

The main goals of the post-mortem exercise are:

1. Review what went particularly well, which establishes a best practice for future projects.
2. Review what did not go well and consider what could have been done differently for a better result.
3. Review the communications and feedback received throughout the project from stakeholders. Consider soliciting specific feedback from key participants in the project who were impacted by the project team's efforts.

I can't underestimate the importance of doing a thorough post-mortem review on the completed project.

Core Concepts

Every project should start with a *charter.*[77] The words "charter," overview, or summary, are terms that get used in similar ways. It comes down to how the project template is designed and what different fields are needed to address to raise attention to the specific parts of the project requiring attention and input by you and from other interested parties.

Some basic things are always present in every project charter. First and foremost is the *project overview.* Actually, the entire charter could be seen as the overview. But this gets into semantics; it is better to think about what is best in your environment and within your group of colleagues, your corporate culture, and your firm's culture.

It's not about the words. It is about making sure it is easy to orient people new to the project so they can quickly get an understanding of what it is about, especially if it is a new idea or new project. It's important that the charter is easy to follow for anyone who is unfamiliar with the project, general project management tools, templates, or documents.

> Charters typically have these sections:
>
> - Project Overview
> - Scope
> - Issues
> - Risks
> - Assumptions
> - Stakeholders
> - Budget/Cost
> - Timelines/Milestones

The project overview is the most obvious place to start and should answer the "what" and "why" questions: Why is this project taking place? Why are we spending time on it? Why did we decide to do this? What are the benefits? Why did we embark on this? Every project requires resources; go in with the mindset of knowing that to run any project, somebody's time or money will be allocated. Therefore, the overview has to be convincing or at least very clear—one that will immediately grab the reader's attention. Once you move on from the "why" of the project, think about why the project is necessary. What is the ultimate goal and purpose for doing this project? What is the ultimate outcome you want to gain?

Scope is a small word but it is an important part of the project charter and the overall project. What are the boundaries that will be addressed within the project? Just as important, what is out of bounds (or scope)? In a project charter, it is often just as important to describe what is out of scope as what is in scope. The same charter document is sometimes divided, as "in scope" and "out of scope," especially if there is a propensity for things to turn into something else or go beyond the specifics of the overview. If that is the case, put out of scope into its own subsection.

What's the difference between a risk and an issue?

Risks *are events that MAY occur.*

Issues *are known events that exist.*

If you are planning an outdoor wedding in Seattle, a ***risk*** is that it may rain. If the venue has no covered area, then the ***issue*** is that there is no option for coverage if it rains.

So what's an *assumption* (sometimes paired with a dependency)?

Once you are aware of the risks and known issues, it is good practice to list out all of the events/occurrences that are required for the project to be successful.

In our example, an assumption would be that the venue can procure a tent from a third party, which would create a dependency on the venue to fulfill that need once the risk of rain becomes a known issue.

Then put together a list of *assumptions, issues,* and *risks*. I placed them together because there is no right or wrong way to write up a charter. Let's rephrase: There is a wrong way if a lot of key elements are missed. But the words used and what is important in a particular project will vary every time. But assumptions, risks, and issues are somewhat interrelated. Sometimes they are also confusing, especially for people unfamiliar with the terms and nuanced differences.

Let's review the terms. An *assumption* is something that is taken for granted. Some contracts come with assumptions in the documents. It is important to state assumptions up front, depending on the risks that might come if they aren't listed. A risk is something that might happen or something that there is concern about potentially happening. It is a good time to write it down if it is an assumption also. Listing an assumption also can potentially lead to listing a risk or vice versa.

Next you'll want to ask: Who are the *stakeholders* in the project? Although this may not be the time or place to list all of the stakeholders, depending on how large and complex the project is, the significant roles or the significant players in the decision-making process of the project should be noted. So, you should be answering questions like, who is the business sponsor of the project? Who is the executive sponsor and do you need that? Who is perhaps responsible for making the ultimate decision? Who is responsible for the budgetary costs? Whose business or practice group is most impacted or whose group is the driver for all of this? Depending on the project, this is a key part of the checklist.

At this point there should also be an estimate of *costs* and *timelines*. These are rough estimates. The project hasn't really begun because a part of the project includes the planning, details, timelines, and cost estimates. As part of planning for the project, charter research is necessary and due diligence needs to be performed to provide a cost estimate. Also enter assumptions and risks that might change the cost estimate as the project goes on but keep it on budget and on time.

Another useful consideration for timeline and budget is thinking about the *approach* to the project. What do I mean by approach? You can give some sentiment or

A GOOD PROJECT PLAN:

Stakeholders and the RACI model (responsible, accountable, consulted, informed): Who are the interested parties and what are their roles?

Timeline and milestones dates: When must certain steps be completed and deliverables provided?

Technology platform: Where do you manage all the project documents?

Communications, report outs: How are others informed and updated?

Meeting cadence: How often are there meetings, and for which purposes, with whom in attendance?

Project plan: What is the overall schedule of key activities and necessary general information?

Budget: How much will the project cost? How is it tracking?

perspective on the cultural aspects of how the project should unfold. Will the approach be rigid or report-based project management where a very strict cadence of frequent updates is followed? Or will there be a more fluid approach where meetings are set as needed and updates held as needed, and stakeholders are moved in and out of the project?

This is likely not a critical part of the charter and there are so many varieties of project charters that one has to pick one that works. A ton of options are available online and through courses.

Moving from the charter, which is one document and the key first deliverable at the beginning of any project, let's get a bit philosophical. Let's move to some higher or more general thinking around project management and the core concepts that are the elements of every project.

I've mentioned stakeholders and how a list of some of the key people involved in the project charter is needed. But now it is time to widen the lens. Assuming the project is approved to kick off and go live, taking time to understand the impacted players is one of the key benefits that a great project manager brings to the team. And until the manager has that experience, it is hard to realize how valuable it is. But knowing who the project impacts will help inform what the change management is for the project. In short, address early on how the change will impact the outcome of the project itself. Similarly, along the lines of thinking about the people who are impacted or those whose inputs and approvals are needed, is moving in a step lower than aligning them into some form of a responsibility matrix.[78]

It is commonly referred to as RACI, which shows who is **R**esponsible and **A**ccountable and should be **C**onsulted or **I**nformed about each task, but there are different versions and formats.

> It is very important to keep people updated on the status of the project and the progress. Did we hit any roadblocks? Did any issues come up? Did any risks become realized and turn into now known issues? A clearly articulated cadence for informing people about the progress of the project is a key concept for every project.

The purpose of that exercise is to take the step of aligning all the people that you have identified as stakeholders, more than the list on the original charter, but the full list of stakeholders in the project. So it includes pretty much anybody, any group of people who can be impacted by the project. They then must be aligned as to whether they are responsible or accountable, and whether they need to be consulted or whether they simply need to be kept in the loop.

One of the biggest challenges with projects is to work through the changes and the communications, and to think through the impacts. How you communicate to all of the different interested stakeholders is about communicating the changes, the specific communications about the impacts to them. But generally, one of the key things the project manager does is plan—not the actual change the project is trying to implement—but the communications about the project itself.

It is critical to create a *timeline* for the project, along with timelines for key parts of the project. These include the events and things that need to occur that aren't necessarily related to the management of the project, but the substantive work of the project itself.

Note about Project Management Technology

The technology platform is another consideration, depending on how large the project is, how complex, and how many players or stakeholders are involved. Answer these questions: Do you need a technology platform to manage a project? Do you need to collaborate electronically, or to store documents and retrieve them electronically, or to push out communications because there is such a large number of people involved? Do you need something that helps you track tasks? Are there thousands of tasks to be tracked or are there just twelve tasks, for example?

So, depending on the complexity there are different types of technology platforms that can help; some are more complex than others and it is important to figure out what is really needed because you don't want to overcomplicate things. That's also a risk. It is necessary to be thorough, but don't cross the line into over-engineering because it becomes a tax on people to stay involved with the platform; so consider more traditional forms of communicating and collaborating.

I mentioned meeting cadences earlier as a part of the *communication process*. It is very important to understand which meetings are necessary, how often, and what kind of updates are needed at those meetings as opposed to a general report out to a communication medium such as email. But it is important to understand who should be there. Is in-person preferable? Is in-person possible? Maybe do video, or is eye-to-eye contact needed? Having an extra touch to your project success could hinge on face-to-face communications depending on the cultures you're dealing with and the culture of the companies themselves.

All of these things are documented in your *project plan*. The project plan is the uber, uber, uber set of all the things mentioned. For those of us who aren't expert project managers, or certified project managers, when we hear "plan," we are more task-oriented and about our plan of attack and how we're going to accomplish things. But really, from a technical perspective, the project plan is the entire compilation of all of these things that we just reviewed.

PROGRAM MANAGEMENT

I've discussed project management, some basics, and the key principles that are involved in it, so now let's touch on another important component of the project management discipline: *program management*. Project and program management are often used interchangeably. It's exciting that anybody uses any kind of project or program management in the context of legal work, but these are very different terms with very different implications.

The main difference is that program management is an ongoing set of processes. Unlike a project, which you'll recall has a beginning and end, programs don't end unless they are formally terminated. A program is a generic term for a series of recurring processes that are run in a consistent way. There is usually a goal that is stated and checked; they are updated to track the progress toward those goals. Another way to view it is as an operation. That is a bit more technical because there are more aspects to an operation than there are in a program, but the concepts are similar. So, you should start thinking of anything that is an ongoing set of recurring processes as a program, not a project.

What program management has that is highly important is *governance*. The program is run by somebody. There are a set of rules and boundaries of what is or is not allowed, and what is or is not covered by the program. Who are the people who are playing key roles? These aren't roles that come and go, these are the people who are doing their day jobs and are dedicated to an ongoing set of processes. Think about a program as having different projects within it.

Financial management is critical to a program, and this is where it starts to be more of a business operation. What are the program costs? It is just as important to manage a program within budget and to its goals, as it is to make sure there is financial responsibility in how the program is operated.

Infrastructure is also critical with more complex programs. Is there a program office? Is there a team that is organized around the program? Are there different types of technologies that may be included in or a part of the program? Again, it is really thinking of it as its own little business.

And then there is planning that needs to happen for the program to be successful. Programs aren't just born—they must be organized and documented. There should be a program plan, and not just a traditional plan. Although it often carries the feel and concepts that are in a project plan, remember they are applied with an ongoing mentality and should contemplate strategy, efficacy, and longevity.

Program management is very common in corporations, more common than in law firms. Law firms should note that in the case of marketing programs, each event is its own project. Each key marketing activity has a start and an end, but combining all of them together makes it a program.

There are many examples where individual projects actually become a program. When firms apply similar expectations and common approaches to a marketing or recruitment program, it becomes a little easier to assess and compare successes in programs that are different in nature, but at the same time are managed similarly.

Real Applications of Legal Project Management

1. Alternative Fee Arrangements

To do a really good alternative fee arrangement (AFA) you have to have good project management. I don't know if that is a natural connection for many people. What is it about an AFA, which is really just a pricing model, that lends itself well to leveraging program and project management?

Planning an AFA is one thing. Let's assume that it is a project where the scope of work must be assessed and priced out. Project management principles are a natural tool, since your main concerns are hours, billables, and breaking it all down to make sure it's a profitable engagement that's also valuable to the client. But really once the AFA has started, a program is starting.

It is a program and not a project anymore because often AFAs are for an ongoing set of services. Ongoing services mean program management is appropriate. This now is an engagement between a law firm and an in-house team or a client group that have come together to receive and deliver services in a different way. Whether it is a big piece of discovery that needs to be done, or a global research project that needs to be done, there's an ongoing business relationship (program) that's made up of all of these different components (projects).

Managing *costs and resources* are key project management fundamentals for AFAs as well. IT enables careful allocation of resources: managing and tracking to defined timelines for key deliverables; sticking to a budget; and leveraging the most capable and appropriate resources. An AFA is the perfect test of how good program or project management is at a firm: delivering on an AFA in a way that is profitable to the firm and delivers the value that the client receives.

2. Litigation

Another practical application is in the *litigation space*. There are two areas that are in common regarding timelines and deadlines, and thus advantaged by true project management: document management and stakeholder management. In a litigation matter, so much is about documents, where they go and when they go, and how to access them when you need them. As most lawyers know, much of litigation is about tracking documents, mainly regarding the sharing and storing of documents that need to be shared as part of the project. Project management principles can tremendously help you stay on track.

Another potential project in litigation is maintaining *contact information for stakeholders*, including lists of parties and people and what their roles are. This helps in managing the costs and expenses of litigation, and keeping all parties as happy as they possibly could be in litigation.

If you are just managing your litigation in a more traditional lawyer approach mentality without project management, it is almost guaranteed that there will be no coordinated documentation in a way that is easily accessible to parties. The information is probably stored in the attorney's head. There is not even clear documentation of the various steps that need to be taken.

But each step is taken organically because an attorney might know that is the next step without really thinking through a timeline and creating a real plan. The attorney is basically engaging in project management through the creation of a project plan, so litigation is a great and common example.

3. Contract Negotiations

Project management also proves to be very valuable in contract negotiations. For those who are transactional lawyers or who have been involved in transactions: Every negotiation that lasts a couple of rounds of back and forth is in fact a project. It starts, as you know, when a negotiation kicks off and ends with a signature!

So, consider tracking the documents and their versions. Schedule calls and meetings, and keep everybody on track and on time and make sure they know who the decision makers are. All of these administrative tasks are part of managing the project. A good project plan has the repeatable calls already set up on the calendar. It has agendas for each call. And notes are taken and shared after each call. So that kind of rigor and hygiene really creates a much smoother negotiating experience for both parties.

I described earlier the post-mortem for a project, but imagine if in every negotiation there is a post-mortem internally, and maybe even with the other party as well. This element is especially useful if you are negotiating with the same party on a recurring basis where there are common opposing sides.

Even if you do not go that far, think internally if you are dealing with multiple people when you have a negotiation. For example, are you bringing in experts or do you have a contract manager or a business stakeholder? Getting together after a negotiation to know what could have gone better is such a critical lesson learned that we only really acquire from thinking through it as good project management hygiene. The project finished. How did it go? This is something we should start doing regularly. We should always look at a post-mortem in any large project.

In Short

Project management and program management are common to almost every other industry. And fortunately this is an area where great progress has been made in legal in the last two decades. In fact, legal project management has become so popular that there are entire day-long courses on the subject. It is often used synonymously for legal ops, which is unfortunate, but at least it is being recognized as necessary in the common practice areas described already.

I don't expect lawyers to sit through lengthy legal project management training (at least not longer than an hour or two, maybe), nor would I do it myself. I do, however, recommend that all lawyers gain an appreciation for what project management can do for their particular practice area. I am a firm believer that every legal practice area can benefit from project management. In fact, I can't imagine any area of the firm's practice that could argue it was not valuable. Sadly, many practicing lawyers look at project management as an administrative lower-level task; this is a misconception that must change.

NEED TO KNOW #3: PROCESS AND EFFICIENCIES[79]

At a time when the legal industry is going through unprecedented change, it is no surprise that many attorneys still don't appreciate the role that process plays in the legal practice.

Process Stigma

Is the practice of law a special, unique craft? Some attorneys think so. They don't think it can be reduced to a process that they see as associated with other disciplines such as engineering or business operations. By calling something a process, some attorneys say it makes their work less meaningful, or less impactful, or that the work does not require intellectual aptitude. Those beliefs are simply not true. Although there is craft in the practice of law that requires deep analysis and judgment, many aspects of it are amenable to process review and optimization.

It is long past time to train attorneys—new and old—to identify the parts of their practice that should be improved and made more efficient. But although the practice of law generally focuses on work that requires unique expertise and training, it is not entirely obvious how process fits in.

The way to contradict this "process stigma" is to demonstrate with basic data and logical analysis how certain functions of the attorney's day job can be broken down into some process steps and how some of the steps can be completed faster.

> *Lawyer down the hall: "Don't you just do that process stuff now?"*
>
> *Operationally minded lawyer: "I do 20,000 contracts a year on a 1.2-day turn-around time. How many do you do?"*

> *A cautionary word about speed and efficiency: For those law firm attorneys who have not yet embraced the alternative fee arrangement and continue to bill by the hour, completing work faster can seem contradictory to the firm's goals. This is a core issue with the current model of hourly law firm services. On deeper analysis, once alternative fees are embraced, it is precisely the efficiency lever that will yield greater profits while revenues may stay flat. Efficiency and speed are the key to increasing profitability for law firms.*

A Simple Example

Process is part of every legal practice at its most basic level. Every lawyer receives work somehow, whether by email, intake portal, phone call, and so on. Those simple, seemingly passive actions, where work lands on the desk of the attorney, are the first steps in the process. For illustrative purposes, I've created the flowchart that follows of the process for supporting commercial contracts (**Figure 7-1**).

Looking at the chart from left to right, it's sort of a decision-making guide. It is not rocket science, but it is something that should be done proactively. It should be done mindfully as opposed to how often we find ourselves working, which is way too reactionary. We react to the incoming work, which comes in at a fast pace and in high volume. An obligation to do something is felt. Attorneys especially feel an obligation to do what lands on their desk because that's what they are there to do—to help the client.

There are other ways to approach it. Sometimes it takes a bit of stopping, stepping back, thinking outside the box, and then taking some smart risks. It might mean some difficult conversations with the client about the work because resources are always limited. After going through a prioritization exercise and the allocation of work—done on an ongoing basis—a complexity matrix and risk matrix can help with these decisions. Think of each step as a decision point where choices are made.

So, once the work comes in, decide whether it is work that needs to be done or not done at all. That's a very big question and a tough one because the instinct is if somebody comes in seeking help, how can I turn them away? Is there a higher or greater value that a law firm can offer to an in-house team by saying, "You know, I'd love to do this work, but I don't know if this is actually necessary work." There is an opportunity at this point to drive a completely different conversation about value.

A decision to "stop doing" is one of the hardest that any attorney can make. It takes a lot of confidence and it takes a very strong relationship

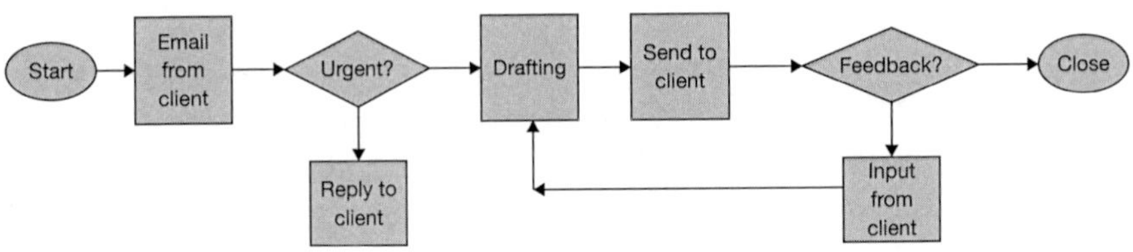

Figure 7-1. *Flowchart*

with the business, whether it's an internal business, the client, or a law firm in a corporate client relationship. But once there is a decision to stop doing, other things should happen. For example, there's probably some client education that needs to happen. Some self-help should be provided, some guidance, materials, things that say, "Hey, while the legal team isn't going to do this work anymore, your businesses actually are enabled and empowered to do this and here's some materials to work through to get that done."

> **Self-Help Note**
>
> As the overwhelming volume of work flows onto the desks of in-house counsel, it is hard to stop and make the time to find recurring patterns of questions or escalations from the business clients. Law firms who are deeply integrated with their clients can be a source of self-help content for the in-house legal team. Law firms should offer their in-house clients assistance to identify opportunities to help enable the business clients, and share that burden with the in-house legal team.

Putting that aside, let's assume we're sticking with the path that says, "You know what, this work must be done. Perhaps it must be done by some legal professional, or maybe it can be done by empowering the business client. Regardless, it actually needs to be done."

At this point, the obvious thing to do is decide whether it needs to be done by an attorney, or whether it can be done by another legal professional. That's a complicated concept because by legal professional, what I mean is a professional who is within the legal spectrum of services. Could this be an alternative service provider? It could be a good contract manager, a great paralegal, an intellectual property (IP) expert, or a patent engineer. It could be a variety of professionals who make up parts of a full legal team but who have a subject matter expertise in the specific kind of work you're trying to accomplish.

It's not necessary that a lawyer does it, so that's one of the big decisions to make.

The flow chart can apply to a request to write a cease and desist letter or another deliverable requested by a client. This is basic, but helps to set the stage of how to help lawyers think of their work as a process. In this flow, it is immediately obvious where the attorney's highest and greatest value is: drafting. It can take quite a bit of back and forth before the actual drafting begins to get the full picture of what the client wants to accomplish. Those loops, which would have appeared between the "urgent" decision diamond and the "drafting" box, are not reflected in the diagram.

Another point in which the attorney plays a key role is deciding if the request is urgent. One may think that the requestor is responsible for making that determination, but that is only partially true. My experience is that most requestors would rather call something urgent than not. Otherwise they risk being deprioritized, and the work getting assigned to a legal "black hole." Accordingly, this decision requires a judgment by an attorney as to whether the request really is urgent. Arguably, except for determining urgency and then drafting, other parts of the process could be handled by someone else. Perhaps some steps could be automated.

Let's dissect that.

Disaggregation of a Legal Process

There is a reason that LPO was born about twenty years ago, and largely in India. There was the notion that certain parts of the legal work were in fact process steps, which could be separated from the core legal analysis, judgment, or decision making that are the best use of an attorney's time. Someone other than the attorney who had initially received the work could perform the process steps. Because these steps were not providing legal advice or otherwise practicing law, it was more accurate to call it a legal process. The outsourcing of such processes became quite common for high-volume practice areas such as discovery in litigation, or document review in mergers and acquisitions (M&A). LPO functions slowly began to move up the value chain closer to traditional legal work. At the same time automation began to impact some of the highest volume, repeatable work—hence the rise of e-discovery tools and systems.

Returning to the example, there are several steps in the process where a lower-cost resource—not necessarily a lawyer in India, but perhaps a paralegal contract manager in a low-cost region of the United States—could handle parts of an engagement with the client. The alternative resource can triage the request and gather the needed details of the transaction the business is trying to accomplish. Similarly, that resource can dig a little deeper to gather the facts that will help the attorney assess the urgency of the request, by asking a similar series of questions of the requestor that will help provide parameters and perspective on urgency. This enabler can also gather feedback from the client after the attorney sends the initial draft, and coordinate changes.

Finally, the entire finalization and closing of the request can be handled by someone other than an attorney. Arguably, that step can be handled by yet another person, who is less experienced (and a less costly resource) than the one doing the triage and feedback gathering.

Automation of Certain Processes

In any process, the many steps involved are often a subprocess or micro process. Anything that has more than a few steps can become its own process. The intake of a request from a client can be a subprocess on its own, assuming there is some information gathering before the attorney starts the work. A subprocess like that can be automated, thus circumventing the need for anyone on the legal side to get involved until all of the intake information has been extracted from the requestor.

By reviewing the data related to the requests received historically, it is highly probable that the intake process can be pared down to a series of questions that the requestor can answer. The requestor can receive the questions via an online form, with some choices and drop-down ideas that will help channel the requestor in the right direction. With a robust online intake form, the attorney steps into the case only once all of the information is gathered. Similarly, the question of urgency can be assessed through an automated process, where the series of questions will provide that determination, rather than simply asking the requestor, who likely will want it "yesterday."

By using online collaboration tools, such as OneDrive, Google Drive, and Dropbox, and other similar tools, the feedback loop can be handled far more quickly, without the risk of people being out of office and losing time waiting for the loops of questions and answers. Online collaboration also allows for real-time resolution of questions, especially when the questions require simple answers or clarification. Online collaboration is not an automation of the process, but a great example where technology plays a key role in creating efficiencies in a process that otherwise could take much longer.

By optimizing the process of serving a client for a contracting need, it is broken down into parts and then aligned with the most effective resources. Through a combination of alternative staffing and automation, the attorney could spend time on only the highest value part of the work that requires specific legal training. Other parts of the process don't require a lawyer to step in. Yet, attorneys are so used to providing the entire service that they do not pause to assess the process.

Admitting that a good portion of an attorney's day-to-day work is a process is the first step to recovery. If it is mappable, capable of being broken down into discrete parts, and easily reviewed for efficiencies, it is a process.

Process Mapping Exercises

It is hard to slow down to go faster, but that is exactly what many practices and engagements need to do. Attorneys should find a way to pause to assess if things can be done better and more efficiently. This exercise is actually quite simple, though it sounds daunting at first. It is a simple exercise of mapping the current process. Any good project manager can typically help facilitate this sort of exercise.

By taking time to verbally describe the steps of a piece of work or engagement, and visually placing those steps into a process chart of some kind, attorneys can quickly identify opportunities for improvement. Redundancies jump out. Suboptimal allocation of resources become quite evident. Bringing in different players in the process also helps ensure that steps aren't forgotten, and all of this increases collaboration.

A valuable exercise that clients will no doubt appreciate is to schedule a process discussion about the engagement. Law firm lawyers should spend time with their clients mapping how the work travels from the originating business owner or client, through the legal in-house team, and then to the law firm. There is always opportunity to make it smoother and faster. Imagine the number of emails and attachments that flow between those three parties, which can actually be a dozen or more people involved in such an engagement process. By just mapping how the work is initiated by clients, there can be very informative discussions that will shed light on improvements.

> *A simple process mapping exercise can signal to clients that law firm lawyers understand the benefits of process improvement and are investing in these activities and skill sets for the ultimate goal of improving the legal services.*

Prioritizing the Work

Once processes are mapped and opportunities are identified, a prioritization exercise needs to happen. This is an exercise that can be done together by law firms and their clients to create a seamless virtual extension of the legal service provider

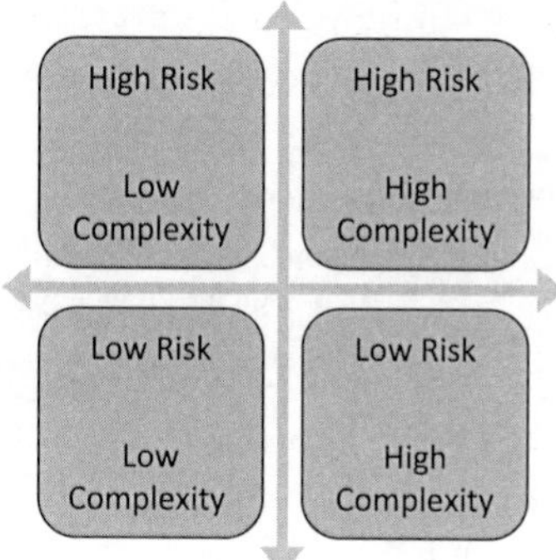

Figure 7-2. *Matrix for Prioritizing Work*

to the client. There could be work that the business client should be able to transmit directly to the external service provider (that is, a law firm) without even stopping on the desk of the in-house legal team. This is one of the more complex processes to arrange, but it's very important. And it does take a bit of a stop-and-think approach, meaning it will likely take time out of your day to put the work that the department is doing in various buckets. This matrix (**Figure 7-2**) works for me in prioritizing work.

The matrix is a fairly common version. There are many types, so think about what makes sense for the department—if you're in-house, or if you're a firm advising a client. It has to make sense for that particular scenario and the culture of the group or company involved. Risk and complexity are two good levers that help firms think about resource allocation.

High risk, high complexity work on the upper right-hand corner is the perfect kind of thing that top internal legal resources should handle (or the most expensive people, if the work is being handled by a law firm).

The matrix is a fantastic exercise that should be revisited regularly, because it is a tool to use for the prioritization exercise. It is worth taking the time to do because it is valuable when considering the resources, and what type of resources to allocate.

Optimize Resource Allocation

Once the prioritization work is done, there's often a reallocation. This just means that some portion of the work is pushed to different resources. In some cases, it actually has not been done for a while and other work is taking its place because resources are always limited. Think about how you can accomplish your goals and work with creative and strategic resource allocation. Reallocation of the work should always be based on what was prioritized.

Similar to what I discussed in "stop doing," there's also an opportunity to empower the business where there is work that needs to be done. For example, it might be a contract that needs to be done. The company needs to have a contract in place, but *just because the company needs to have it in place does not mean that an attorney has to do it.* Somebody else can take the task of filling out the contract, sending it along to the other side, and potentially even negotiating it.

There are options. Let's break down each one and what that means in terms of the further choices that need to be made. Once there is a determination that an attorney needs to do the work, the big question is, "Is it one of the internal attorneys or should it be sent to external resources?" If you're in-house, the work might have to go external because the subject matter expertise may not reside in-house. If you're in the law firm environment, perhaps a certain piece of work should be handled by a different professional. In either case, the costs are very different; it all comes down to a budget and that includes bandwidth and skill sets.

The root question is: is it really legal advice that's being provided? Or can this work be done more cheaply with a different professional or ALSP? This is where the line starts getting somewhat gray. For one, ALSPs don't go to court. They can't represent clients in court. But there are many steps they can do that attorneys are doing, and they are just as capable of doing those tasks—they may actually have people that are experienced lawyers.

They aren't under the umbrella of a law firm where they're authorized to practice law. Consider procuring the services of not just a law firm, but also the services of ALSPs. Possibly it's an attorney staffing company, and there are licensed attorneys who are authorized to practice law in the way that a staffing company is incorporated. Think about the way that the internal team will oversee that work and technically be the ones practicing law. You can be creative by going external, even if you need an attorney, and still not have to rely on the traditional law firm model.

Now, if you say, "You know what, we actually don't need an attorney to do this, we just need somebody who's really skilled and capable at this subject or this topic or this issue." Then opt for other legal professionals, such as a good contract manager to negotiate a contract. Could a really good business analyst do this negotiation of this contract? Is there an expert in

IP who can assess the benefits or the issues with this litigation matter over a license, or a disagreement about a license? Those professionals could be internal depending on the size of the company or firm and the types of skill sets available, or you can go external, in which case you really are most likely going to use an ALSP.

If the decision is that there is no need for an attorney, the work can be done by somebody else or with some other sets of skills; this is common, for example, in contract negotiation. It's a very common, logical step to have an external provider do overflow work. Maybe you just need a second set of eyes with a good depth of experience, not necessarily legal skills, to do that work.

Decisions are available at every point in the process. They hopefully are made mindfully and proactively so the organization can stop and assess the right work and see if it needs to be done.

Is it the right work? Is the work being done by the right resource?

Monitoring + Continuous Improvement

After that exercise is complete, shift your mindset to monitoring. You always are watching how it's going; you've reprioritized, you've reallocated—well, how is it going? By learning and assessing how it's going, you may notice that adjustments might be needed. And after adjusting, it's time to review if that was the right adjustment. Then the cycle starts again. It's a very logical approach, and it seems natural, but these are the kinds of thoughts that should be going through every leader's mind when they're inside a legal environment with a significant staff.

So, think about improvement and reallocation as a continuous loop. It's not an exercise that should be done in a vacuum that requires you to stop your day job and stop your work to focus on it. It is something that should be done on a natural cycle to the extent possible.

Continuous improvement is a process engineering concept that should not be underestimated and should always be applied to law firm engagements. It sounds generic and something everyone should be doing. We should always be continuously improving, because it's a core facet of efficiencies.

To assess if a change is actually an improvement, there must be a baseline of how things are working in the current state. That baseline is grounded in some sort of data point. A common data point that is useful for everyone is understanding the time some steps in the process take to complete. The timeliness of legal support is always a point of concern for clients, and understanding how long things take in the current state is a great metric to track as improvements are made.

Conclusion

There is no easy way to get to the best and most efficient process. It is constant tweaking and assessing, learning from what's been happening to make it better going forward. Measure how things are going now to test how they will get better after processes are changed. Creating a data-driven culture and driving decisions based on data is a core facet of what it means to have an operationally efficient engagement. Data and the ability to make a decision based on an objective or an empirical set of information as opposed to a very subjective or anecdotal set of information is critical. Not only does it create a sort of a baseline or a common set of information that people can ground themselves in, but it instantly creates credibility because it turns new initiatives based on opinions or conjecture into fact.

A fact is a fact and it's very hard to argue with certain facts, especially when they are reflected in key data points. So, driving decisions based on data creates a credibility in the operation that is necessary if companies want to push the envelope and create new efficiencies and processes, and manage change.

NEED TO KNOW #4: AUTOMATION[80]

When people talk about innovation in legal services, they often confuse it interchangeably with legal technology. They are not one and the same. Technology is one aspect of innovation.

The legal industry has come far but still has far to go with legal tech and especially automation of functions and services. Automation is happening and it is happening in various parts of the legal industry.

The pressure to automate is compounded by the fact that there is so much discussion about technology that people are skipping over the importance of process optimization and efficient resource allocation. People and process are the most important and first steps that need to happen before any automation can occur. Automation exists to help enable the most optimized processes run by the right people, the right resources, the right skill sets, and functions. But there is no magic button; automation can't be the answer until you spend time understanding processes and whether the right resources are allocated to running those processes.

Nevertheless, automation is an obvious goal when thinking about innovation and efficiency. No doubt, automation is a way to become more efficient. It only works if processes are first optimized. The best processes enable the automation. Don't automate a bad process, because that incentivizes more bad behavior.

The hype and excitement around technology is forcing a much bigger discussion about innovation and for that we can all be very grateful. Technology is critical and I am a big proponent of anything that can possibly be automated.

But a word of caution: Law firms should not jump to automation before they are ready. Still what is happening is real: Investments in legal tech have skyrocketed, with over $1.6 billion in 2018 alone—up from just $233 million in 2017.[81] These investments are coming from venture capitalists, who for many years or even decades have ignored the legal industry and ignored the legal space in general. Unfortunately, the law industry has been considered an area that is not ripe for automation or technology. It has been considered a dormant sleeping giant. In fact, that is what it has been. The legal industry is a giant, but it is no longer asleep.

> Technology is making its way into the different parts of legal practice, of legal service delivery, and of the legal industry; all of those terms are starting to blend together as automation plays a bigger role.

Investments in automation are happening in areas such as identifying *legal resources*. Imagine from the consumer perspective that someone is looking for an attorney. There are now resources available to help find the right lawyer online. There is also the *automation of legal work*. Consumers who needed the help of a lawyer in the past, besides not knowing how to find the right lawyer, now can skip over finding the right lawyer and do certain things on their own. Online solutions, such as Rocket Lawyer and LegalZoom help lay people do their own legal work and not have to go to an attorney at all.

Automation is also moving up the ladder into more complex areas of law. It is already happening in the back office of legal departments, law firms, and legal aid entities and foundations. Both in law firms and corporate departments, the back office has experienced a significant amount of innovation. What are some of the areas where automation is happening?

Billing, timekeeping, invoicing. Managing and sharing information. Managing documents, managing knowledge. There's also the general information learned over years of practice that attorneys are used to keeping in their brains and then passing down to junior attorneys verbally; it is now managed in online documents and through information management systems.

Those infrastructure/back-office operational functions have seen innovation and technology take off. Technology has enabled the optimization of certain processes that were occurring in the back office in a way not seen before and in a way that is very necessary. This includes the billing and invoicing process, and timekeeping: the amount of data that now is first collected through automation and technology and then disseminated. That information is now coming in formats and ways that is consumable not only for the law firm or the in-house department, but the ultimate business client, whether a corporate client or a consumer, a personal client. Data is being extracted more effectively and efficiently from LSPs and shared with a client in a way that really helps optimize service delivery.

But what is happening in the legal service delivery, or what is called the front office? We know that the practice of law is being automated for certain consumer legal services already (note the reference to Rocket Lawyer and LegalZoom). We know that people are going online and creating their own landlord-tenant forms. They are creating their own divorce forms and bankruptcy forms. A lot is happening in the consumer area. But how are automation and technology playing a role in automating and optimizing the delivery of legal services? For commercial legal practice, is there a parallel phenomenon occurring with regard to innovation and technology?

The answer: All sorts of technologies are invading the legal practice, supporting the actual work that the lawyers are doing.

Let's look at a really good visual that can help orient us around this topic. This topic is very broad. **Figure 7-3** is a graphic from Continuing Education of the Bar (CEB).[82]

The graphic is a framework around how to think about technology and where people can orient themselves. It also illustrates that there is no one way to operationalize in legal or to do legal ops.

There are many, many options that are helpful in legal departments, law firm management, and the actual practice of law. Starting in the top right of the graphic, note that it shows the depth to which there is automation happening in different areas; the outermost circles are more general

LEGAL DEPARTMENT TECHNOLOGY ROADMAP

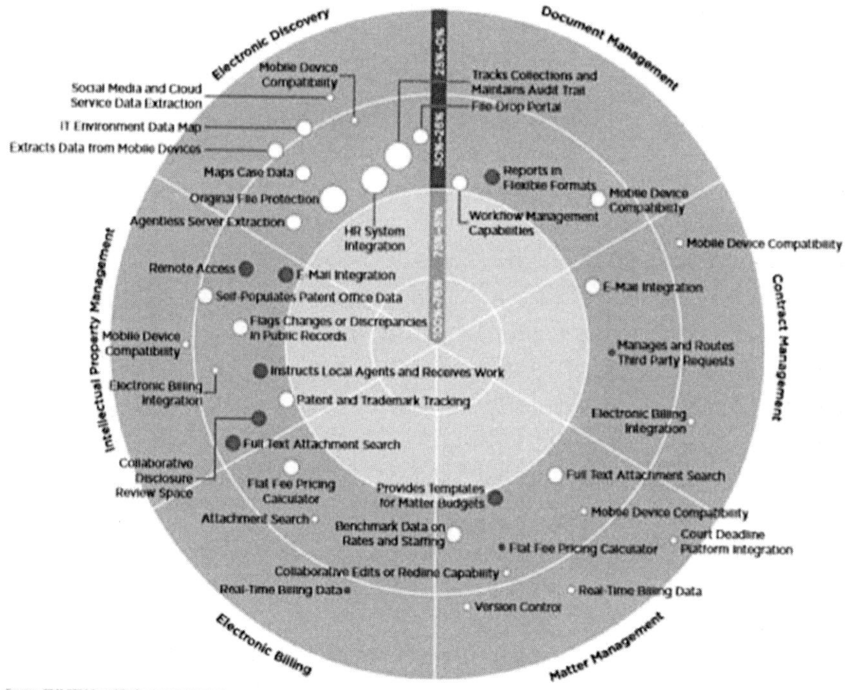

Figure 7-3.

automation, and the innermost circles are about concentrated efforts of automation.

From document management to contract management, just go around the circle: *matter management, electronic billing, intellectual property management,* and *electronic discovery.*

What first jumps out is that there is a push and pull happening. Where is the chicken and the egg? Document management, matter management, and electronic billing are generic functions. Every legal practice must manage documents, whether paying for their creation or invoicing clients for the work to create them; the same occurs with receiving, invoicing, and billing. Again, these are generic and necessary for everyone.

The other three—*contract management, IP management*, and *e-discovery*—are specific to certain domains within legal or subject matter expertise. IP is its own legal practice area. Contract management is associated with the commercial transactions practice, and perhaps M&A. Electronic discovery is connected to litigation. There is more innovation and technology in those three areas.

The question is: Was the technology created because there was a need and a pull from the market? Were lawyers in the IP practice area and commercial transactions practice area and litigation, seeking a technology solution? Were they demanding it of service providers, or are they starting to automate themselves? There are some firms that stand out, especially in the IP area, and that realize there is an opportunity. They created their own technology solutions within the firm, and then realized their customers had a need for that or for their clients.

So, there is an interesting dynamic happening in the legal industry as it relates to market needs and good old-fashioned supply and demand. Are there areas where supply is bursting but there is no demand? That could be. But there are certain areas of demand and I think that is evident. Clearly these were three areas of demand that were really front-office lawyers talking and saying they needed a better way to do a certain part of their transaction practice, a better way to handle IP transactions, and certainly a better way to do discovery in the course of large litigations.

Document Management

It is interesting to think about what is happening in the market holistically. But now let's jump into a specific area: document management.

What is it? What does it do? What does it mean? I want to mention some really basic concepts.

First, there is no common taxonomy. There are people who would say document management means something slightly different. Some consider contract management a subset of document management. There is also something called enterprise legal management, which encompasses everything. That is, managing of the entire legal day, legal workflow, and legal processes.

But let's go with some generic concepts again to help orient this discussion.

What is the legal practice, if not creating documents? By documents, I'm talking broadly: letters, pleadings, contracts—the list goes on and on.

Practicing attorneys all struggle with managing document versions. How many times have you saved a document and had to be creative in the file name so you remember which version it is?

> Is this a possible file name? *CompanyA_MasterServiceAgreement_05242019_LBcomments_(redlined)(final)readyforsig*

One of the biggest values of a good document management system is that it automatically tracks versions; you are not saving as a new version every time. By virtue of updating a document it knows to give you a new document version number and all the history. Everyone knows they are working from the latest and greatest. That is by far the No. 1 benefit.

Modern document management has been around for about a decade. It started with sharing infrastructure and tracking files in a way that keeps sequential order neat and tidy. Then there is mobile access: Everyone is working on the go, whether using a tablet or smartphone.

Lawyers must access documents anywhere and anytime, and they need to access the right versions. Mobile access is becoming a key functionality, and a key sales pitch for the document management system. Most of these are moving into the cloud even if they used to be on the premise, which meant that they were living within the boundaries and confines of the enterprise or the law firm. Things are all moving to the cloud. Document management is one of the first beneficiaries of cloud-based adoption because access from any device is key.

Searching is a big reason for a document system. We spend so much time searching for documents, for the latest version, for past versions in case we need to compare something. Search time is expensive. Are lawyers even the right choice to do the searching? Even with the best document management system, sometimes the searching takes too much time. Is it right to bill clients for searches by an attorney? Probably not. We have moved on from that role in some cases, but in many cases we haven't.

Then there is *retrieval*. Once you have gone through the search process, there has to be a way to retrieve information and document it in a way that is easy to use. Considering most people still do their documents in Word, for example, a key consideration is making sure the document management system is easily accessible through your favorite word processing system.

Contract Management[83]

I confess I have a soft spot for contract management. Every function of legal ops and every skill set capability discussed in this book was tested and experimented by me within the context of contracting.

For some, the term contract management sends a mixed signal of managing only the document and its life cycle. But think about it more broadly as contracting. And there is an explosion of technology happening in contracting.

The most basic place in which technology has moved forward at a faster speed is with the management of contract documents. For instance, think about contract life cycle management (CLM) (**Figure 7-4**). A document is created, it goes through a negotiation process somewhere outside the system usually (though many systems offer a platform for two parties to exchange negotiated drafts of the contracts inside the system); then there is an approval process, a signature process, and then it is stored. The storage and subsequent management of the document includes the expirations, amendments, document modifications, and contract renewals.

That is where the CLM systems are quite progressive and impactful. A CLM system comes in many flavors. Some are really good at creating contracts. What is the contract creation automation opportunity? What are the processes that fit in there?

Contracting technology falls into three general categories: (1) life-cycle management, (2) analytics and data extraction, and (3) review. Purchasers of contracting systems can easily become confused by the different types of solutions and some features can overlap, creating even less clarity on how to select the right one. To pick the best solution, the buyer must identify the problem they are trying to solve. It is easy to want to solve all the possible issues faced in the contracting process, but

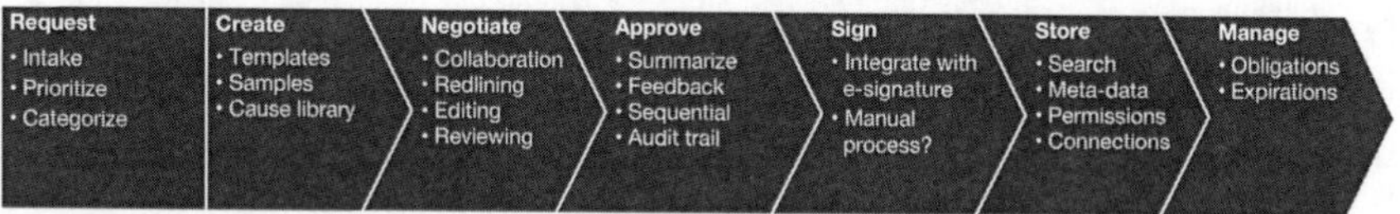

Figure 7-4. *Contracting Process*

because there is no one-stop-shop solution (at least as of yet), it is critical to identify the problem first with some specificity, and then seek out the right solution.

To make it easier when looking for solutions, buyers should understand the three categories so that they are empowered to ask precise questions of the potential vendors that home in on the real strengths of the solutions.

Lifecycle Management

CLM provides an infrastructure for contracts to flow through from creation through signature. It has a broad range of features; vendors are stronger at some features than others. CLM systems provide functionality to create contracts by building them from clause banks or libraries. They can walk users through a decision tree to add the right provisions until a full set of terms are compiled into a contract template.

At the other end of this process, CLMs are good at creating searchable repositories for contracts by creating a database of basic (and or detailed) facts about the contract that the customer considers important, such as start and end dates, the value of the contract, type of contract, and business division. These systems usually have workflow and rules-driven actions that can make the flow of the contract for approvals and then plug into an electronic signature service seamlessly. CLM systems can be used for the most basic functionality and then enhanced as the processes mature.

Analytics and Data Extraction

Contract analytics and extraction solutions dive into the contents of the contracts, usually post-execution, to locate pertinent terms and compare them to other contracts. These solutions are common for M&A, where large numbers of executed contracts must be researched for specific terms related to the proposed deal and flagged for further analysis by legal professionals. These systems are also great for locating obligations in executed contracts and extracting critical information about deadlines and other time-bound terms, for easier compliance by the business.

Review

Finally, the contract review solutions are the newest to this landscape of contracting automation. As of now, there are only a few solutions in this area. These solutions use advanced technology to automate the legal review of the contracts as part of the negotiation cycle. They effectively serve as an assistant to the lawyers by flagging provisions in contracts that don't align to the preferred positions of the company reviewing the contract, enabling the attorney to focus on those disagreeable terms only, rather than reading the contract in its entirety.

Other Contracting Automation Opportunities

Drafting

When we write a contract, it is likely that it is not starting from a blank page. That would be silly. We look to find samples; we want to use templates. The time we spend on templates is a critical part in any contract optimization project. At least samples of clauses or samples of full contracts are needed that we can use as the contract is created for the particular transaction at hand. Why reinvent the wheel and why charge clients for that kind of time?

So, a lot of automation has happened and continues to happen. A great example are the "clause libraries" that are live. They allow contract creation to happen in real time in one clean experience with clauses that are built and sourced from different areas. Contrast that with the typical workflow—typing into a blank Word document, trying to extract pieces from other Word documents that one has to search for, open up, find that *one* clause that you were hunting for; suddenly there are twenty or more different contracts scattered on desktops in the law office.

Negotiation

Obviously there has been a lot of progress made in contract creation. In contract negotiation, however, progress is not as broad. There are many, many users who need a better way to create a contract, and they are more concerned with that and are happy to continue to negotiate the way they always have. Typically, the engagement kicks off, and we start with a draft. We redline. We edit. We review everything within the document itself. We send these different versions back and forth. Many times, all of this is done over email.

There are some great collaboration technology solutions out there that can help reduce the back and forth of negotiation. With contract collaboration solutions, people can collaborate on anything, but to collaborate a negotiation on a technology platform somewhere where parties from different entities can come in and edit together in real time is a brave new world. Parties can have a conference call while editing in live time. That is really progressive and saves a ton of time rather than trying to track emails back and forth. So, there's proof that the automation of negotiation is happening. It is probably not quite as widely adopted as some of the other aspects of contract management or contracting automation.

Approval and Signing

Approval and signatures often go hand in hand. They don't have to, but, depending on the size of the entity, often a person who is signing is also the one who is approving, and by virtue of signing it means they have approved it. As corporate clients get bigger or firms are dealing with large corporate clients, there could be many layers of approvals for people who aren't the signatories.

So, automating the approval process provides a great audit trail. You can now track who has actually provided approval and it doesn't have to just be about the signature, but it can actually be the five or six others involved: Imagine the finance lead that has to approve a contract before it actually goes to the signatory—and that signatory is the CEO. Perhaps the CEO's business manager approves every contract before the CEO signs. An approval mechanism that is automated creates a nice audit trail, and is beneficial for a lot of clients and companies.

Electronic signatures have made a big splash in the last five to six years and it is a very common place to start with automation. As you think about how to innovate in your practice area in your firm or in your department, electronic signature is a great place to start. It is now widely accepted, so the adoption process isn't nearly as painful as it once was. It is actually accepted globally as well, so not just within different functions within a corporation or law firm but entities around the globe are starting to accept electronic signatures. The days of running around with a pen and trying to chase down signers are quickly becoming something of the past.

Storage

Storage is probably the No. 1 problem with contract management, especially when companies cannot find their contracts. Even some of the best, most organized contracting functions in some of the best companies have trouble finding their contracts! On one hand, it makes sense that the bigger the company, the harder to find. On the other hand, it's also common that the smaller the company, the faster they are growing and the less time they have to prepare for infrastructure, making it harder for them to find their contracts as well.

So, good storage or a good repository is often the No. 1 most utilized functionality within a CLM system. Companies who are investing significant time and resources into launching a contract management system are probably doing it for one key business problem: to find their contracts.

A good repository will have a lot of features. You want an easy search. That is the number one requirement, especially if an entire enterprise is searching, not just a handful of attorneys or a group of contract managers. For every employee in a company to be able to search, that capability must be really clean and slick, because virtually everyone is used to and adept at the Google and Bing search experiences. They are used to Amazon and buying something in a matter of seconds. With that in mind, creating a complex search experience is not going to be very helpful as people work through the changes.

One technical requirement of a good storage/repository system to consider is what kind of meta-data (data that describes the information you're storing) is collected. Imagine a filing system—which is what these storage systems are—that is, electronic. It is nice to have a few basic pieces of information in that file: entity names, for example. Who are the contracting entities? Start date. End date. Type of purchase.

Another technical requirement is a bit more complex, with more technical thinking about the permissions. Which kind of information is going to be accessible to the person who is searching, especially if it is a firm-wide solution? How do you differentiate between attorneys, paralegals, or an administrative assistant sitting across the firm? That can easily become more complex and or require a bit of a deeper technical expertise.

Then think about the integrations with other solutions across the firm as well. Do you want the contract management system to feed into the customer tracking system? Do you want it to feed into the procurement system? Is there a compliance tool that a contracting system could plug into? Those become very complex very quickly. My advice is to keep it simple and try to prioritize the most important ones first before going down too deep a path in integrations.

Notifications

To amend a contract, it is critical to find amendments as they are related to the original document, and find termination letters as they relate to the original contract and when it expired. Just managing the expiration date of a contract can be a problem. That will often go unnoticed until something comes up and . . . you realize a contract has expired.

So the ability to create notification systems is fantastic and highly useful, especially when dealing with a broader set of people who can't manage the contract hands-on. Those reminders are helpful for them.

Matter Management and E-Billing

These are areas that are particularly important in corporate legal departments. For law firms to understand how and why these solutions are being implemented it will only enable them to better serve their clients. The ability to empathize with the in-house client is a critical skill for today's law firm lawyer. There is a huge amount of progress that continues in billing, timekeeping, invoicing, and in the infrastructure that helps in-house teams manage the bills they are getting from their law firm. Creative ways of billing their clients through AFAs and value-based billing are needed. The good news is that it's happening; the bad news is that it is not happening very quickly, and there are not yet as many firms as there should be that are doing it.

At least it is happening. There are some creative law firms that are trying to push new ideas to their clients, on how to bill their services to clients, and in-house teams are pushing for creativity, predictability, and value-added services from their law firms.

Matter management and e-billing systems go hand in hand—but think about the better ways to track spending. From an in-house department perspective, we are no longer at a place where GCs can go to CFOs and say, "I don't know, it depends this year. I don't know about the budget I need. I don't know how much I will spend. What if a big litigation matter comes and I am not prepared for it?" Preparing for the unknown is a lot of what needs to be done, but law departments now more than ever are being held accountable like other lines of businesses across the company. And that is pretty new; it wasn't the case a decade ago.

Tracking spending is becoming a No. 1 priority for in-house teams; and the rise of legal technology helps enable in-house teams track their spending better, and calculate AFAs. These insights are great for firms handling the work, but it does require law firms to adopt that structure. Supporting your clients by having the data available through automated tools gives those firms an edge over others doing it as they always have.

We are not yet at a place where project work is sold by law firms on a regular basis. There's not yet a complete understanding of how billable time relates to a project, the deliverables, and the outcomes. There is still a lot of work that needs to happen on the back end and in understanding the real profitability in time spent on an AFA and the output of the value that is coming from this new way of billing for services.

For example, you won't have two-hundred associates at a law firm saying they spent time doing a research project, and describing that work in one-hundred-and-fifty different ways—now there is a predefined way to say it was research. More detail, but now we know exactly how much time was spent on research because that work was not hidden in other descriptions of billed time. Which leads to the next benefit: the ability to track that time, assess it, and sort by different spending areas. This is real analytics.

Automating time tracking and using metadata gives firms a deeper insight into their own work. With these systems, lawyers can ask how much time is spent on research versus how much time is spent on drafting a document without having to look line item by line item in six-minute increments and trying to figure out the math. Now there are ways to categorize, sort, and filter the money that is spent. Similarly, by creating categories of spend that can fit into a template or some sort of a standardized approach will help operationalize the practice. That's a fact. Anything that can create some consistency using templates, a consistent way of capturing information or recording information, is going to help a ton.

When matters are created or when attorneys create new budgets and they are defining a matter and a description, having just an open definition is very complex when there are large legal departments involved and every attorney thinks about what they're doing very differently.

But if you give all transactional attorneys a set of choices—what kind of transaction, what type of contract negotiation, what type of contract—you have created data that is traceable, auditable, and reportable—that is the most important thing. So, as consistency is built up over time, a foundation is created from a starting point and then you know how to improve from that.

> **AUTOMATION WARNING:**
> With most contemporary automation tools (based on human-constructed rules and standardized data), there is no way to automate until tracking is done with consistency and the current status is known.

Matter management e-billing systems are creating a great foundation of fantastic solutions out there. There are also a variety of probably less fantastic solutions and that is where the selection process becomes very important—more on that later. Until now, you've been collecting basic data that historically has been collected in a completely haphazard way. Now it is being organized. And that continues to evolve and is getting better and better and more useful. Similarly, for budget caps and tracking, the same thing applies. The same concept creates ways to report and track information that we never had before.

There has been a ton of progress in this space.

IP Management

It has become obvious that IP needs to be managed more efficiently, and automation has certainly helped. Just the ability to link into public filings, and public information available on trademarks, patents, and on copyrights is great progress.

Beyond public records, there's information readily available that was traditionally hard to get to—and if accessible, extraction was completely manual. Emailing, faxing, calling, or asking for somebody to send a clerk somewhere to search has been replaced with technology solutions that people have on their desk. You can search in various systems and more importantly, you can retrieve and access information that then feeds into your own system to manage workflow and workload. For example the tasks of tracking filings or calendaring of events can be integrated into Microsoft Outlook (still the most popular desktop calendar application and the place attorney do most of their tracking or appointment, events, and deadlines).

Workflow is a generic concept in document, contract, and matter management (basically any kind of management that exists), because what even *is* workflow? When most people say workflow, they're referencing the bouncing back and forth between people and systems of information and documents. Automating workflow to avoid using faxes or emails or, heaven forbid, snail mail is critical to optimize efficiencies. And a closer look at the tools that automate these processes reveals that many are simply really robust collaboration tools.

For example, an opportunity for engineers and attorneys to collaborate together on a patent filing is priceless when work is done in real time. Time is not wasted bouncing documents and emails back and forth hoping somebody checks their email and responds efficiently. That is an immediate time-saving measure. If you haven't experienced it yet, whether IP management or other types of legal practice, real-time online collaboration is really something to get hooked on.

E-Discovery

E-discovery is most widely known because of the progress it has made in legal technology. It started within this past decade and has exploded. Actually, it became obvious about fifteen years ago that what junior associates are doing in law firms is (1) not fun for them and (2) extremely expensive and not effective for the client in the final analysis. Electronic discovery was born out of that need; it is the result of a supply-and-demand market reaction.

What does electronic discovery do? Basically, it is a way to jump into all those emails and start threading out the related ones in a way that even somebody with the best brain and eyeballs would have a tough time doing and tracking. It connects and threads out emails, matches them, maps them, and puts them into buckets. There is easy keyword searching across millions of documents. Imagine how valuable that is; imagine the amount of time it took to do that manually in the old days.

Mapping case data, creating audit trails—these are the things related to electronic discovery that have become standard tools in every firm and legal department. Beyond that, this is the area with the broadest range of choices, functionalities and capabilities. It is worth exploring further for organizations with a very high-volume litigation practice.

A Little Bit More on Artificial Intelligence

The LawGeex graphic shows examples of the different areas that AI is infiltrating, as well as some of the key vendors and service providers in this space. AI is a big topic in the legal sphere and every day it seems to get

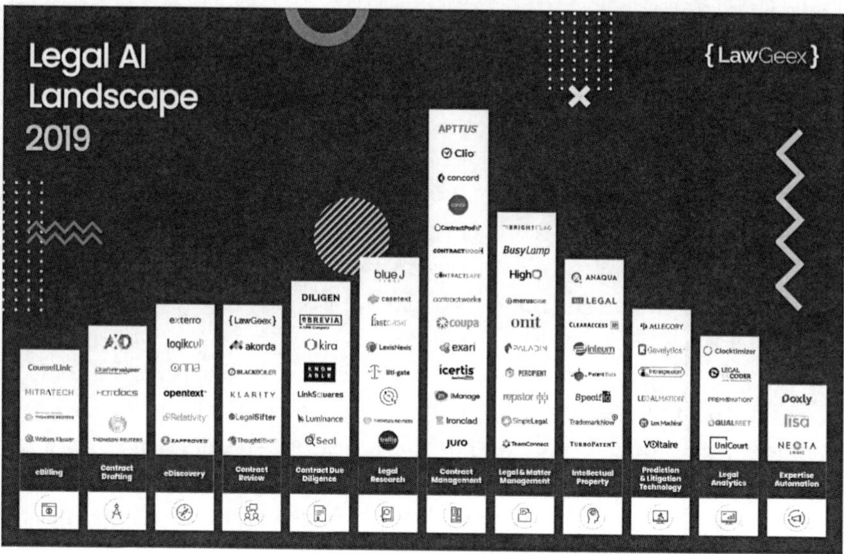

Source: LawGeex.com

bigger. It's very exciting, but there's also some hype. So, care is needed when selecting and looking into AI.

It's helpful to start with a very simple definition of AI. If you recall chapter 5, you'll remember that we touched on three general AI concepts: broader AI, machine learning, and deep learning. The point to bring home is that AI is essentially the ability for machines to perform human tasks, beyond general computing. It includes high-level judgment-making or decision-making skills that we rely on humans for. That is true of even the most basic class of AI. But the real magic is happening in machine learning and in deep learning.

"So again, artificial intelligence is any ability for a machine to do a task in a smart way, but you can do that by programming these tasks," said Olivier Colle, an engineer in Microsoft's Research in Artificial Intelligence division. However, when it comes to machine learning, it is really the ability for machines to learn how to perform these tasks without being programmed in advance. That makes a huge difference because it's very similar to how humans learn things by being exposed to situations and reacting to it. "With machine learning, they're going to get exposed to data, to examples, they are going to learn how to perform these tasks and complete these tasks."

But deep learning, a subset of machine learning, is the closest we are getting with AI that simulates the human brain. The one advantage deep learning models have is they are very efficient and they learn what's important in the data to solve tasks. Now the downside of these deep learning models is they are very hungry in term of data. They need tens of thousands, often millions of data points to learn and they need a high computing power. So data is extremely important for deep learning.

"The analogy that sometimes you hear is if deep learning is a rocket, well your fuel will be data. And without data you know your rocket, your deep learning model, is not going to work. It is very important to manage data and you find all types of data can be interesting. From the meta-data you find in contracts, unstructured data from documents, raw documents, it could be contracts of course. It could be data that's surrounding that legal process, customer data, enterprise resource planning data. So you realize that when you work in the legal space, there is a lot of data, unstructured and structured data that you can leverage."

Colle encourages people to think of the type of data they have and then throughout the process of the contract, have data in a structured way so that it will have provisions. It will have types of clauses, termination by date, and additional data because you're going be able to draw insights from the data.

For instance, you'd be able to predict what kind of clauses and what kind of contracts are more likely to succeed with the other party so maybe you can speed up the negotiation process, and you can optimize the financial aspect of it. Throughout the contract life cycle, you're going to see data in the contract, but you also have iteration on the contract. Managing data is definitely a challenge, but it's important to start managing it in a structured form as much as possible so that you can leverage it to get insights and predictions, detect anomalies, detect trends.

Are robot lawyers coming to take over human lawyers' jobs? Will we even need lawyers anymore? How far away is technology from replacing the contract lawyer, for example, and the negotiations we spend our hours on? There are no specific answers yet. However, what we know is that as more and more of the legal processes are automated over time, I believe that AI will help to augment attorneys rather than replace them. Once the right AI models are trained with the data that has been gathered, AI solutions will allow attorneys to focus on only the important tasks as opposed to the more repetitive and predictable tasks.

Buying Legal Tech

In most cases, if you're looking to automate a process or task, you'll start looking at buying new legal technologies to help you accomplish your goals. So, what does it mean to buy legal tech? There are so many options out there and it's hard to understand the difference between the hype and what's real, but a couple of basic steps will set you on the right path. For a quick reference guide to buying legal tech, see the appendix section.

Step zero of this endeavor is making sure you're ready to begin the search. It's critical to know what problem you're actually trying to solve, as opposed to simply buying some technology because of a persuasive sales pitch or shiny new features. Listen to your employees' problems and investigate the root cause of that problem. In the long run, having your team's input will help ensure sustainability and generate buy-in. Once you've done that, you'll also want to start your market research early and give yourself time to evaluate products against your needs and wants.

After you're *sure* you are ready, you will want to define the current-state process that touches on your identified problem. Technology is here to enable and optimize process. To do that, you'll want to start by understanding the sequence of steps: Who is doing which steps of the current process, and what are the potential opportunities to automate some of those steps, or how can technology simply enable those steps to become faster?

Understanding your processes and then gathering clear requirements for improving them takes a significant amount of time; it's something that organizations should be prepared to invest in. Understanding how to gather technical requirements is really its own discipline and skill set. Involving the right people can't be underestimated. It's not just about the people helping you run a project, whether it's those who are helping you to find the process, or those who are helping you gather business requirements or advising you on the available technology solutions available or who will work within the firm's existing technology infrastructure. It's also thinking about the right stakeholders, potential users, or the people who are going to be impacted and expected to play a part of or use the technology in the future.

Prioritizing needs is, as with project management and scope creep, the biggest risk with technology implementation. For example, if a firm is trying to solve two or three problems and automate two or three processes, once it starts assessing the technology and then realizes it can automate much more, it's very tempting to want to go all in and automate as much as possible. My advice is to stay small, stay focused, get some wins with those automations, and then there will be a road map on how to expand the automation possibilities in the future.

Prioritize the things to accomplish. Alignment is a really good project management approach. A project in technology implementation and selection should be tightly run. A professional is likely needed, somebody who knows how to manage a project of technological complexity and or size. This is not something that attorneys are often very good at.

Many in-house teams are being accustomed to issuing RFPs for buying technology and other services. They think about what can be leveraged in RFP protocols that already exist within the company, within IT departments. Other experienced professionals around the company can help gather requirements and enable the selection process inside the legal departments. An RFP has its own rhythm, its own best practices and rigors to follow to optimize experience and selections. (See the resource guide for more about the RFP process.)

Then consider the security challenges that might reside within the firm, what kind of access issues exist in the technology solution, and the tech stack that the firm uses. Don't underestimate the importance of having the right people to help make the correct selections. Then there is implementation, which is another separate project.

Now that you're comfortable with your project mission and the team you've assembled, fast forward and imagine what it's going to be like being attached now and involved with the technology for a long time. What is the ***support and maintenance*** offered? Imagine if you find a really beautiful, wonderful technology solution. It does what you need and has all the functionality you're looking for, but then you realize through research or through feedback from peers and colleagues that the support experience has been terrible. Or the maintenance is slow. Communication is poor. That becomes a very bad experience very quickly, even though the solution itself might, from a technology perspective, be very good and viable. So think ahead about the kind of support needed.

A lot will depend on the kind of resources available internally. What are the existing teams, and what skills do they have from a technology perspective to solve problems? Maybe you don't have to rely so heavily on the support provided by the tech provider; maybe you can leverage some support or technology experts within your organization. If you don't have that internal support, it becomes that much more important to think about the post-implementation services provided by the tech provider.

It's also important to consider the ***ongoing enhancements*** expected from the solution. Are continuous improvements on functionality expected? Make a list of things wanted in future functions and features that maybe the tech provider promised that is shared on a road map.

Although technology enables a process, there is no doubt that even the best, most fitting technology solution will require some tweaks. So, think about the impacts of the technology on the processes that are optimized and that will require change management and extensive communication.

And finally ***success metrics and measures***: how will success be measured? Is it purely a turnaround time issue—this process before took X amount of time and now it's moved down to Y amount of time. Is that a success measure? Perhaps documents could not be found easily before, but now it takes a shorter amount of time. Or are fewer people needed to manage documents, to input information about documents, because now there is an automated system that extracts certain data?

Actually it's not necessarily about immediate success. Sometimes it's really about answering the question: was this worth it? Implementing automation means spending a lot of time and resources, in financial and human capital, during the course of a significant technology journey.

In Summary: What Really Matters

1. **Process first, automation later.**
    - Before considering automation, make sure that processes are optimized.
    - Streamline what is done today and make sure it is most effective before automating.
    - When selecting technology, make sure it works with the process.
2. **No magic bullet.**
    - If there are issues with how things are going today, automation may not solve the problems and could actually make things more complicated.
    - Implementing technology takes a lot of work on the side of the customer, with dedicated resources who are experienced in implementing solutions.
    - Gathering the requirements for a solution is the most important step in the implementation.

3. **Features are exciting, but may not be necessary.**
    - Create a list of prioritized features that fit the main purpose.
    - Don't cater to peer pressure when other stakeholders suggest features that were not on the priority list.
    - Get clear timelines from the vendor about when promised features will be available and how they will be tested before availability.
4. **Consider implementation services and ongoing support.**
    - After the sales pitch is closed, vendors bring in new contacts to handle the implementation. Make sure to check qualifications and experiences.
    - Get references from others who have implemented the solution.
    - After "go-live" quality support is critical to successful use of the solutions. Demand high-touch white-glove service whenever possible:
        - 24/7 help hotline
        - Dedicated customer success manager
        - Specific timeline for responses to inquiries
        - Clear escalation path to solve problems
5. **Use what you already have.**
    Before investing in a new piece of technology, consider if a significant portion of the automation needs can be satisfied with existing technology, for example:
    - Microsoft Word: Create simple macros for contract clause automation.
    - Microsoft Outlook: Create reminders and use tasks to organize simple project plans.
    - OneDrive, Box, DropBox, Google Drive, and so on: Share documents online and exchange drafts through linked files, rather than attaching big files into emails.
    - Sharepoint: Create simple internal "websites" to share knowledge and materials.

NEED TO KNOW #5: VALUE AND THE LAW FIRM MANAGED SERVICES MODEL[84]

It's good to be the client. Clients dictate what they want from law firms, and when they want it delivered, right? That may have been true for decades, if not centuries, but now it is more complicated. As pressure continues to mount on internal legal departments to do more with less, and as legal professionals are functioning more and more like business professionals, lawyers have to think differently. Legal departments need to ask for different outputs from their outside counsel firms, and law firms need to deliver legal services in a different way.

In-house lawyers love their jobs because they are close to the business and contribute to how it works. They know firsthand how businesses operate and how they outsource non-critical work. So why don't they learn from their business colleagues about how to operate the legal practice? Because it is, after all, a business.

I submit that in-house lawyers are indeed learning, and that is forcing a change in how legal services are delivered in-house and in the expectations we have of law firms. We can and should expect operational excellence from law firms, just as we expect it from professional service providers.

It is time for law firms to deliver services with the quality of a law firm and with the operational excellence of an outsourcing company. In addition to high-quality legal services and advice, in-house legal teams need to get insight into the work of the law firms in a way they have never had before. Law firms are full of valuable information and data about the legal services they offer, which could inform in-house teams about the business of the company they work for. Yet, that information is not harvested and business is continuing as usual: deal by deal, legal memo by legal memo. Besides doing away with the billable hour, in-house teams need to get more back than they have received from law firms for the same amount of money.

Change is afoot. When I worked at Microsoft, we stratified legal services for procurement contract review in a way that allowed for the optimization of external and internal resources, and to learn about legal transactional practices in a way not previously done. The most radical change was to move law firm contract review and negotiation into a managed services-type engagement. As with IT managed service arrangements (which have been around for decades), Microsoft began to engage law firms to deliver value to the in-house department as a managed service. It was the same contract review service they had done for Microsoft for years, but in a very different way. What follows is a case study in what I believe to be the most valuable way of delivering services in a practice area where the work is recurring, somewhat predictable, and without end in sight.

Stratifying the Work

Before considering what work to outsource and to whom, legal departments should assess regularly if any legal involvement is necessary at all. We reviewed work prioritization and resource allocation in the earlier chapter on Process and Efficiencies in great detail. Sometimes legal becomes a sort of a crutch for the business and finds itself overloaded. The graphic that follows, **Figure 7-5: Stratification of Work,** was my view on how work might be allocated and resourced between in-house employees and external resources based on the complexity of the transaction. I created this several years ago when I first began to consider outsourcing legal work in a different way, and before AI was anywhere near the sophistication it has today. Although this model has evolved since then, the general concepts still ring true in this simplistic assessment.

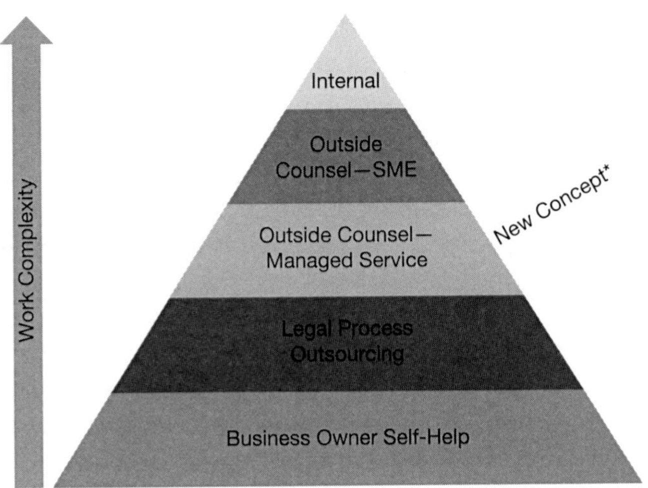

Figure 7-5. *Stratification of Work*

At the base of the triangle is the large volume of work that is not complex and requires no involvement from the legal department. This type of contracting work can be handled by business owners by following some simple guidelines and prepopulated templates. The next level up is the work that in-house legal professionals, either junior attorneys or paralegals, should actually *stop* handling because the work is predictable and not challenging. That work is conducive to documenting in a playbook and is rather easily outsourced to a LPO company, which uses low-cost experienced legal professionals across a variety of skill levels. Read more on that in the chapter on ALSPs.

The next level combines high-level law firm legal services with the operational efficiencies of an LPO. This type of work should be commonly handled by law firms, but could benefit from the recurring themes and learnings that make the delivery of legal services more predictable and efficient. Although playbooks are helpful, the law firms are in a position to make judgment calls and legal advisory assessments such that playbooks are not the only basis for the work delivery.

Finally, there are those transactions that require the subject-matter expertise of legal experts and the unique business insight that only the in-house legal team can bring.

Regardless of changes in the legal services delivery models, there will always be a need for experts at law firms or by legal advisors closest to the business to handle the most complex transactions. Note that this visual is about what type of resources makes most sense and distinguishes clearly between internal full-time employees and externals.

An even more progressive view that I came up with more recently is depicted in **Figure 7-6,** which demonstrates a real blend of internal and external resources as a virtual team delivering a holistic solution. In this model, the business clients don't even feel the difference between their in-house lawyers and the law firm lawyers. Yes, this is still largely a vision, and one that I am experimenting with now. I firmly believe that this is where law firms should head, especially for certain types of recurring work (in this example, commercial transactions). As law firms become more connected with the work of the in-house teams and closer to the ultimate business client, this sort of solution becomes the most logical resource model, and ensures work is done by the most effective and efficient resource, including AI, leveraged by the law firm. In fact, real outsourcing presumes that the service provider is the one leveraging technology to be more efficient and

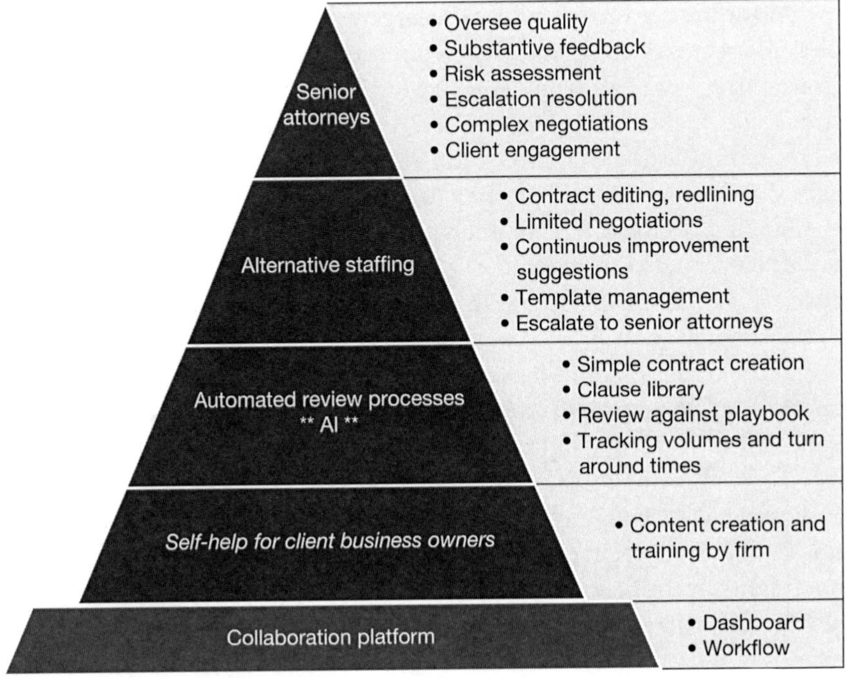

Figure 7-6. *Holistic Resourcing Solution for Commercial Transactions*

it is not expected that the client has to procure their own technology and layer it into the mix of resources.

The Myth that Managed Services Won't Work for Law Firms

Outsourcing has a unique concept buried within it: managed services. A managed service is a type of delivery model for outsourced services. Think broadly about outsourcing. Companies pay for service providers to deliver services across a variety of areas. It is *the way* in which the services are delivered that defines if it is regular outsourcing or if it is a managed service provided by a third party.

Many companies outsource janitorial services, real estate maintenance, catering, and other non-core work needed to run the business. Typically, those are outsourced as a managed service. What does that mean? The buyer relies on the supplier to deliver the service end to end without getting involved in *how* they perform their duties. The buyer has no say about what workers are deployed, how much those workers are paid, or how those workers perform their tasks. The supplier handles all of the "how" details; in return, the buyer expects outcomes. The outcomes have to be agreed upon and documented, but really it is all about answering the following question as a customer: "Are my objectives being met?"

Recently it has become more common to see companies disaggregating and outsourcing certain segments of core work. Manufacturing companies hire manufacturers overseas and shift entire operations to them. Tech companies are hiring software development service providers across the globe and trust them with delivering core testing functions. Like those companies, legal departments have historically outsourced to law firms, but they have not really taken that outsourcing practice along the continuum to a managed service, like other industries have.

The one area where we have seen some examples of managed legal services is in the models delivered by LPO companies. LPOs have been providing "back-office" services for law firms for well over a decade. Back office can be anything from pure word processing up to some services related to data management of a firm's financial processes, such as overseeing e-billing, or managing procurement. Slowly, LPOs have moved up the value chain to do work that is closer to the "core" of legal services, like document review and discovery. LPOs have stepped in to provide lower cost resources for high-volume, tedious work. Most of that work was handled offshore, in India, and proved to be quite successful. Still, there was a reluctance to outsource any work that was considered core to law firms.

With the onset of the 2008 Great Recession, and along with it, the increased pressure to do more with less, there was some expansion in the use of LPOs. Microsoft was an early adopter in a way and pushed the envelope of what could be outsourced to an LPO. When other legal departments and law firms were outsourcing only document review or contract extraction, the company chose to outsource the legal analysis and written negotiations of contracts. This was "*real*" legal work that is core to in-house practitioners. It was work that was handled by internal paralegals and lawyers, and some of it was done by outside counsel. Microsoft made significant changes to how this contract review work is handled and redesigned the internal legal support model within the in-house department.

Outsourcing, though, is not something to jump into. It is not a bunch of work that is tossed over the transom to an LPO, with the hope of a neat and tidy outcome. In fact, it takes a lot of work on behalf of the client to prepare for outsourcing, and then a significant amount of work to manage the relationship. That work is very different from the work of actually doing the substantive legal analysis. The work to be done by the client after outsourcing is all about managing expectations and reviewing the results together with the service provider. It requires project management skills and business operations experience.

What's In It for the Client?

For decades, legal departments have bought services in the way they were sold by law firms. There is nothing to say that the client can't or shouldn't dictate the services it needs and how to receive those services, within the limits of the current legal market. In fact, now is precisely the time for clients to redirect the law firms and ask for more, and different services. It is time we get more value for the money.

But moving to a managed service is not necessarily done to save money. Actually, cost reduction should be secondary so that law firms don't get scared away by the thought of lost revenues. The goal is to get more from the law firms for the same amount spent. For example, there is arguably a body of work done today by junior associates that can be done at lower costs, and the savings can then be applied to delivering different skill-based professional services.

Legal departments that have enough volume going to law firms can require that law firms provide additional services traditionally not considered within the expertise of legal professionals. For example, data analytics, associated with spreadsheets and "people good at math," is becoming a common request from clients. In-house teams are hungry to know more about their own companies' business, and much of that knowledge sits with the law firms. The in-house lawyers know what legal work is being handled outside, but they lose sight of some of the business problems and issues that are associated with that legal work because the outside lawyers are working directly with the business owners. Over time, law firms that provide a significant amount of recurring work for companies begin to learn valuable insights about that company's (also known as their client's) business and legal needs. In fact, it is that unique insight that makes those law firms valuable to the companies and why in-house legal departments become dependent on their outside counsel. The truth is there are many scenarios where law firms know more about their client's business than the client's in-house legal team.

So, why not demand that knowledge to be shared with the client? It is not enough to hope that the best partners will see the benefit in educating the client about the law firm's learnings, but it must be a requirement of the engagement. In-house legal teams should request that the law firms provide some basic information about the work handled outside. For example, in a transactional practice, the law firms should, as standard practice, provide the following basic data points on a regular basis: how many transactions were handled, some breakdown on types of transactions, feedback about the documents/templates used, common negotiation topics, and so on.

This sort of information is already in the hands of the law firms; it needs to be gathered and collated in a consumable format. That is where data analytics comes in. Once foreign to law firms, it is now developed and nurtured across the industry as more clients begin to request these insights. The client benefits immediately from such information because adjustments to templates are available, as is training to internal business clients who are misusing or abusing the outside legal services.

A perhaps easily overlooked benefit in receiving this sort of data is that the in-house team discovers the gaps in knowledge within their company. Often it is the outside legal team that becomes familiar with the business contacts within the client company and can relay back to the in-house legal team where there are gaps in experience where training or further education would help. Senior business leaders will be better informed by their legal counterparts about trends in the industry. In-house legal teams would no longer pay law firms to educate business clients on matters where they could be trained by the in-house team. This presumes that the in-house attorneys can consume such data, and act on it effectively.

Training opportunities are just some of the many benefits of receiving data analytics information from the law firm. A more tangible benefit is the learnings from the repetitive work handled by law firms. In a transactional practice, law firms are often doing similar types of deals over and over again. Each one has its unique aspects, but all deals start from some sort of template, or sample used before. As law firms try to accommodate and please their corporate clients, they often fall into the trap of using the client's preferred forms and may shy away from telling the painful truth that the templates are outdated or they regularly waste negotiation cycle time on the same issues. Experienced and confident partners may raise these concerns, but it is not systematic in how law firms deliver services. So, corporate clients pay for the repeated use of "bad" templates. Once law firms get into the practice of providing this sort of feedback, as would be required in newly documented engagement letters and statements of work, in-house teams can update their documents more regularly, reducing cycle time of negotiations significantly, which results in savings.

If these benefits are not enough, then the one that is sure to convince even the biggest skeptic is the benefit of predictable fees.

What Does the Law Firm Get Out of It?

For this section, two law firms[85] that have partnered to deliver a managed service together to a global client have provided their perspective on why they have invested in this new managed services model.

1. **Sustainability** (chosen over short-term profitability)

The challenges facing law firms since the 2008 banking crisis are widely reported. For the most part, there are simply too many corporate law firms whose business models have been too reliant on customer loyalty and unchallenged hourly rates. As in-house legal departments face the increasing pressures of tighter budgets and greater workloads, coveted work is secured through points-based procurement assessments that place sometimes disproportionate emphasis on price. It is a race to the bottom that law firms cannot afford. It is also of no benefit to clients who want to secure long-term supply partners.

What this means, in short, is that the lawyer/client model has to change, and it will. It needs to move from one of winning on price to a sustainable, mutually beneficial outcome. In the new world, the winners will be the law firms offering real value and quality service to legal departments by reducing in-house workloads while containing risks and costs. The managed services model offers exactly that. Those law firms who can offer managed services alongside a sustainable pricing model (for the law firm and the client), and who do it well, will have a clear and compelling point of differentiation.

Lessons learned by the law firm from one particular engagement translate into other work for the same client by showing that law firms do take seriously the charge to do more for less. These lessons can also turn into new work for other clients as the use of this new delivery model yields more learnings. Further, if the client is willing to speak publicly about the successes of the managed-service delivery model (or allow the law firms to do so), there is a great advantage when competing with other law firms for new work. There is a big competitive difference between saying "we know how to improve processes and provide greater value, and we hope to do this one day soon for a client" and saying "we have a record of success improving processes for clients, and here is what Client X says about the additional value we have provided."

2. Relationship building

Law firms providing managed services have a unique opportunity to be part of a client's "business as usual" in addition to their big-ticket deals. This day-to-day contact (otherwise achieved only through often costly and precious secondments) leads to much tighter and more focused client relationships—and with it, to a competitive advantage of winning big-ticket deals. Such relationships are also formed through multiple touchpoints between a law firm and its client (at all levels: senior and junior, business, and legal), which affords much more stability than the traditional overreliance on a single point of contact. Clients welcome a team-based offering.

Law firms learn a great deal from these types of managed services arrangements. It might involve the client's policies and positions, or something more specific about how individual in-house attorneys like to work or their views on particular issues. An added benefit is that the law firms also learn about their own processes and how to cut waste and increase value as perceived by the client. Developing greater skill in listening to the client and designing solutions in close collaboration with clients to deliver greater value helps law firm lawyers become better lawyers.

3. Opportunities for a broader service offering

Law firms delivering managed services will usually sit in the "engine room" of the legal function, dealing with the volume of day-to-day contracts that drive the productivity of the business. With this position comes a unique insight: Law firms can identify opportunities to add further value and win further work. Many in-house counsel underestimate the value that outside counsel place on becoming more of an integral part of the in-house team. Law firm lawyers like to solve real problems for their clients; they also like helping in-house counsel succeed. This includes helping in-house lawyers move up the value chain within their own organizations. Managed legal service lawyers find this to be enormously satisfying and believe it will help their relationship with these clients and in-house lawyers for years to come.

Successful managed service offerings should set continuous improvement (legal and non-legal) as one of its goals. In this regard, law firms are given a platform not only to suggest improvements but also to deliver them. Law firms can and should use this opportunity to widen their service offering to new categories of work—and revenue—beyond traditionally "legal" work. Examples of such new categories of work are process mapping, legal project management, risk management, horizon scanning, document automation, and AI. All of these services are complementary to the core managed service and can drive further growth for the law firm and the client.

Financial Benefits of the Managed Services Model

Switching from a traditional by-the-hour billing model to a managed legal services model yields business benefits for both sides of the engagement. One immediate benefit is the predictability of a recurring monthly billing cycle. A flat fee for services eliminates the peaks and troughs of normal hourly billing, making forecasting easier and more reliable for both parties. In **Figure 7-7: Billing Cadence**, Microsoft examined its monthly invoices for legal services for this particular piece of work during 2014.

One can see that there is no discernible pattern to the hourly billing, in stark contrast to a flat-rate scenario. To be sure, the nature of flat-fee pricing means that at times one party will see financial favorability, since fee-setting is not always an exact science. For instance, in the example

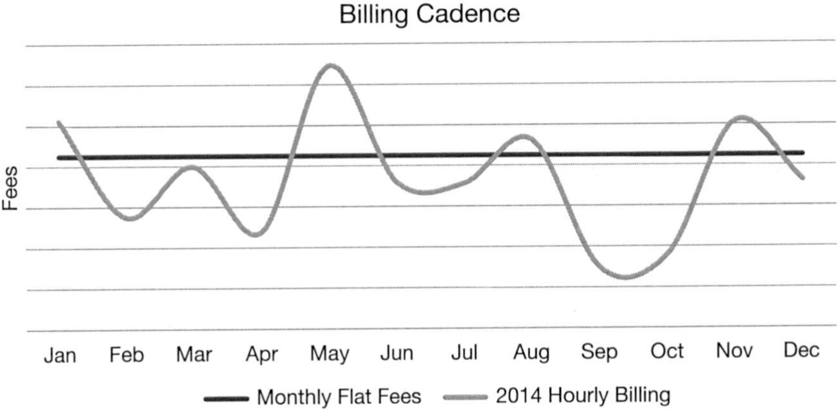

Figure 7-7. *Billing Cadence*

noted, a managed services provider would have come out of the year more favorably than Microsoft would have, as the total flat fee for the year would have exceeded the total paid under traditional billing. However, the full-year variance would have been within 15 percent of the flat fee, and there would be the added benefit of forecasting accurately under a flat-fee model, so it would have been a win-win for both sides.

Law firms moving to a managed services model also can see a windfall resulting from the base fee calculations. If the fees are based on total hours of anticipated work, typically a blended rate is used to calculate the annual fee. Blended rates are often calculated as the average rate of all legal staff who are expected to provide services. This can run the gamut from contractors and paralegals up to partner-level attorneys. There are a couple of financial benefits that a managed services firm can realize. For one, this calculation sets aside non-legal personnel who are required for a managed services model to run smoothly. Project managers, administrative staff, and technical staff are all critical to start up, manage, and improve the outsourcing program. By excluding non-legal staff, blended rates end up higher than they would be otherwise. In the hypothetical scenario depicted in **Figure 7-8**, a $35-per-hour windfall is built into the blended rate. Although it may seem small, a large-scale arrangement will magnify that favorability over the course of the work.

Another benefit of the blended rate is that it assumes that some number of senior-level resources will be required. Early assumptions about the amount of senior level involvement may shift, however, as the law firm gains familiarity with the client and the incoming matters. The initial startup period may indeed require the expertise of senior level resources,

Sample Blended Rate Scenario				
Legal/Non-Legal	Position	Hourly Rate	Number of Resources	Total Cost
Legal	Partner	$ 550	2	$ 1,100
Legal	Associate	$ 350	5	$ 1,750
Legal	Paralegal	$ 200	3	$ 600
Legal	Contractor	$ 150	5	$ 750
Non-Legal	Project Management	$ 85	1	$ 85
Non-Legal	Administrative	$ 50	1	$ 50
Non-Legal	Technical	$ 75	1	$ 75
Legal	Total	$ 280 Blended Rate	15	$ 4,200
Non-Legal	Total	$ 70 Blended Rate	3	$ 210
Combined	Total	$ 245 Blended Rate	18	$ 4,410
	Delta in Hourly Rate	$ 35		

Figure 7-8. *Blended Rates*

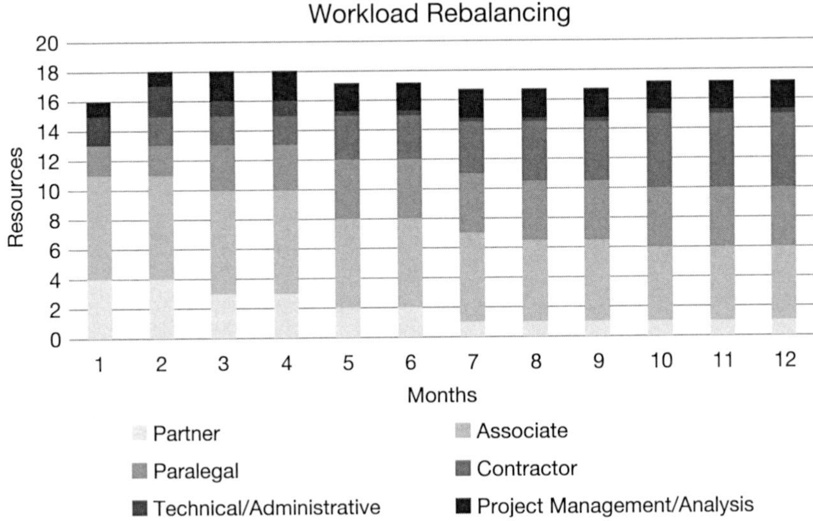

Figure 7-9. *Workload Balancing*

but over time, the law firm should be able to assign the work to less costly resources, all while billing under the preset fees based on the blended rate. In the sample (**Figure 7-9**), the client still has access to all levels of resources, but the balance of work should evolve so that the bulk of the work can be provided by lower cost resources.

Since the commodity purchased by the client is the managed service, it does not matter what level of resource is providing the service, provided the quality meets the designated service levels. This allows the law firm to have scalability and be better able to handle a client's varying flow of work without overly relying on a handful of resources. For these reasons, it behooves the managed services firm to aim for a higher margin by quickly ramping up and distributing the work to less costly resources.

Note that an increase in a law firm's efficiency is made possible with data collection and analysis, two key components of a well-run managed services program. Although business intelligence (BI) may seem a buzzword more apt for other industries, it is a concept that is well suited for the legal services industry. Data can reveal such information as how much time a transaction takes from start to close, what level of resources are used, what types of contracts are most common, and which contractual provisions are consistently problematic. This type of data can inform the law firm and the client where there might be room for improvements,

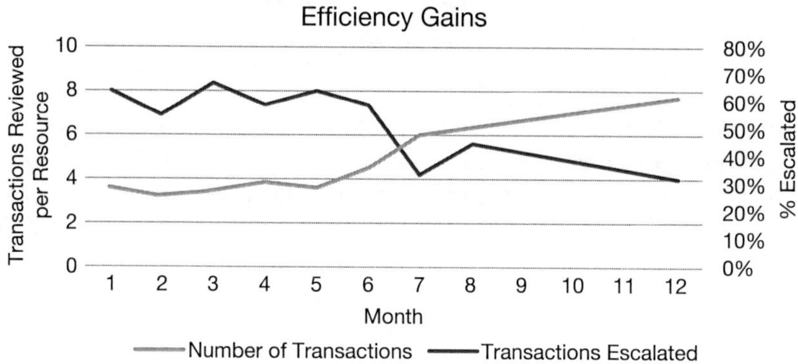

Figure 7-10. *Efficiency Gains*

or even demonstrate the success of the program. BI also quantitatively revealed the benefits of Microsoft's program. For example, in **Figure 7-10**, data shows that the outsourcing partner was able to increase volumes per resource while decreasing escalations back to in-house staff.

The overall improved efficiencies shown here give Microsoft more confidence in the service and the value that the outsource partner provides. The more efficient the program is, the more likely it is that a larger quantity of matters will go into the program, even if the matter would not have previously risen to the level of sending it to outside counsel. Increases in volume can increase revenue for the law firm, so efficiency gains are a win for all.

Whether the fees are built on annual transactional volume or annual hours, the managed services model provides business advantages for the client and the law firm. The new client-firm relationship is not just about the law firm providing more for less; it is the intersection where predictability, positive efficiency incentives, scalability, and smart use of the client's limited resources drive a mutually beneficial relationship.

Law firms also provide their perspective in the challenges that law firms face as they try to move in this direction. Although the rewards are great, the "change curve" will be steep.

There is no template for delivering managed legal services by law firms. This offering has to be crafted in a partnership with a willing, invested client. It cannot be overstated how important it is for the consumer of an innovative service (or the in-house team) to be willing to invest the time and insights necessary for a law firm to be successful. Everyone must

For those law firms looking to offer managed services, there are at least a few key challenges to overcome:

- **Mindset shift.** Law firms (and their finance departments) should reassess how they measure "profitability." For almost all firms, this means focusing less on hours-based realization and near-term profits and more on guaranteed revenue and long-term sustainable relationships. Still, successes with great clients (including projects generating substantial fees on a recurring basis) pave the way for additional innovation by and within the law firm. There is nothing like a client win to get the attention, interest, and support of the partners.
- **Delivery.** Implementing a managed service will require a significant investment in operational and technological efficiencies, which quickly distinguish between legal/non-legal work and "triaging" matters as (1) standardized; (2) specialist; and (3) bespoke, so assigned appropriately at the outset. This is particularly critical for recruitment/retention because good lawyers don't want repetitious low-level work.
- **Sourcing.** To be agile to clients' needs, law firms will need to establish a flexible approach to multi-sourcing through a combination of both legal and non-legal personnel such as project managers, paralegals, consultants (flexible resource), or external specialists (for example, tech partners).
- **Measuring success.** Finally, for any successful managed services project, both parties need clear objectives and incentives. At the outset, law firms and clients should not be afraid to discuss the metrics of success and what the rewards will be (for both parties).

be committed to making the transformation successful. The law firm and in-house legal teams must align interests and goals to jointly develop a successful managed service delivery model. Law firms can't market this sort of delivery model in the abstract, without specific experience already in progress, and in-house teams can't demand this delivery model without clarity on the desired outcomes and planning. What law firms can market is a willingness to try something new and curiosity for experimentation.

NEED TO KNOW #6: ALTERNATIVE LEGAL SERVICE PROVIDERS[86]

Anyone thinking about optimizing processes should consider the resources they have, what the legal department looks like, who is doing what kind of work, and whether the work can be done by somebody other than an attorney. If so, what about the law firms? Or can this work be done by somebody other than a law firm?

As initially discussed in the context of the legal ecosystem, the ALSP, also known as legal process outsourcing (LPO), or legal service provider (LSP) (and whatever other name these companies can be called) are critical to the future of legal practice. Some take issue with the use of the word "alternative." I don't blame them. As the legal industry evolves, these service providers are no longer alternatives; they are key players. ALSPs are core service providers, just like law firms are for many corporate legal departments.

ALSPs can pretty much do anything that a law firm does except practice law. The hard line is that from a regulatory perspective in the United States, only attorneys can practice law. And ALSPs don't cross that line.

But then this means that once legal services are unbundled or disaggregated based on the process components of the work, there are many parts of the lawyer's job that somebody else can do which don't involve the practice of law. ALSPs have stepped in to take some of these functions off the desks of the lawyers. Corporate legal departments are turning to them to provide different staffing models, different staffing solutions, and to lighten the load of their lawyers. They are also turning to ALSPs in some cases to pull back work from the law firms that do repeatable, recurring work.

Smart law firms also use alternative providers to help reduce their own costs for certain functions that don't need legal expertise or licenses. First, they are using them for back-office functions—for example, for word processing or things not traditionally considered "lawyer" work. And as the legal practice continues to evolve, law firms are beginning to use ALSPs for some of the legal work in document review, e-discovery related to certain steps in the e-discovery process, litigation matters, and even in some of their repeatable contracting work. As ALSPs move up the value chain, law firms are realizing that it is better for them to play *with* them and *use* them than it is to lose revenue to them.

Still, for the most part, law firms have been giving up potential revenue to alternative providers because in many cases, law firms have looked at the work done by the ALSPs as something that is, for lack of a better word, below the quality of the type of legal work they want to do. Contrarily, the quality of the ASLPs is typically quite reliable, but the type of work they do tends to be at the junior level. It's the work most attorneys, especially senior associates and partners, don't want to spend time on.

To be clear—law firms' revenues are by no means declining, but they are leaving revenue on the table that is gladly being gobbled up by ALSPs. It's worth noting that that seems to be changing. Every client wants holistic solutions, so firms are being forced to integrate their own offerings with outside providers to improve the legal buying experience and retain clients.

LPOs AND ALSPs: WHERE DID THEY COME FROM? WHERE ARE THEY GOING?

> "You had this market event, the explosion of electronic information in the growth of the e-discovery industry, you had providers in India who were already doing objective coding of emails, Bates stamping, etc., and other providers, who were somewhat ingrained in the legal market, were doing back-office and middle-office support for the law firms. So, it was very much a natural progression for these organizations to go and meet this new demand and start providing E-discovery and document review services from an offshore location."—*Mark Ross*

My friend and colleague, Mark Ross, executive vice president and global head of Contracts, Compliance, and Commercial Services at Integreon Managed Solutions, is an authority on the ALSP space. Having been in this business since it was first a possibility almost twenty years ago, Ross has identified a number of overlapping and interrelated factors leading to the emergence of this player in the legal ecosystem.

First, Ross notes, was the explosion of electronic data particularly as it related to e-discovery, litigation, and document review. "In or around 2004 and 2005, what we saw in the marketplace was corporate legal departments who had outsourced their HR, their IT, their marketing, and often their finance and accounting, were faced with exploding legal bills because of this exponential growth in electronic data impacting the scale of the discovery exercise." They reached a point of total frustration with traditional providers (essentially the Am Law 200[87]), he says, who were charging $200 to $400 an hour for young associates to sit in a conference room, or in the law firm's basement, to stare at a computer screen hour after hour and simply click whether a document was relevant or confidential. At the same time, a number of providers had set up shop primarily in India and began to leverage lower cost resources for certain work.

These conditions created the perfect opportunity to reimagine the "how" and "why" of those pieces of legal work, and ALSPs were there to capitalize on the frustration.

The Evolving Dynamic Between Law Firms and ALSPs

The relationship between law firms and ALSPs is a complicated one, but seems to improve over time. Ross said there are four stages of law firm acceptance of ALSPs:

1. In the early days there was a "kicking and screaming" phase where law firms had been on this e-discovery and document review gravy train for a number of years. That gravy train came to an abrupt halt when their corporate clients demanded that for this specific area of work, firms should engage with an LPO or ALSP. Most firms are unable to get away with completely ignoring alternative paths to completing these tasks, but this painful phase was a necessary stepping stone to the deeper reliance on ALSPs we're seeing now.
2. From 2008 to 2009, law firms reached a phase that many are still in—the "checking the box" phase. This is where ALSPs are recognized by law firms as being an offering that they have for corporate clients. Unfortunately, it never goes much further than saying "yes, we have a relationship." Often it seems that law firms falling into this category are exceptionally skilled in marketing that they have innovating approaches to service delivery, but *also* rationalizing why they did not use those new techniques.
3. Some more innovative law firms are at the stage that Ross views as being where the market should be, one of "strategic collaboration."[88] Some firms have not only built up their own alternative delivery

platforms, but they have entered into well-publicized partnerships with ALSPs. Ross notes, "They have welcomed these providers into their firms, and have invited these organizations to look at their different practice areas and see what elements of the alternative legal services providers create a combined offering with the law firm that's essentially greater than the sum of its parts." This is the sweet spot (for now), reserved for firms that are truly looking to add value for their clients and keep pace with the evolving market.

4. The fourth stage, which has not been reached as of yet, is what Ross calls "bifurcated ownership." That's where the lines of ownership between ALSPs and law firms become increasingly blurred, with law firms owning ALSPs and ALSPs potentially owning law firms. As we all know, law firm ownership issues are complicated and don't necessarily lend themselves to this relationship just yet. But the whispers of expanding law firm ownership rules are growing louder all the time.

Corporate clients want the right resources that use the right technology, at the right price point—and importantly, all of this is based on the complexity of a given task at hand. Those law firms that embrace legal technology and ALSPs "will gain a greater share of the client's wallet, of that I have absolutely no doubt," Ross asserted.

On the legal technology piece, if there is one legal services ecosystem participant that is embracing legal technology and bringing it to bear for the benefit of clients, it is the ALSPs. They were the first to bring predictive coding to Big Law. They were the first to start leveraging their technology relationships in the name of streamlined services.

Now, we're seeing the same dynamic play out in the field of AI for automated contracted extraction. More mature ALSPs have deep relationships with some of the leading AI technology providers. As the demand and use of AI and legal technology continues to grow, the ALSPs will follow suit.

Engaging ALSPs

So, all of this begs the question: What is an easy or smart starting place for law firms to start engaging with an LPO or alternative provider? Ross asserts that one area that is perfect for collaboration between law firms and alternative providers is project-based work in response to, for example, a regulatory event. If you look at a particular regulatory event or requirement to support compliance with that event on behalf of your client, you should be able to deconstruct the end-to-end process and plug in an ALSP.

Right now, in the world of financial services, Markets in Financial Instruments Directive is one of the hot new regulations.[89] The impact of this regulation is that a number of financial institutions need to "repaper" their derivatives agreements. A range of different tasks are involved in this repapering or amending exercise, and many of these tasks are relatively straightforward in nature. At the same time, these efforts benefit from a law firm wraparound for subject matter expertise and compliance.

Another similar example is arising out of GDPR compliance, where companies are finding they may need to review or even amend potentially thousands of contracts. That sort of project to review existing contracts and provide some sort of template amendment is a great project for an ALSP.

Ross also cites the M&A practice as having great potential to leverage ALSPs. A significant proportion of the overall cost when a law firm provides end-to-end M&A support services to a corporate client is in the legal due diligence component. It is increasingly common to also see large corporations requesting that their law firms provide a fixed fee for the provision of end-to-end support across the entire transaction. By providing end-to-end support for an M&A transaction on a fixed-fee basis, it is not only easy, but economically sensible for the law firm to segment out elements of that end-to-end process and have them undertaken by a provider that (1) is used to performing this type of work, (2) has resources across the globe that can do this type of work easily, and (3) understands the technology platforms that are used for this type of work, the data rooms, the workflow, and so on. This helps improve the law firm's margin because the ALSP can

> "My perception of this," Ross says, "and I think the market's perception of this, has changed over the years. I still recall vividly, probably in 2007-2008, talking to the managing partner of an Am Law top 50 firm who turned to me and said, 'This whole LPO, alternative legal services provider thing, is win-win-lose. It's a win for you guys, it's a win for our clients, and it's a loss for us at the law firm.' I disagree with that vehemently. That presupposes a zero-sum game, that every penny of revenue that is diverted to an alternative legal service provider is somehow or another a penny of revenue that is lost to the law firm."

undertake a discrete element of the M&A transaction, the legal due diligence, at a cheaper price point than the law firm's own resources.

LESSONS LEARNED:[90] OUTSOURCING CONTRACT REVIEW TO AN LPO

The chapter on outsourcing, Need to Know #9, goes into great detail about the mechanics. In this section, I want to share a summary of the key lessons learned from my experience outsourcing to an LPO, which began in 2008 and continues today with my successors. What follows is a description of that specific engagement, as it still continues to be an industry-leading study on the benefits of outsourcing.

For many corporations, the traditional staffing model for procurement-contract drafting, review, and negotiation is based on a method that is labor-intensive and cost-prohibitive through the reliance on expensive in-house legal resources. Many of these resources are overpriced, especially for tasks that involve the review and negotiation of repetitive, lower complexity contracts. Given the constant need for these services, however, in-house lawyers and contract specialists often find themselves overwhelmed, with unrealistic demands on their time.

> There are enormous economies of scale that are gained by having the same people do the same work over and over. They become more efficient and more experienced. The more they learn, the higher the level of work we can give them. If they do really good work at the lower level, we'll raise the complexity a little bit, which allows the LPO to provide a greater value as they move up the value chain, so to speak, and we extract a greater value because we get to offload more work that would have had to be done in-house.

Often there are no formalized workflow processes, standard templates, accepted language, backup provisions, or guidelines for turnaround times. In this scenario, overburdened in-house lawyers cannot meet the tight timelines demanded, creating a conflict between the business client and the legal department. Often, the legal department will then engage external law firms to help on an hourly rate basis—leading to an unpredictable and potentially inefficient use of internal legal resources, and an overpriced dependency on outside counsel.

A major point is that the investment in time required to negotiate high-volume, but routine contracts can adversely impact the ability to review and manage the more important, higher risk contracts. The potential consequences to the business are clear: Either incur increased risk resulting from the business avoiding the legal department to expedite purchasing, or suffer delays in the procurement of goods and services. The need to balance risk and expedited legal services led to what became the first major outsourcing of core legal processes for Microsoft's legal department.

Lesson #1: Understand the Processes

I emphasized the importance of process earlier in the book in the context of technology, but it is equally important when considering outsourcing. Before engaging in contracting transformation, take time to understand the "as is" (current state) process. Map this out and identify areas for improvement. Determine what activities, if any, are redundant and can be eliminated, what can be outsourced, and what should be kept in-house.

Microsoft took on this challenge and initiated a dual-track effort to study its internal procurement contract review processes while assessing the opportunities afforded by an LPO provider. It was understood that contract review involved repeatable steps, and that the high-volume and low-risk nature of these contracts made the work ideally suited to LPOs.

Lesson #2: Create a Comprehensive Playbook

Outsourcing contract review effectively is predicated on successfully transferring knowledge from internal stakeholders to the LPO provider. Integral to this is the "playbook"—an outline for best practices that includes approved templates, negotiation positions, and sections outlining standard operating procedures, escalation protocols, and decision matrices.

In May 2009, following a rigorous selection process, Microsoft selected its LPO partner. The relationship started with a team of seven paralegals in Fargo, North Dakota, supporting procurement contract review. The LPO and Microsoft worked together to define the key performance indicators that would underpin the engagement and created a playbook—an extensive manual—that documented the entire process.

Initially, Microsoft outsourced only the legal review of vendor contracts, but as the Integreon team gained familiarity with Microsoft's processes, the engagement expanded to other types of contracts. The expansion also included Integreon becoming the first point of contact for Microsoft's internal business clients. Whether an issue should be escalated followed a process documented in the playbook. The result was a dramatic reduction in the time spent by Microsoft's in-house legal team reviewing contracts and answering basic questions, freeing them to focus on higher value work. The collaboration and integration of the LPO and Microsoft teams ensured that the engagement realized short-term successes and laid the groundwork for program growth for similar types of high-volume contracts and related contract administration tasks.

Lesson #3: Innovate Through Automation

Sometimes the hardest part of automation is understanding what platform is the best fit for the environment, budget, and tolerance for change. Enterprise-wide, multifunctional platforms may serve some best, while others may find such systems far too complex and expensive for their needs—especially if the end result is that only a fraction of the platform's functionality is used.

For Microsoft's lawyers, in addition to realizing the benefits of lower-cost LPO resources and the process improvements that result from working with an LPO provider, they understood that the technology underpinning CLM played an equally important role in driving further efficiencies. Although ahead of the pack in many respects, true transformation would still lie beyond Microsoft's reach without a revitalized technology supporting the process.

Microsoft already had some experience automating a contract process when it launched an NDA tool for its global employee population of more than 100,000 several years earlier. This offered a streamlined way for employees to create an NDA quickly and without the legal department's involvement. The tool's success was dependent on a good, simple template and efficient electronic signatures, and was a perfect smaller step in the larger contract automation journey.

In April 2013, Microsoft embarked on an effort to select a scalable CLM platform. The company understood that to reap the benefits of a new contracting system, it would need to scope precisely the functions to be automated and control the input of data into the system. After selecting the new platform, Microsoft asked the LPO to provide the ongoing administrative support for the platform, including: managing the intake of contracts for storage and ensuring the consistency and accuracy of information. In essence, a new contract "help desk" was born.

Concurrently, Microsoft focused on automating other aspects of the process. It leveraged its own Office 365 capabilities and Azure (technologies that most large companies also already have in their "toolbox") scalability to build a sleek yet simple online intake system for its employees, allowing for collection of critical contract data and visibility to the business on the status of their legal requests. This way, Microsoft could track how many requests were pending, what types of requests they were, and where they came from. Expanding on the help desk managed by the LPO Microsoft now had a one-stop shop for a variety of contracting services—from legal review to electronic signature and storage. By leveraging a combination of technology, improved processes, and creative resourcing, Microsoft was a trailblazer for the future of contracting in larger in-house legal departments.

Lesson #4: When Everything Is Great, Stay Involved

Although many corporate legal departments start the outsourcing journey with the best of intentions, over time the internal champions get pulled on to other pressing engagements and the level of involvement can wane. This can prove detrimental to the longer term success of the relationship. The involvement of key Microsoft personnel with the LPO and the continued focus on efficiencies within its legal department encouraged the expansion of outsourcing in scale and breadth alongside enhanced automation. This has directly translated into time savings for legal professionals and faster contracting for the business.

> Once a steady state is reached, the inclination may be to say, "Job well done," and call it a day. But this is not a recipe for success. Stay involved and continue to look for opportunities to innovate and work with the LPO provider to drive continuous improvement.

The results of Microsoft's relationship with the LPO were transformational, with the average turnaround time for legal review decreasing from three days to less than one, and the percentage of contracts reviewed within the agreed upon turnaround time increasing from 86 percent to 99 percent. At the same time, Microsoft's costs for contract review are now predictable, and the operating model optimized for future scaling.

Looking Forward

The last ten years have seen significant change in the sourcing and deployment of legal resources, particularly with growth in the adoption of LPO. It has become clear that the most effective model is a symbiotic ecosystem in which legal departments and LPO providers play crucial roles. Under this new model, with legal departments embracing process improvements, technology, and resource redistribution to providers like LPOs, efficiencies can be driven not only into the contract review process, but across the entire legal department.

LPOs are growing, especially in the type of work that they're getting. They used to do only very basic types of work a decade ago, and now they're handling more sophisticated pieces of work on the legal services spectrum. Successful ones are even nipping at the heels of some of the law firms. It's not an explosion as of yet, but time reveals a steady evolution as these providers demonstrate quality and build trust.

NEED TO KNOW #7: DATA[91]

Data is the secret sauce to innovation. It is also the gateway drug to get lawyers addicted to the benefits of technology.

Data is the secret sauce, the key, and the keyword. There is a growing realization that we all can and should seek data as a prime part of the business. Corporate legal departments and law firms face major challenges that will force them to rethink how they do business. Factors reshaping the landscape of the legal industry include: increased globalization, growth of the internet, automation of legal processes, emerging technology, and developments in data security.

This means that legal teams must reinvent their processes and use technology to help them increase efficiency and productivity by handling the vast amounts of data they handle properly, no matter where they are.

For a law firm to be a valued partner to its in-house clients, at the basic level, every outside counsel should provide certain data points: on their costs, their timelines, the level of resources they're providing, the volume, and response times of communications; expect these as standard. If a defined set of data points is expected to be delivered promptly and regularly, it will slowly become the norm of the engagement. If firms struggle, then it becomes a competitive advantage for those who

Imagine the optimal legal ops world where work flows smoothly to the right resources as its progress is tracked. A piece of legal work arrives on the metaphorical desk (the email inbox) in-house. It's then allocated immediately and automatically to the most cost-effective and efficient resource, whether that's a legal assistant, a junior lawyer, the GC, a software platform, an ALSP, outside counsel, or even self-serve. That engagement progresses at the optimum rate, and afterward, reporting on its progress and success is delivered to key stakeholders. This information makes the right-sourcing of work even more targeted next time. The business gets maximum bang for its legal buck; the legal department as a whole is freed from the low-value flood of work that clouds its effectiveness every day; and business and legal are free to partner on high-value strategic work that takes the company to the next level.

are comfortable with this notion. Why would clients pay for less value once they see what is possible? Particularly with the arrival of business-savvy ALSPs, there's no excuse for a modern LSP to be data-illiterate.

The scenario just mentioned isn't remotely possible without good data analytics. Similarly, all the mind-blowing benefits promised that will arrive with AI, blockchain, and any number of other hype-heavy game-changing tools won't get off the ground without good data as the foundation. Without proper analytics, it is impossible to identify areas where new solutions would be truly beneficial, and we can't evaluate the efficacy of new tools we implement. Gathering and deploying data is what every other rational, sensible business function does. If legal is to be a business partner, its time getting by without data is gone.

Fundamentals—Data for Better Relationship Management

Every attorney, whether in-house, law firm, legal aid, or other area can use data to improve the quality of the service or the relationship with the client.

I want to start with this concept because it is the easiest data to gather by the service provider. Basically, it is data that can be gathered manually at any point.

- Information about how many items of work or matters have been done by the firm within any given period of time (month, quarter, year). In data speak this is *volume.*
- Information about the actual work is always interesting to the clients. Even just being able to show the categories of work helps inform the client at a more macro level about the kind of legal work that the business is requesting. Think about the types of work and creating natural and logical buckets to align.
- Patterns about the work is the next level of the categorization of the work. For example, consider if there are seasonal spikes that would be informative for the business to appreciate why legal responses may be slower at certain times.
- The ultimate value, as perceived by the business, is data about the timeliness of the legal support. How long things take in legal is always valuable data when the business (inevitably) complains about how long legal review takes.

For firms not accustomed to tracking any data points at all, data harvesting and tracking can be a bit intimidating. Firms shouldn't run before they can walk, and there are a couple of low-hanging fruits that can help them get accustomed to gathering, managing, and analyzing data that will help them make more informed decisions.

First Step: When firms are considering how to become more operational, *measuring the cost of servicing a client* is the first thing to do. It sounds logical and simple, and something that every experienced lawyer should have the basic skills to do—particularly with the advent of matter management and e-billing software—but the reality is different. In the Big Law setting, where numbers of clients and touch points are high, it's easy for cost tracking to get out of control. Losing control might not mean a catastrophic collapse in operational capability, but the volume and complexity of this effort can take so many hours that the team doesn't have time to analyze properly, meaning that planning goes out the window, and the legal team becomes reactive.

Basic costs per client or matter is black and white, and should be easy to measure, so start there. Once that basic data is gathered, then they can start to add more metrics: historical trends, payment cycles, and so on—these will unearth helpful insights. For example, if payment cycles are fast, can better rates be offered for prompt payments? To help prepare for resource allocation, is there a particular event or season that typically generates additional work from the client? These are questions that firms can begin to ask to help themselves *and* their clients.

Next Step: The next must-have dataset relates to how business clients engage with their internal legal department. The only question that the client really cares about, more often than not, is *how long a matter will take*. The quality and indeed any other aspect of the advice is almost irrelevant to them. They assume the quality is high and that legal issues are covered by the legal professionals. So, all that matters to them is timeliness. They want predictability and certainty so they can plan for a matter, engage legal on it, resolve it satisfactorily, and then move on. This means that tracking the time from a matter being requested to its outputs being provided is the very least that business partners should expect, but far too few firms provide this insight. Although this data has a profound impact on customer satisfaction, it helps legal to resource properly, too. Is work going to the wrong person? Is the time spent on uncomplicated matter the best use of the legal resources? Tracking data properly is the only way to answer these questions, and to provide the level of service that the client has the right to expect.

Legal Data 2.0—Data for Quality Improvement

Even between those two critical data sets, cost tracking is actually more of a crawl. Firms are already crunching the numbers on profitability, but they can learn a lot more by paying attention more closely at different levels. That is the first place to start.

Data used to improve the quality of the legal service is a bit more advanced, and can be a goal for future innovation, once basic data about the relationship (as described already) is being collected.

Of course, my favorite in-house subject matter perfectly illustrates the effect data and analytics can have on the law practice: contracts. Every company deals with contracts—they're the foundation of business—and an increase in the volume and complexity of contracts is often the decisive factor that compels a growing business to hire its first lawyer.

Capturing contracts volume is black and white at the start; there are a finite, knowable number. Ask the sales team how many deals they have, and they'll know immediately how many sales they've made. Similarly, HR will know straight away how many people they've hired. But ask legal how many contracts they've produced in a given quarter and there might be disappointment. This must be rectified first to avoid embarrassment and make sure nobody knows more about contracts than legal does. Whether employment contracts, sales agreements, or other type of contracts, the business is likely more in tune with volumes than the legal department that is supporting all those contracts.

But smart in-house teams move beyond this headline figure to capture turnaround time, type of contract, involvement of outside counsel, monetary cost, most and least negotiated clauses, and so on. These might seem like softer metrics but the lessons they bring will allow delivery of actionable insight to the business. Helping them close, procure, or onboard faster has a direct impact on the bottom line, and works wonders to boost the reputation of legal internally.

Armed with that data, leadership can make sure the right people see it and use it to make strategic decisions.

In this context, I often advise communicating spend or costs monthly, as financial data always has a keen audience—no matter the setting. Workload and workflow-related data is better suited to a quarterly strategic meeting, where it can be presented to the relevant senior leadership. Key indicators like contract volume, headcount touched by legal matters, turnaround times—these are headline figures the GC needs to know. It's important to arm the GC with hard stats for the tough conversations she or he has to have at their level; it's likely the CFO is grilling them for information, and historically legal hasn't always been able to provide it. The era where this was acceptable is just about over.

In fact, those firms that are doing this sort of transactional work for clients can be invaluable in providing data about the substantive elements of the negotiations they do on their clients' behalf. These firms are in a great position to educate and inform their clients about negotiation trends and pitfalls. They should be tracking which terms are commonly negotiated and how those negotiations resolve themselves. They can analyze deviations from standards and preferred clauses and demonstrate to clients how negotiation cycles can be improved by adjusting the default positions. Law firms will need to invest some time and resources in collating this data and organizing it in a consumable format for the client. This is precisely the kind of work that can be performed by the contract manager and other paraprofessionals. Also, this work would lend itself to some great technology that is readily available, for analyzing negotiated contracts and summarizing clauses. Most in-house teams function on anecdote and experience when it comes to negotiations, and many have built guides off of their experiences. But how many have the data to back up why they changed a certain provision, or why they are changing their risk appetite? Not enough!

So, from an in-house and law firm perspective, data is a fantastic tool that helps legal teams make consistent quality improvements as time goes on:

- Collecting data about the terms in negotiated contracts will help to inform the position of the legal department and will increase speed of negotiations going forward. Sample terms and standard templates can only be improved upon once data shows that the existing terms are constantly negotiated, and resulting terms show a pattern.
- Litigation data is similar, when litigating similar issues. Tracking outcomes becomes critical, so that mistakes are not repeated. Surely this is not novel, but *how* the data is collected is key. It should be searchable and reportable in an easily consumable format.

Some Law Firms Get It

Law firms are investing in different types of professionals, whether it's the firm or a legal process outsourcer—whoever it is that's delivering the service. They don't just have attorneys. They have Six Sigma professionals. Project managers. Program managers. Marketing professionals. They have data analytics—data analysts, data scientists, you name it. That's all in a very hot evolution right now. You're seeing the more forward-looking, forward-thinking service providers are already staffing in a different way.

LeftFoot Podcast, March 2018

- Other areas where there is recurring work (patent applications, employment law questions, acquisitions, and so on) there is always data that can be collected and informative for future similar work. Even basic information is helpful and the right place to start. Something is better than nothing.

Bridging the Skills Gap

To become data-driven, and data-enabled, lawyers will have to overcome inertia and a skills gap in the profession. Although some progressive law schools are catching up and the number of law schools teaching skills like forecasting and data manipulation is growing, much progress is still needed. Most worrying is the huge cohort of mid-career lawyers who were never taught any data skills as part of their training, and now face another twenty years of practice without them. To stay competitive in the job market, it's crucial for lawyers to try to address this, and in a way that holds their interest. For example, a transactional lawyer might find a financial management class interesting; a more process-driven lawyer might prefer to learn Six Sigma. However it is addressed, it's important to keep up with the kind of role that the twenty-first century lawyer is becoming—not just what it is today, but five or ten years from now.

To underscore a theme echoed throughout the book, please remember: Change management is driven by leadership. The tone at the top needs to be mindful and proactive, creating and maintaining the kind of operational rigor where data tracking is natural. That might mean setting annual numerical targets, instituting client engagement metrics, or even enforcing a monthly reporting requirement.

The mix of carrot and stick required to make good data a reality will be different for each department and its law firms, but the key is to get started. So many firms and companies throughout the world are undergoing digital transformation across the board—whether moving publishing online, bringing case management to the cloud, or automating marketing. The legal profession must be part of the technological revolution and as a point of pride, collect and exploit data to enable a more efficient, digital future—or risk being left behind. Aren't we all tired of the negative expectations that the world has of this profession: slow, old-fashioned, unpredictable, and so on?

NEED TO KNOW #8: THE MODERN LEGAL WORKFORCE[92]

Throughout this book I've highlighted the many changes that are affecting legal service delivery. As more firms and legal departments experiment with new techniques and find great results, the composition of the legal workforce is undergoing a more permanent transition: (1) business professionals are being incorporated into legal service delivery within legal practices, and (2) practicing lawyers are demonstrating aptitude in business skill sets. As mentioned in various parts of this book, new skills are needed to enhance and improve legal services. Whether those new skills are procured from other professionals who are not attorneys, but brought into the legal practice to provide their expertise in data analytics, financial modeling, project management, operations, or another business discipline, or whether attorneys are expanding their own skill sets to include business-type skills, the important news is that the great outcomes from these skills are impacting legal services in a very positive way.

> *We hear so much about diversity and inclusion in the kind of more traditional topics, but it's really a type of inclusiveness that the legal profession has just not been good at. We just haven't been. I think that's kind of your first starting foundational thing. I think that would really transform legal services from every angle, right? We have to let others in that can look at things that are so obvious to them where, for practicing attorneys, it's just not in their skillset.*
>
> *Legal Ops Rising* Podcast—December 2017

> It is a paradox. Innovation officers are specifically hired to implement change, yet when they try, they don't seem to have great success at the pace they might expect, given the high level of support they received during the recruiting process and the title they were bestowed. This is perhaps the greatest internal tension in law firms today.

"That's not my job."

An emerging development in law firms centers on the growing number of roles dedicated to innovation in one form or another. But these innovation officers and partners face great challenges, or are tasked with innovation yet meet significant silent resistance. There is usually the external perception that a law firm embraces innovation, yet practicing attorneys often have little interaction with those innovators and don't know how or even when to engage them.

In-house and even in some firms, there has recently been a significant focus on legal ops. Sometimes the role of legal ops is clear. Other times it is a function that is less defined, but it typically does fit within the description. Legal ops across law departments and firms includes myriad capabilities and skillsets: from project management to technology implementations, from data analytics to process re-engineering, and from vendor management to creative law firm pricing negotiations.

No matter how legal ops are defined, it is becoming more obvious to many lawyers that these skill sets are critical to the future success of legal

By creating an us (practicing bar members) vs them (everyone else) distinction, we are potentially alienating extremely valuable and highly skilled professionals. We don't mean to, but I'm afraid it is happening. I don't know when this concept was first uttered or in what context, but somewhere along the evolutionary path in legal services, we devolved many other professions into one non-descript group. Some have survived as independent professions among us, like paralegals and contract managers, but others have morphed into some unclear and attorney-driven new category of "non-lawyers." The funny thing is that modern thinkers agree how much these "non-lawyers" are needed. We rely on them, and we learn from them every day. Law firms and in-house legal departments are posting new positions daily, which is a great sign of change in our profession. More and more, we are delegating parts of our jobs to them and enhancing the legal service we deliver thanks to their skills. So let's change the lingo to match our intentions.

Take the pledge: Promise to stop calling these amazing professionals without whom we could not be successful "non-lawyers." To all the program managers, operations managers, business and data analysts, and all other allied professionals who work with lawyers daily, thank you for your patience with our profession and thank you for always trying to put on your best lawyer speak around us. We appreciate you!

services. Most often these functions are performed by business professionals who have not practiced law, or those "recovering" lawyers who realized they really did not enjoy the practice of law and preferred the process of delivering the legal services. But the relegation of more "innovative" or non-traditional attorney functions to *those people* showcases the ultimate challenge the industry faces today: Changing lawyer behavior is hard anywhere—in-house or within firms.

The good news is that law firms do hire for these roles. They realize the need for these functions, and are putting their money where their mouth is, to some extent, in taking this first step. But the problem is that the rest of the lawyers apparently feel excused from innovating because there is someone down the hall with the word "innovation" in their title. Law firm lawyers proudly parade their innovation "people" at pitches and client meetings, yet they are not ready to include them in the discussion of the engagement. It goes back to a lack of understanding and appreciation: Practicing lawyers just don't appreciate what these innovation experts can do for their practice.

The news is not all bad. Law firms are trying, even if it's at the macro level. They are investing in new and different professional roles. They are enhancing their marketing with new terminology and creating new lines of services for certain practice areas. There is not yet a wholesale overhauling of firms, but it is good to see the various pieces of the puzzle appearing.

Make Way for the Unicorns

Similarly interesting is the changing nature of the attorney role. There are lawyers who are embracing the new era in legal and enhancing their own skills outside the practice of law, but still related to it! It's time for in-house lawyers and law firms to make way for these unicorns. By "unicorns" I am not referring to the next great tech startup, where the word usually appears.[93] I'm talking about the mythical creature that lurks (or does it?) in law firms all over the country and around the globe, in corporate legal departments at some of the world's best companies. Instead, I mean the lawyer with an appreciation for process and who seeks out data—the lawyer who is frustrated by the inefficiencies of the legal practice and is emotionally torn between perfecting the craft of law and breaking it down completely into an objective set of processes and metrics. There is a new breed of lawyers who are standing up and speaking out. They realize that there are better ways to get their jobs done. They are curious about technology and process improvements, and they have a natural thirst for data about their practice.

Those who still love the practice of law but are eager to innovate the way they practice can take a page from the "Unicorn Lawyer" handbook. This is a beautiful opportunity to combine skill sets into a new operationalized legal practice. I use the term "legal practice" and not legal service or delivery model, or any other popular concepts, because my focus is on operationalizing the practice of law and moving legal ops into the front office.

As we've already discussed, there has been great success in back-office legal ops: e-billing, time tracking, conflict checking, matter management, and so on. The real challenge for the legal industry is to operationalize the practice of law. To significantly impact the way lawyers practice their craft, a movement by lawyers, for lawyers, is needed. I've been called a unicorn (I interpreted that as a compliment) and I've been told, "You don't talk like other lawyers." But while I've come to learn that I'm not alone in this respect, there are not yet enough of us to make a significant impact, such as the impact being made by legal ops professionals in other parts of the corporate law department, and or law firms.

> I used to think that I must have a mutated gene of some sort that makes me "different" from other lawyers. I realize now that many lawyers have that dormant gene, and if allowed to develop, it can become a powerful influence on how legal service is delivered. That's when the unicorn is born!

> **Lawyers must lead the way.** When it comes to changing the way lawyers do their jobs, we listen to other lawyers first. Ask any legal ops professional who has tried to influence change in the front office, and they'll be the first to tell you how hard it is to break through to the legal practitioners. Lawyers who have practiced law in a certain way for many years, in a profession that has gone mostly unchanged for more than 100 years, are hard to convince to adapt. There has to be a compelling reason to change and it must pose minimal risk to the business client.

Let's examine the sort of lawyer who could be defined as a "unicorn"—or perhaps more precisely, the new "operationally inclined lawyer." Lawyers with the following traits or skills are likely to qualify.

Business-Minded

The best lawyers have often described themselves as business-minded. This means they are focused on delivering the legal services and advice needed for their business clients to get their business done. Keep in mind that commercial (transactional or litigation) lawyers exist only for that purpose—to help the business clients get work done. Without businesses, there would be no need for commercial attorneys. So, why do lawyers need to describe themselves as "business-minded"? Well, there are those lawyers who get so focused on delivering the most perfectly researched legal advice or the most risk-mitigated document that in fact they forget the ultimate business purpose; they are the types that businesses label as "blockers." To break away from the perception that "legal blocks the business," lawyers have had to demonstrate they are keenly focused on business objectives while practicing their craft and delivering services.

What is needed is a new type of business-minded lawyer—the type who is focused on the business of practicing law. Those lawyers who treat their practice like a business will be the ones who can bring legal practice into twenty-first century. In every business, there is talk of timelines, costs, efficiencies, data, targets, goals, and many other concepts that are usually absent from the discussions of legal practice. In-house lawyers are more likely to bring these concepts into their practice as they spend more time closely aligned with their clients (the business). They realize the legal practice is directly linked to business goals. These lawyers are, in effect, an extension of the business and often end up absorbing these business concepts into their legal work. As the legal work moves further from the business, that is, to law firms, these concepts become more distant as well.

> The attorney's job is still to deliver legal advice from the law firm. They don't need to be process experts. They don't need to be green belts in Six Sigma. They don't need to know how to architect solutions, but they do need to know when to bring in all those people who know how to do that other stuff. Let's just call it other stuff for lack of a better word because that's the only way they will improve and enhance the engagement experience with the in-house team that's moving at a faster pace than ever before. That pace will only increase.
>
> Lucy Bassli on Chad Main's *Technically Legal* Podcast

The business-minded lawyer thinks about turnaround times for their legal work and wants to set expectations with the client about when they can expect to see the results. This lawyer balances legal risks with business goals to give the business a response that will enable the outcome rather than provide the perfect legal advice. Legal advice will be provided with an understanding of the business processes within which the advice will be taken and connected to the goals that the business has set. Engagements with law firms thus will look different: Deadlines are set, expected outcomes and deliverables are discussed, and risk tolerance will command extensive conversations. Decisions will be made to prioritize work and accept more risks to increase efficiencies and the effectiveness of the legal work delivered. Feedback about timeliness and quality will become an ordinary part of the engagement, backed by data and examples.

> *Some firms just really miss the mark on making you feel like they really care. It shows in lack of preparation. It's shown in coming to a pitch with your standard, glossy materials, having not read up on our latest, publicly available information. I'm not talking about sifting through quarterly SEC filings, even. We're just saying, "Hey, read the recent blog that our chief legal officer recently wrote."*
>
> *LeftFoot* Legal Business Development Podcast—March 2018

Data-Influenced

As I have stressed in this chapter, data will be the best friend of the new "operationally inclined lawyer." Data will be used to support smart risk-taking and advice about the types of deals or cases that may be worth the expense of legal advice. When lawyers start saying "no" to certain lower value work and push back certain parts of their work to the client/business, they will support those recommendations with the data that shows how much time such pieces of work take, and how much that work costs. With historical data providing a better lens on reality, the business will be more receptive to accept this work for the benefit of speed.

A good example of data-influenced decisions is found in the tracking of turnaround times. Gone should be the days that lawyers say "it depends," when asked how long a piece of work should take. The "operationally inclined lawyer" is to analyze the mountains of data related to past work experience and give a good estimate of when the work will be completed.

As in other types of services, there can be caveats for unexpected scenarios or complications, but there must be a set of expectations for clients.

Lawyers can easily figure out how many and how long: how many [fill in the blank] have they done in the past certain amount of time? Data around the number of contracts, pleadings, memos, or other deliverables is easily counted. Similarly, lawyers can figure out how long those deliverables usually take. For law firms this is much easier when they are, for better or worse, still tracking time. In-house lawyers may have a tougher time accessing hard data about turnaround time historically, but after enough experience, it can be done. The macro point is that data is key, and will help, among other things, determine what work should be handled by lawyers, what work should stay in-house or go to firms and allied professionals, and how long things should take.

Process-Focused

Process is what it comes down to. Operationally inclined lawyers know and appreciate that what they do is actually a process. Key functions can be broken down into a series of steps, some of which are simple and some that require great judgment and thought. The operationally inclined lawyer will naturally seek ways to make the various steps of the process more efficient, and then spend their time on only those steps that require their attention and unique judgment. This is another way of thinking about what is commonly known as the debundling or disaggregation of legal services. There are steps in the legal process that can be handled by the business, by paraprofessionals in the legal team, by automation and by external legal providers—whether lawyers at a firm, or related legal professionals at other types of companies.

For example, when the business can handle its own contracts, like NDAs, by reviewing some self-help guidance and using a template that the legal department provides (ideally web-based), the business is self-reliant and can move at its own pace. There is no need to wait on legal to be part of that contracting process. Even when negotiations are needed, if the legal team can provide negotiation guidelines, the business can handle things on its own. This does require that some risk is assumed: the business may not follow the guidelines, so legal must accept that risk. This is also a great example again where data is critical. The data will reveal, for example, the number of disputes there have been over NDAs. If very few, then this is where smart risks should be taken and data will create courage for other lawyers to accept that they don't need to be involved. If the lawyers are still concerned, then at a minimum they can consider outsourcing the negotiation process to lower cost legal professionals to save time and money.

Conclusion

The new breed of lawyers will have a combination of all these skills and other traits. They will have new skills beyond what is currently taught in many law schools. They will push their lawyer counterparts to think differently about how they practice law, and they will delight their business clients with their focus on data and process. Over time, these unicorns will become more common and visible in most firms and legal departments (**Figure 7-11**). There will likely be a greater percentage of these unicorns in the millennial generation than in prior generations, and they will befriend robots and automation. Just like there is no reason to fear robots, there is no reason to fear unicorns. In fact, they should be embraced. These new, operationally inclined, unicorn lawyers will easily bridge gaps with technologists, serving as great translators for those who are not comfortable with technology or change. So, make room for the unicorns . . . in fact, you may be one!

Figure 7-11. *Image of Signage Used by Law Firm Seyfarth Shaw, Which We Co-Developed for Their Booth at the 2018 Annual ACC Meeting*

The Millennial Factor

There is so much written[94] on millennials joining the legal practice (see the appendix for list of helpful articles) all of which is actually quite easy to distill, for the purpose of this book, in a very unscientific summary:

1. How they want to work
   - *Technology.* Yes, they are more adaptable to technology, but that does not make them legal tech experts. They will, however, quickly learn whatever technology enables them to be more flexible in where they work if it allows more of a "freelance" lifestyle where travel is made easy and supported with technology.
   - *Flexibility.* I stopped talking about work-life balance a few years ago and accepted the concept of work-life integration. I've heard millennials refer to "work-life blending." In this view, the definition of success and happiness intertwine professional achievements with personal accomplishment and fulfillment.
   - *Options.* They leave if they are not happy. Switching jobs is not uncommon, and longevity at one firm or corporation is not perceived as a badge of honor. In fact, it may seem a little boring and uncreative. They do not feel stuck in their jobs. If unhappy, they just change jobs. They also aren't as attached to titles as prior generations. Even the defining title of "attorney" may not mean as much to them, creating tons of more interesting career path possibilities.[95]
   - *Feedback.* They are not fans of cold empirical rating and rankings as ways to be evaluated. They want live-time input and guidance to improve their performance. There is preference for mentorships and informal coaching. Relationships are important.
2. Type of work they want to do
   - *Purposeful.* The work must have some broader purpose or benefit to the community or world beyond the immediate client project goals. The work should feel impactful at a bigger level. Social consciousness is high on the agenda.
   - *Engaging.* Millennials are deeply aware of the capabilities of technology. With the explosion of legal-focused productivity tools on the market, they want their seat at the table in handling substantive and meaningful work.

3. Who they want to work with
    - *Culture.* Enjoying colleagues socially and feeling comfortable among peers is critical to millennial happiness at work.
    - *Diversity.* They demand equality and appreciate difference of perspective that diversity brings. They are not fans of the traditional hierarchy of law firms.
4. How they want to learn
    - *Experience.* Theory and principle are no longer enough. Millennials are demanding experiential learning and hands-on work opportunities that provide benefits to the community around them (see *Purpose*). Legal aid opportunities while in law school seem to be attractive.

NEED TO KNOW #9: OUTSOURCING LEGAL

Outsourcing Generally . . .

As a follow-on to the ALSP dynamic and our review of the managed service model for law firms, let's examine some more practical aspects of outsourcing legal services, because it can be overwhelming.

First, the notion of sending work to somebody other than a law firm is a novel concept for many corporate departments; but that is fine, it is all part of the needed evolution.

Secondly, outsourcing is a form of business operation that is uncommon in legal, and certainly not a natural experience for most practicing lawyers. A review of some key principles of outsourcing and then some basic steps will set a good foundation for any attorney planning to outsource or planning to deliver services as an outsourced service provider.

> *Future Vision Note*: Although most references in this chapter are about ALSPs, consider replacing them with law firms—those moving in the direction of delivering managed services. Those same principles that are common for outsourcing to ALSPs can also be applied to those future scenarios for managed services by law firms.
>
> It may not be common yet, but it will be. It has to be!

Why Outsource?

So first and foremost, the *business case*—**why outsource**? It's crucial for anyone proposing outsourcing to leadership to develop a business case for outsourcing. This must be the clearly understood and explained reasons for outsourcing. It's where you describe the benefits and the goals. Some of the likely reasons are scalability, efficiency gains, and potential savings. Convincing others of this change will require that there be significant improvements to their own experiences, so you've really got to sell it to get everyone on board.

Scalability

There are a couple of things to think about. The kind of work that is most suitable for outsourcing, even as the outsourcers are moving up the value chain and providing more judgment-based work, is work that is scalable. When I say "scalable" I mean work that increases and decreases in volume over time. It fluctuates, sometimes without a clear pattern. These can be difficult to staff internally, because it means that at times the teams assigned to them are completely overloaded, while at other times the company may be temporarily carrying headcount because the volume does not require as many people as are on staff for the work. Or the work process is changed, requiring more human resources, or changing the types of transactions, which may need different skill sets at times. The solution the ALSP provides means they can flex to those functions, whether it is volumes or skill sets, but they're able to go up and down and stretch and that is a huge benefit as opposed to internally managing team of employees.

Think of an ALSP as a rubber band: it stretches and accommodates the work on an as needed basis, at that moment in time. It's a much more scalable option, and it should be sustainable if you imagine replacing or enhancing the roles of the existing full-time employee team, and or core team people, if they are doing the same thing over and over. Think about it: How many years could your internal team member do that piece of work? How long until they want to move on to other things? This is about sustaining those people and continuing to increase their interest and excitement in their work while you are using the ALSP to scoop some of the more tedious or repetitive work off their plate. This really helps make the internal team more sustainable.

Efficiencies

An ALSP's business model is completely focused on the bottom line. It's all about profits. The more work they can do in a certain amount of time, the more money they will make. They have figured it out: It is about profitability, not just about revenue. The incentives are built into the model to be efficient. Although the business model for law firms is still different, many firms are wrestling with the notion of efficiencies and passing those onto clients (while internally dealing with their own compensation model restrictions, billable hours, and so on).

If the ALSP makes a certain amount of money from a fixed-fee arrangement, the more it can squeeze outputs/deliverables within the allocated resources, and the more profit it gets to keep. Since the fee is fixed, the ALSP is incentivized to use as few resources as possible. This need to be efficient means that ALSPs will be employing technology to enable their speed and enhance their own data gathering, so they can continuously improve.

Potential Savings

Often, switching from a law firm to an ALSP brings immediate savings. If work done by a law firm is lifted and shifted to an ALSP, there will be immediate and significant savings because the cost of the ALSP resources is much lower than law firm lawyers. A lot of work is being done by firms today on the traditional billable hour that can be done by other skilled workers, who are not licensed attorneys, therefore drawing a much lower salary. That is basic math, so think about what the opportunities are to demonstrate savings.

Frankly, cost savings shouldn't be the ultimate goal right out of the gate because a buffer should be included. It may take time and money to train the ALSP on work that the attorneys do not need training to do. They'll need time to improve their quality and will need to spend more time on the work initially. Still, even with those unavoidable transition costs, the price of the resourcing will always be lower, likely resulting in savings if not immediately, then shortly after the work has been transitioned and the processes stabilized.

What to Outsource?

As ALSPs climb up the value chain, we've seen the scope of their services increase, as discussed in the chapter on ALPs. Still, there are some common characteristics of work that are easily outsourced and most likely to be successful as you experiment with this type of resourcing structure.

The work to outsource should be **repeatable** for a number of reasons. It is like a sport—the more you practice, the better you get. For those who are not sports enthusiasts, think of it within the context of your own work. The more you do a similar type of work, the better you become at it. It can be done much faster over time, and there are lessons along the way that are applied to make it more effective as well. Since the ALSPs are built around cost-effective resourcing, those lower cost resources will need to be trained with specificity and cannot spend time making complex judgment calls. Steps should be clear and predefined, so repeatable work gives you the most bang for your buck.

Generally, **high-volume, lower risk** work is the best for outsourcing. Why lower risk? Because trying to convince lawyers to outsource their work to anybody but themselves presumes that quality is a big concern; there is a presumption that things will go wrong. So mitigate that risk because this is a very big change, and to start, it's important to build trust in the process. Go with high-volume work where the ALSP can learn very easily from many transactions or a lot of interactions and hopefully at lower risk levels so if something does go wrong through the process it's OK—people can assume that kind of smart risk.

How to Outsource?

Once convinced that outsourcing legal work to a managed service provider (whether a law form or other LSP) is the right option, some key steps must be taken to achieve measurable success. These are not logistical steps necessarily, though I provide some practical guidance. Some of these steps are philosophical, too.

Clients must understand what they are outsourcing.

There is no faster way to fail in outsourcing than to expect the service provider to take on processes that internally the client team cannot understand or explain. It is critical for the client team to spend a significant amount of time learning their own process. This step is something that does not come naturally to attorneys because they are used to doing what lands on their plates. A problem to solve is received, or a contract to review, and the work begins. There is no time taken to review how to get to the end results. To outsource effectively, the current process must be clearly documented with some detail. Specifically, pay attention to the "special" cases that arise, and unique scenarios that are outliers, but should be noted for full transparency.

Once the current state is defined, that is the perfect time to identify inefficiencies and process gaps. There is no reason for the processes to stay the same in preparation for outsourcing. Make as many easy changes as possible at this point. Revise the process maps to reflect a better process than what you started with. There will be ample opportunities to refine it once the service provider is engaged, but for now it is important to have as clean of a process as possible to share it during the RFP engagement with potential suitors.

> **NEWSFLASH**
>
> Things will go wrong. We should be more forgiving of our own internal resources than we are of those we trust externally with our work. A real outsourced and managed service relationship is built on mutual trust and joint skin in the game. It is a virtual team!

Process maps are not common to the practice of law. We discussed this in greater detail in the chapter on process and efficiencies, chapter 7. This exercise may require the help of a Six Sigma[96] or other process expert. Many project managers have this skill set, and there are automated tools that can help as well. Documenting a process in prose using Word would be very natural to an attorney because they live in Word documents, but real process efficiencies are best analyzed in a visual representation that shows the various players involved and the key steps taken in each role. **Figure 7-12: Sample Process Workflow** depicts seven stages on the NDA process touched by six different roles before a process improvement effort. It demonstrates the complexity that can become apparent when breaking down what otherwise would appear to be a fairly simple process of creating and executing an NDA. Needless to say, the process was simplified tremendously!

Deciding on the Outcomes

It is important to determine exactly what is intended from the outsourcing process. These outcomes will be unique to the client and firm depending on what the goals are for outsourcing. Understanding whether the goal is to save money or free up the time of internal employees can dictate how the engagement will be arranged. Similarly, whether there is a goal to gather deeper insights into the legal work currently handled can be a great driver for a managed service. Of course, it could be a combination of these and others. Regardless of the stated goals, the desired outcomes must be reasonable and within the scope of capabilities sought from the providers.

It is very easy to come up with a grandiose wish list of goals, but care should be taken that the goals are actually achievable. The service provider plays a key role in helping wishful clients be practical about their expectations. No one wins when there is over-promising and under-delivery. Naturally, a good service provider will advise on the goals and should honestly describe what is and isn't possible. An easy trap for clients to fall into is the "metrics buffet"—all the data you want for one set price. This is not as great as it sounds, and not always very helpful. Often the client is so overjoyed with the prospect of receiving data about the work that for years has been unmeasurable, that they want everything tracked and measured. This is a cumbersome task for the service provider and often yields data that the client does very little with. As discussed in Chapter 7, consider which data will actually inform changes within the firm or the outsourced process.

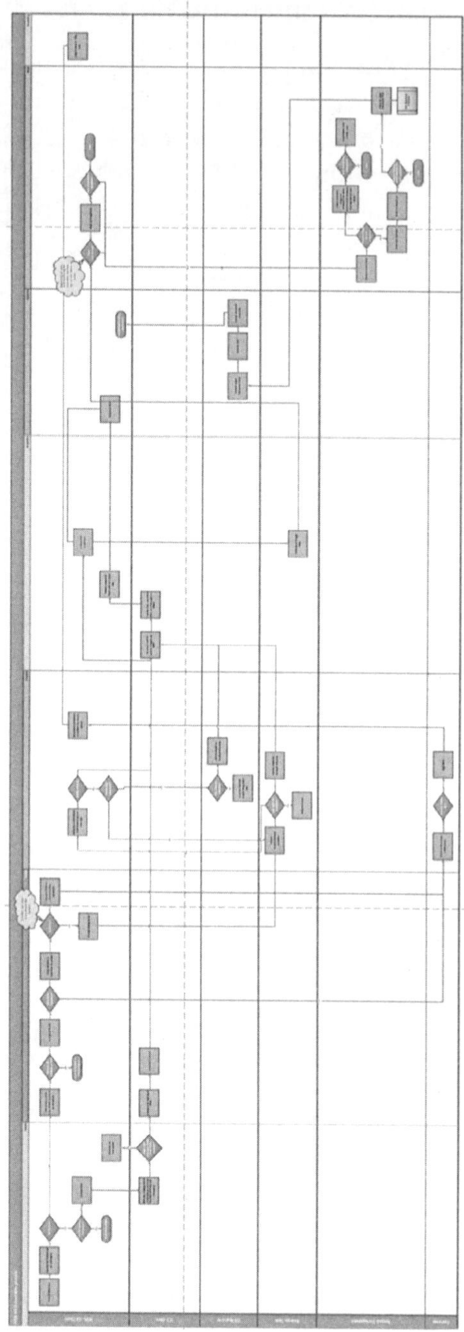

Figure 7-12. *Sample Process Workflow*

Selecting the Right Partner

Although most attorneys are familiar with RFPs, because their business clients do them, they are still not quite the standard in legal services. Only recently have RFPs for legal services from law firms become more common. Law firms are getting better at responding to them, and legal departments are getting better at issuing them. Still, there is a long way to go. Legal departments should engage their company's procurement team to leverage best practices for sourcing services. There is still the perception that legal services are unique, but there is a lot that can be learned for the standard procurement process of running an RFP. The legal team should modify the RFP documents to make sense for the purchase of legal services, but certainly can benefit from the more generic process well-established by procurement professionals. (See the appendix for more on RFPs.)

Clients should spend time with the respondents and learn about their capabilities and innovative solutions to deliver legal services, but also spend time getting a sense of their culture. Will the law firm's culture match the culture of the legal department? Preferences for communication styles, drafting styles, and risk tolerances are just a few of the attributes that can quickly signal whether there is a match. Also, an important factor is the law firm's policy for conflict checks and seeking waivers. That will become critical, and is unique to law firms, since most ALSPs can provide dedicated teams walled off from other clients, so that conflicts are not an issue. With law firms, it is critical to define alternative solutions where the law firm will have a conflict, and to set timelines for the conflict checks to avoid delays in processing.

Planning the Transition

Figure 7-13: Transition Timeline is a sample timeline for outsourcing a sizable operation. Granted, this was a first-time outsourcing contract legal review, and subsequent processes were outsourced on a slightly compressed schedule, but the steps taken are all quite similar. This sample reflects the timeline used for outsourcing some of the lower level repeatable work to an ALSP, but all these same steps apply when outsourcing to a law firm for a managed service.

Once the light at the end of the tunnel is seen be careful not to skimp on the transition plan. Work backwards with the service provider from an agreed-upon go-live date, and focus on the communication to the

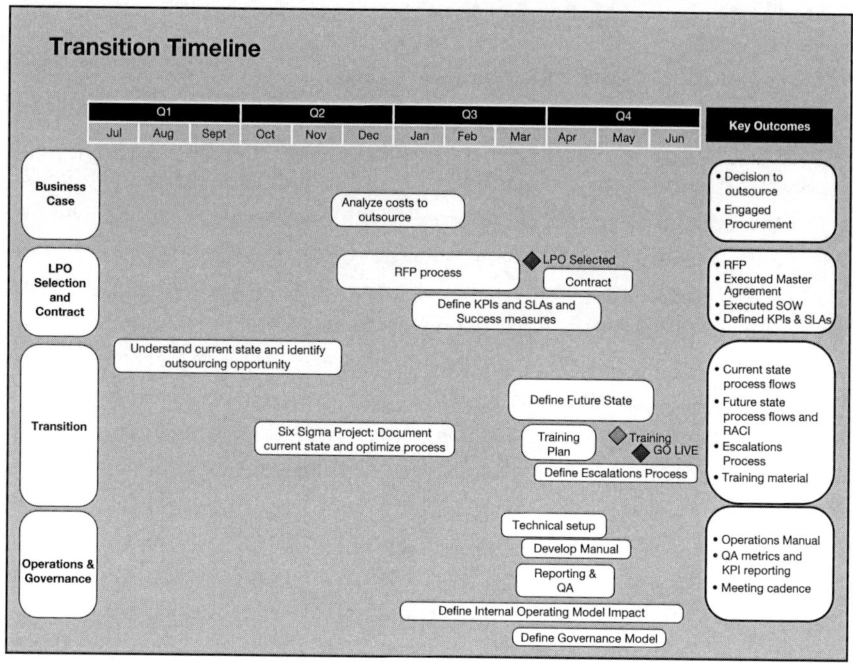

Figure 7-13. *Transition Timeline*

impacted business owners across the company and the hand-off between the client and the provider. There will be questions thrown back and forth, and both parties have to agree on timing of those exchanges and set SLAs, so that no one holds up the other, especially in the early days after the transition.

Another critical ingredient for success is a clearly documented governance framework that will guide client and service provider interactions on a regular basis. At a minimum the following must be agreed upon: (1) How will success be measured? (2) How will issues be resolved? (3) What is the escalation process back into the legal department to resolve inquiries from the service provider? And (4) How will the process be reviewed for efficiencies and improved upon continuously? There are many more questions to consider, and the service provider will likely suggest some goals for the governance model as well. This is an opportunity to have the service provider share best practices from the industry and learnings from other engagements.

Governance Framework

Establish a joint *governance framework*. How do you know if things are going well? How do you know the ALSP is delivering what it should be delivering? Think through what that could and should look like, because it is very different than the traditional way of engaging with a law firm.

The governance model plays a really important role. Consider what a big change it is to go to an ALSP, especially if you are going from a law firm; everything about the engagement is different, the kind of people at the table, the skill sets that the people have, the work they are accustomed to doing, the way they engage with their clients, what they perceive as a client meeting, how the client meeting is run, and how they perceive themselves to be successful or how they are measured on their success. Almost every aspect of that engagement will be different than what is experienced in a traditional hourly engagement with a law firm.

So, why a governance framework? Simply put, it's how the relationship is governed; it's going to work once it goes live. I cannot stress enough the importance of transparency in each direction. How it is going on each side must be answered honestly. That means giving critical feedback if you are the recipient, you have to be willing to "take it" if you are the service provider and vice versa.

We sometimes forget how much of this is on us as clients to really make this successful. But in-house has to be just as ready to provide feedback, to be a part of the escalation process as the provider, to live within its SLA. Every time an ALSP has a question they take in-house, it is unacceptable to say, "I don't know. It depends. I'll get back to you." Because that ALSP is measuring themselves very tightly on SLAs and turnaround times. They can't have something sitting back on the client's side even though it is the "client."

Transparency back and forth is critical. What are the rules and responsibilities to the overall engagement? Who talks to whom and at what level are we speaking to each other? Is there a team lead at the ALSP, is there an account manager at the ALSP; are they one and the same? It depends on the size of the operation. Who within the in-house is handling this? Is it the attorney who still has a full day job? Is that the right person with the right skills? It probably is not. It's where someone with operational rigor and experience, and program management, is needed.

For example, what are the weekly meetings? These are the tactical meetings where you are going to discuss how things went that week. Were SLAs met? Were the measures the right measures? Is the turnaround time

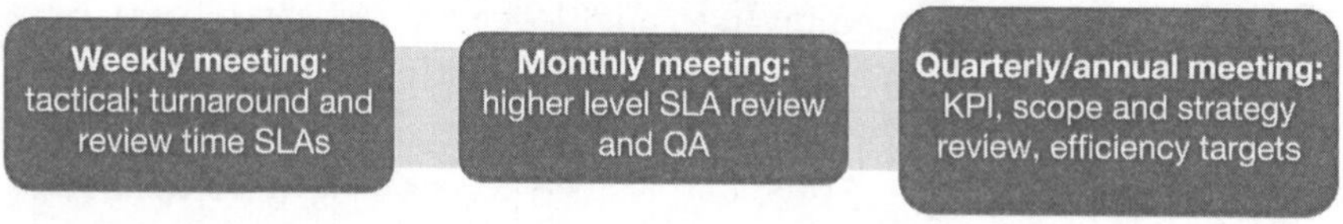

Weekly meeting: tactical; turnaround and review time SLAs

Monthly meeting: higher level SLA review and QA

Quarterly/annual meeting: KPI, scope and strategy review, efficiency targets

Figure 7-14. *Meeting Cadence*

as good as it can be? Was it completely wrong? Did you completely misjudge what the turnaround time should be? All of these things should be going on in recurring weekly meetings. Monthly meetings will be a higher level review of the data that was collected during the last month. That means more data than seen in a weekly meeting: How do you measure quality? What was the quality of that work over the course of that month? Key topics and quality measures? And what can be learned or improved from the metrics (the "actionable insight" aspect)? Quality measures are one of the most challenging things to define in this kind of a model. It means something different to different people, but it is something that needs to be worked through, with a transparent, open conversation about what is and isn't possible.

Quarterly or annual meetings are a step higher than the monthly meetings. **Figure 7-14** is an example of a governance meetings cadence that works in this particular scenario. Other engagements may not need weekly meetings; others may need twice-a-week meetings, especially for the first six months. It has to be customized, obviously, but it should be a standard approach that there are recurring meetings and in those recurring meetings there is a set agenda with sets of data that will be reviewed on an ongoing, recurring basis. It is only getting to that recurring rhythm that you start seeing benefits, opportunities, and continuous improvement. If it looks different every time, with different metrics every time, getting the needed consistency for continuous improvement will not occur.

Spend time figuring out the governance model, and spend time thinking about what happens after going live. This is a huge transition process that could take easily six weeks to six months depending on the scale of the operation or the scale of this engagement.

Stay Connected

What happens once live? That is when the real work starts; it is not enough to have a go-live party and celebrate that particular success. It's not successful until a couple of months in and the parties are actually tracking to the measures set out in the goals that were jointly agreed upon.

Once the go-live celebration is over, the client and provider must stay closely connected. The first "problem" is likely to arise within hours. Someone will be confused about the new outsourced process, and complaints will begin. Understand that complaints about any change are natural and not a sign of failure. In fact, consider preparing a survey for key stakeholders within the business who will be using the newly outsourced service. Track those survey results and identify patterns.

Most importantly, clients should be careful not to blame the service provider for failures when there is a good likelihood that the client had something to do with issues that arise. Do post-mortem reviews and alter direction as needed. Be agile and open to critical feedback. Work through problems with the service provider as one unified team, and over time, the relationship will yield results beyond those anticipated.

SUMMARY: BEST PRACTICES FOR SUCCESSFUL OUTSOURCING

Best Practices: Before the Transition

To summarize, let's go through some best practices before the transition.

Let's be clear: **plan, plan, plan!** Take the time and bring in the right resources that will help determine the right solution provider. How will this service provider be trained? How will the internal team be told what is changing? Changing management when work is outsourced is its own work stream, so think about the sensitivities involved.

Then know the processes, map them, and define the areas of opportunities, while removing waste, simplifying, and clarifying to ensure everyone is on the same page on what can and should be outsourced and what needs to stay in-house.

What can you stop doing? Why outsource to a supplier work that no legal resource should be spending time on? Map the processes, and think about the operating model and the governance framework and how the two interact with each other.

More questions to resolve at this stage include: What roles will change? How does the operating model of the in-house team look different now that it is actually in operation, going from just legal practice mode to a more operationalized engagement? Communicate as much as possible about this transition, because it is a big change.

Culturally and emotionally, it's a lot for some people to absorb and understand where they will fit in the future. And there's a whole technical aspect to this depending on how robust of an engagement is wanted, or what the ALSP can deliver. What are the technology interactions that need to happen between the ALSP system and the client system? Are they living in one, are they living in another, and is there integration and high-tech skill sets that are needed to make those things work together? These are all things to consider before the transition.

1. **Plan, plan, plan.**
   - Time to review vendor options
   - Time to train the vendor
   - Time to explain to the internal team what is changing
2. **Know your process.**
   - Map it, identify areas for improvement, clarify, and simplify process.
   - Decide what can be outsourced and what needs to be kept in house, and what can be stopped.
3. **Define a new operating model.**
   - Manage the impact of outsourcing on full-time employees—how will roles change?
   - Prepare and *communicate* to support a positive transition.
4. **Set up technical for the LPO.**
   - Plan early and have the appropriate support.
   - Discover options for collaboration on work.

Best Practices: During the Transition

Then, during the transitional phase, this is a bumpy time and you have to be prepared. Know what you are getting into, eyes wide open. Just like moving houses can't go 100 percent smoothly, no big transition like this can go 100 percent smoothly. Be prepared for bumps, think about how to manage those bumps, and think about the tone to set between the service provider and the internal client team on how bumps are dealt with. You don't want to go into the transition phase blaming each other. This has to be an all-hands-on-deck time.

So how do you best transfer the knowledge, from a very logistical perspective? All these in-house people (or perhaps the legal team has been

- **Think about how best to transfer knowledge.**
  - Create an operating manual with clear black-and-white rules.
  - Define escalation process.
  - Devote time to creating good training.
    - Who will present?
    - What is the best format?
    - Keep the vendor engaged.
- **Develop and manage an outsourcing transition plan.**
  - Need project management help!
  - Continually reassessing
  - Transition continues after go-live.
  - Do a "post mortem."
- **Establish clear objectives and key performance indicators.**
  - Define what the vendor is accountable for.
  - Set clear expectations.
  - Make sure they know you are still involved and interested.
- **Feedback loop.**
  - Feedback on LPO, and vice versa

relying on law firms who know this work best) know how things work and over time they know it better and better and better. That makes the transition to an ALSP that much harder. How do you do a really robust knowledge transfer exercise? Sometimes this requires third-party help, somebody who can come in and help document all this knowledge and create desktop procedures.

The escalation process is also critical. Just because it is handed off to an ALSP doesn't mean they won't have questions. There will be transactions, deals, or parts of the process that perhaps should be handled back in-house (or that the ALSPs are going to *want* to send back in-house). How does that look? How is it handed off? All of those are details worked on during the transition as everybody learns about the process.

Every ALSP engagement will require an outsourcing transition plan. And to develop and manage an outsourcing transition plan, help is needed. Whether it's on the legal service provider side, the buying side, or the lead operations team, bring the best project manager into the fold for this. They will be the best point of contact for all stakeholders and will have eyes in the sky on how the project is unfolding. With that, they're also able to continually reassess the situation and offer feedback or modifications to the process when necessary.

Clear objectives and key performance indicators are vital during the transition. What will success look like? That is the most important question—and the answer should be as data-driven as possible so that it is an objective, measurable standard.

After the transition plan is created and implemented, begin thinking about the post-mortem and start taking notes. Make sure the project plan is as tight as possible because it is certain there will be things to discover along the way. As discussed more thoroughly in chapter 7 on project management—the post-mortem process is often forgotten, but can be invaluable. Think about creating a feedback loop because both sides need to know how they're doing. Both sides includes the in-house team as well, because the in-house client needs to know if they are not stepping up and making sure it is successful from their end. Otherwise there is no way the service provider can be successful.

It is a dangerous game for the service provider if they feel they have a checked-out in-house team. The client must be open to receiving feedback from the ALSP, just as it should be comfortable giving feedback. The cadence, rhythm, and process of how that needs to happen is part of the transition plan.

Best Practices: After

Finally, post-transition: do a post-mortem on how the transition went. Find out what did and didn't go well, because some of those same factors or dynamics that may have crept up during the transition will probably creep up again during other parts of the engagement, which is an ongoing relationship.

If there are things that didn't go well during the transition, it is probably a sign that things will not go well again at some point. This is the right time to clean up those issues. Stay in close contact—especially initially—because there's no such thing as too many meetings in the first few weeks. Check in, even if it is for five minutes; get things on the calendar so that you know people are accountable for being on the phone at the same time to ask, "How do you think it's going?" Neither side should be shy to ask for more check-ins rather than less.

- Stay in close contact.
- Make sure both parties understand the long-term visions.
- Monitor performance.
- Discuss improvement opportunities.
- Expect efficiencies to grow.
- Consider expansion of outsourced duties.

> In a robust outsourcing model, what you're hoping for is that the outsource service provider is balancing resources in the most cost effective and efficient way, since they're balancing the time, the language needs, and the skill sets that they have and spreading that work, potentially, across multiple jurisdictions.

Monitor performance. Make sure everyone is on course and aligned with the vision. It should be a uniform vision clearly understood by the provider and the client. What are the improvement opportunities? What are we learning along the way so that we can get better?

Efficiencies should be growing, so you should be watching not on day two or day five, but on month three, month six, and month nine. Set markers on both sides on what efficiency should look like.

If things are going well, consider outsourcing more; the outsource providers likely will offer other areas where they can help because they will start seeing more opportunities. In a really good relationship, the outsource team becomes an extension of the client team; they start to see more about the business and can inform the in-house team of things about the business that the in-house team possibly wasn't capturing by themselves. There is now a real opportunity to expand the relationship, which is a great carrot for the outsource provider, and a huge value for the in-house team that is constantly going to be inundated with more and more work. So, this is the way to approach outsourcing to an ALSP.

NEED TO KNOW #10: CORPORATE LEGAL MANAGEMENT: PEEK BEHIND THE CURTAIN

To really move the dial on how services are delivered, we should take a deeper look at how corporate legal departments manage their spending with law firms. Traditionally, outside counsel spend has been focused on tracking the billable hour, the firm's timekeeper, who is working on a particular matter, and how many hours are spent on a particular matter. Other considerations: what level is that person, what's their billable hour, is there a discount on that billable hour?

And with this approach there is also a known delay between when the work is done and when the bill is received (and then further delay until the bill is actually paid). It's called "work in progress," which is time allocated to certain work at a firm to a client (or already accounted for) and maybe the internal law firm's systems, but that hasn't been transferred to the in-house team to review the bill and make payment.

What I've just noted are steps in a process that often is antiquated: the time that it takes just to transfer the bill and the information about time spent on which matter, plus the time to transfer it so that the in-house team can assess it and actually issue payment. That adds up to a significant amount of time, especially for the medium-size or smaller firms that are more tightly watching their revenue flow or for the in-house teams that are watching their budgets. That delay of work in progress can really get in the way of having accurate information and control over the situation.

Ping Pong Engagement

Ping pong engagement is not a technical term, but it is how I perceive the billing and invoicing relationship between a law firm and an in-house team. The relationship is like a ping pong match. It starts with the client initiating a request for help or initiating a call or an email to the law firm, needing something. Review this, research this, and answer that question. A law firm then does the work and responds. Then it goes back and forth on the inputs and the outputs, and then there's a final product or final deliverable handed to the client.

At that point the law firm is ready to issue their invoice and the work in progress is reduced to a final bill. Then another ping pong match begins—the bill review is done by the in-house team (or I hope it is being done!).

Part of that process is to review write-offs, write downs and discounts, and all the other variations of ways in which bills are adjusted.

Law Firm Lawyers, Pay Attention!

For even the best leaders of the most innovative in-house teams, while they want the legal operations function to be impactful and legal operations professionals to enable and assist the attorneys to make the decision on which law firms to spend, it is still the practicing lawyer who's going to make that judgment call. They're going to decide which law firm to engage. They're going to decide which attorney they want to spend money on.

Once that happens, there is yet another process that begins, and again it is the ping pong engagement. The bill was too high, or what does this item mean or why was this rate applied, or what happens at that point in the conversation; so, there is more back and forth that likely will result in some sort of an adjustment. Sometimes those adjustments are made by the firm in advance of the bill being sent. The core issue is the client is not happy with the bill they received.

Sometimes the firm reviews it. They may realize that possibly too much time was allocated to a project. For example, a junior attorney didn't quite know how to approach something with a bit of a discount, and so an adjustment is made. It is more back and forth and a very manual process to adjust the bill to a final bill that is actually agreed upon by both sides.

With every back and forth, time keeps ticking. That ping pong kind of experience creates a lot of opportunities for things to fall through the cracks. It can add up to a lot of time and a lot of frustration on both sides. There are opportunities to improve that process, perhaps through automation and technology, or even something as simple as a more routine evaluation.

Law Firm Services Buyers and Sellers

Another factor affecting how this spend is managed is that the seller (law firm partner) takes a job in-house and becomes the buyer. In-house lawyers are essentially engaging law firms in the same manner in which they used to be engaged when they were at a firm.

We need to remember that those in-house attorneys (and therefore legal service buyers) started in a law firm and are used to providing service and billing for it in a particular way. That's what they were taught. It might not have been detailed training, but somehow they acquired knowledge at a firm on how to bill and how to review time sheets, how to edit inputs and entries of time, and how to eventually communicate with the client on a discrepancy in a bill or a question about a bill. So for those who transitioned from law firm practice to in-house, they are receiving or buying the service, or reviewing the bill through the same lens they had when they left the firm.

There is typically no training on this after the transition in-house. Somehow, these lawyers are expected to know how to buy from law firms and review value of what they received. There's no guidance on the appropriate ways to push back or ask questions. Most in-house lawyers are not comfortable providing critical feedback to firms they came from or have long relationships with. These can be very uncomfortable conversations; again, the transition from a law firm to in-house doesn't magically create a different perspective on the billing process or expectations of value.

We're all in the same boat whether it's a law firm or in-house—we're just on opposite sides of the table in the game of invoice and billing ping pong. To change these practices, it takes both sides coming together, realizing a change is needed.

This is a very important point and sheds light on some of the issues we see at the root of engagement problems. There are differences of opinion on how successful it would be to apply standard procurement processes and centralize spend management to control the decisions of which law firms are used. That probably isn't the fastest path to success.

Maybe some in-house teams have been successful with that, but for the most part, the culture is still that of respecting the autonomy of the practicing attorneys and their decision making. The belief is that they're going to be best positioned to know which law firm has the core capabilities and legal expertise to provide the service needed. The budget owners and the in-house team are still going to be the ones that will make the final decision.

What wrapper can we add around it to help provide some oversight to help provide guidance and set guardrails? Here are some ideas I suggest.

One Way to Enable Better Selection: Convergence Program

One way in-house teams are trying to manage spend is through *convergence programs.* A convergence program rationalizes spend across the number of law firms that in-house teams are engaging. It's a term of art, but really it is about reducing the number of firms. It's thinking about how to bring together certain types of skills, identifying those in a way that then limits the pool of law firms legal departments are engaging with. Is there certain work that is done by a handful of firms and that's all that is needed?

Why are there so many other firms doing lower volume, less frequency work, but that require a lot of oversight and management? The volume of work sent to a firm is not in correlation with the time and effort it takes to manage that law firm relationship. Meaning, a firm that does only small pieces of work still needs to be managed: Invoices need to be reviewed, rate increases need to be monitored, feedback should be provided, and so on. Not to mention when work is done with gaps of time in between and in lower volumes, the learnings are slower and there is more need for substantive engagement from the in-house team on risk tolerance, preferences, and internal business goals.

There's some substantive benefit that comes from engaging a smaller number of firms because in-house teams will have more concentrated work in a smaller number of law firms that will provide expertise and learn so much. With that expertise comes efficiency gains.

Engagement Guidelines Help Create Consistency

Another pragmatic tactic legal departments use to manage spend is a set of *engagement guidelines.* These will answer some important questions: What are the general rules around engaging? What can the law firms expect when they are doing business with the in-house team? And what are the expectations from the in-house team when doing business with a law firm?

These can be basic guides, such as:

- We will not initiate any conversations until you sign a set of policies.
- We will not open a matter until we have an agreed upon budget.

- We will put a clear work description in place before we actually authorize the work.
- The law firm is not allowed to begin actual work until we have made some sort of a clear, designated marker of authority from the in-house team that says the work can now begin.

Note that this is much easier to do when there are a limited number of law firms used.

Taking that a step further, the in-house team won't pay any bills that have time tracked or billed in the calendar before an authorization is issued from the in-house team.

It comes down to establishing rules of engagement. They can be simple to begin with, some very basic rules like sending invoices within a certain period of time of the work being completed. Or making a clear policy that says certain invoices after a certain date simply won't be paid.

It's really hard on the in-house budget when firms invoice such late payments, so engagement guidelines are recommended for those who want to avoid the challenges of unpredictable late payments. This keeps things for firms on track rather than waiting six, seven, eight, or nine months for payment when, at that point, the budget for the in-house team has already been allocated or repurposed.

Stratification of Work—It's Worth the Effort!

Stratification of work is a third way for in-house teams to take control of spend, but it can take a bit more hands-on work. This isn't just about reviewing the bills. What I mean specifically is that work stratification is aligning the list of firms to the work being done, to understanding what kind of work they actually are doing for the in-house team by type of work, geography, or teams within the legal department. If the department is big enough, certain teams will begin to work with certain firms, potentially doing similar work as other teams do with a completely different set of firms.

It is an important exercise to create a matrix around the type of work, geographies, and firms that are doing it; also the business unit that is the ultimate beneficiary of the legal support, or however it makes sense in the corporate environment to organize the work. This exercise becomes more challenging in big complex corporations, certainly. The more established a department is, the deeper the engagement needs to be to do this stratification exercise. It requires interviewing many of the in-house attorneys who are making the decisions on what they spend and with who, so it takes a more manual assessment—especially if the technological infrastructure for the billing and invoicing isn't as robust as some would like it.

Differentiating among legal work opportunities is probably one of the first places to start. It's simple, because it comes down to whether the right firm is doing the right type of work. If you think about it, not all firms should be doing all kinds of work. At the same time look at how many generalist firms there are. It seems like every major firm is a general firm, right?

There are always some specialties, but it's pretty interesting if you look at how many firms there are doing the same kind of work. It's amazing how many of them have not just the same client, but the same client in the same practice area.

At first blush, it seems odd for legal departments to hire multiple firms for the same work. But it's easy to see how that happens—clearly there's something missing since work is spread across so many firms, and every firm has experts in just about every area. The truth is that there is often plenty of work to go around, but no firm can manage it all, and no one firm is good at everything. For law firms looking to outsource some of their work, it's no different.

To get started with work stratification, legal departments think about overflow work as its own bucket and then start subdividing that work.

Routine Work

For general recurring overflow, that kind of work is sent out to law firms because there's just too much of it to be done in-house, and the in-house team needs a release valve. It could range across several practice areas. For example, you might see it in litigation, commercial transactions, or maybe some IP or employment work. Another bucket in the more general recurring work includes the bet-the-company litigation. That's a great example of where there should not be too many firms involved. But how do you really set apart that bet-the-company litigation? Who should that go to? Take some time to assess who the right providers are and how many are needed as the ones your firm turns to for bet-the-company type of litigation.

There is something to be said for putting some tension in the system and spreading the wealth. You also learn by having different experiences coming from different firms. Just remember, there's no one way to slice and dice this. Go for the option that resonates the most for you in your particular setting.

Just a note—there's a risk when there is only one trusted firm advisor; they become so embedded and so part of the corporation's culture, and tendencies and policies, that they actually forget one of their biggest values: They bring in an external perspective.

Specialized Services

Then there's heavy, subject matter-specific advice that is needed on particular legal issues. Not everybody can be an expert in privacy law and not everybody's an expert in patent matters litigation or prosecution. There are very unique spots and room for paying top dollar for deep expertise. But not every firm should be claiming to have deep expertise and if they do, that means there are quite a lot of experts. So it follows that if there are, that market condition should drive costs down—but we know that that's not happening.

How do you identify the real experts and focus on those? Once you've done that, the level of service obtained should be quite different. Not only should it be top advice from a substantive perspective, but now expect a trusted advisor role from the subject matter expert because there will be much more engagement time spent with them to educate them about the business.

Why spend time educating more and more providers about the deep knowledge they need to support the business for some very unique and narrow legal issues? It really benefits everybody to have the best advice provided by a small number of experts within a small number of law firms. So then why is the work continuing to be billed in the same way? It always happens. If you've spent time now thinking about the right firm delivering the right kind of work, isn't it also the perfect time to say, OK, we know we're now committed to a handful of firms? We're going to have deeper relationships with these firms. We expect them to be experts in the particular type of work where support is given, whether it's the recurring overflow of the bet-the-company litigation or other types of work.

This may be the right time to talk about the billing structure and whether tracking the billable hour in six-minute increments is the best way to pay for recurring overflow work. That is a loaded question. Simply put, it's not. You don't want to have to pay for it that way, especially if it's recurring and especially if you have some predictability. It's just a good reminder at this point when thinking about differentiating the work: Once it is differentiated, it is the right time to think about whether to pay by the billable hour.

Managing Law Firm Performance

Managing law firm performance is important but not a common practice yet. Some companies are doing it but not nearly as many as should be. The quality of legal service is still very much a subjective measure.

It's very hard to explain to a client in a quantifiable way how "good" is defined, but it is an assessment based on experience because those who are procuring the service have likely worked in that area before or delivered a similar service when they were at a law firm and have some understanding of a qualitative measure or a qualitative assessment, without necessarily having the data or metrics behind it.

Think about all of the corporations without established legal departments. Or if they do have a young department, maybe the legal department is only focused on one particular area of law and other company divisions are allowed to engage law firms on their own. Those who purchase law firm services might be the finance team that spends on legal, or maybe a procurement or sales team (or in a small company, the CEO or COO).

Trying to manage the performance of a law firm is nearly impossible without having some quantifiable measures. This is where a scorecard is recommended, doing some benchmarking with other companies, and benchmarking with the firms as well. Quantification will take a variety of shapes. I'll mention a few because much of the way that law firm performance is handled is directly related to the culture of the in-house team. For example:

- How far are they willing to go to seek and solicit feedback?
- How far are they willing to go to rate very objectively and aggressively the skills or the services that were received from the law firm?

This will depend on culture. This is an area where the legal industry has a very long way to go. It is quite far behind compared with many other industries, including other areas of professional services.

So, this probably isn't one of the first places to start if you're starting on ground zero with law firm spend management. But there is a ton of opportunity in this space. It's something that, frankly, some law firms are really open to, and most of the better law firms are open to receiving feedback. They actually *want* to get feedback. That's just not something that is ingrained in legal practice, whether it's the lawyers at the law firm or lawyers in house.

It also requires deep partnership between the in-house team and the law firm they are engaging. For example, there should be an open conversation around the expectations of what a project will cost. Moving away from the billable hour is an underlying theme, whether we talk about management services, alternative legal providers, or legal tech. It has been a hot topic for many years.

Yet for some reason it is still the most common way in which legal services are billed. Other professional services have managed to move away from it. But why haven't the law firms? There are some viable reasons and answers as to why the billable hour remains so popular. One is the lack of consumable historical data at the law firm to budget and plan for an alternative fee. It's very hard to look back at data that hasn't been collected in an effective, useful way to structure something more creative.

Similarly, on the client side, the in-house team often lacks data around what it actually expects to send to a law firm. How is a law firm expected to propose something, if it's not based on the billable hour and if the client has a tough time articulating expectations on what the work will look like in the future? There's a lack of insight that may be coming from the client in many cases.

Along the same lines, there's work that is unpredictable. Often the client simply doesn't know what's coming next; they don't know what's going to land on their plate, and whether they will need a law firm. Without that predictability, how is a law firm expected to have some sort of a creative pricing structure or pricing proposal?

There is also the uniqueness of matters. There's a tendency that every matter is unique, that every engagement is slightly different. The opposing side is slightly different. Documentation looks slightly different. That creates enough insecurity and lack of confidence in doing something creative with pricing that people will fall back on the reliable billable hour.

Finally, there are those special skills that are needed from certain lawyers based on their deep expertise, just as sometimes I just need someone to come in for a couple of questions or review a couple of items. And it should take a couple of hours, and that's probably OK to bill that way.

These are just some reasons to continue to hang onto the billable hour. I'm not saying they're right or wrong, but this is in fact what is happening.

Until the work becomes a recurring engagement and those special skills become less special in the context of how often they're procured, they might be special in the context of how available they are. There is enough uncertainty that the billable hour ends up being the easiest way to procure those services. But that doesn't mean they can't be subject to some sort of an alternative fee structure.

Our job is to think about creating the conditions that will help drive different conversations. How do we create insights? How do we create predictability? How do we remove some of the uncertainty? And the answer to that is largely data, some technology, and a lot of process.

Finally . . . The AFA!

What we're really talking about once we think about moving away from the billable hour is AFAs. There is no one definition for AFA—arrangements come in variety of flavors. At the most basic level, an AFA is any billing method that is not based on the hours worked.

In many cases, even if a firm and client agree on an AFA, somewhere at the firm, hours are still being counted and then multiplied to create some sort of fixed fee. But the bill that results is not split into increments of time. So, it's really an alternate way of invoicing, just not based on six-or fifteen-minute increments. In these cases, the fixed fee is really not much more than basic math.

Hourly rate × set # hours per week × 4 = Monthly fixed fee

This is not what I like to call an AFA—it's more like the billable hour in disguise. There is nothing alternative about tracking time and multiplying it out for a month. The only alternative thing about this AFA is that it is a predictable for the client.

When I hear AFA and then realize it is just a flat or fixed monthly fee, I see nothing more than a calculation of hours. Even worse—often firms are asked to produce their "shadow bills" so the client can see if the fixed fee is close to the actual hours worked (and would have been billed if not for the fixed fee). This is terrible incentive. It actually does nothing about the value being delivered, services being provided, and insights being gathered. And, ultimately, the method of engagement doesn't change. The same things are happening with contingency fees. In those arrangements, there are not real incentives to change service delivery.

Real change is happening when we think more broadly and better understand that we are trying to get to a place where a different type of value is extracted from the law firm. For me, a real AFA is based on a different set of measures than time, and it includes other valuable services beyond just the actual legal work. That value is created when service delivery is no longer driven by the pricing structure but driven by client needs. In a real AFA, law firms are incentivized to provide project management, incentivized to provide data, incentivized to stratify their work, to have work done at lower cost and with lower cost resources, and to automate some of their processes. They focus on delivering a holistic service, leveraging various skill sets across their firm, and actually using the very expensive systems deployed by their IT departments. Even more, they're engaging attorneys across all experience levels because they are delivering a service—not a piece of advice from one expert to a client in a ping pong match. (See the discussion on law firm managed service in chapter 7, for an example of an AFA.)

An interim step is a fixed fee per transaction. There are some creative things being done in M&A for global expansion advice on employment or regulations, where the fixed fee is provided per deal or per country analysis. This arrangement does create incentive to be efficient and pass the benefit to the client where work is reusable. This format allows for predictability and enables law firms to be creative with their resources.

I suppose that in the end, anything outside of the mysterious monthly bill, with no predictability and no creative use of resources, is progress forward. Any such progress requires a leap of faith and trust in the relationship. There needs to be open communication and opportunities to revise the terms. Both client and firm have to accept that sometimes the firm will do really well and sometimes the client will get a great deal. If both can be accomplished, then that is ultimate success!

Conclusion

It is hard to know where to start for concluding thoughts on such a broad topic as legal innovation. It means so many things to so many people, and sadly means nothing to many others. The reality is that there are innovative things happening across the ecosystem. They are in clusters of projects across the U.S. state court systems, in groups of professionals making their mark in legal ops, inside high-tech corners of law firms, and among creative professors at law schools. Progress is clear, but still slow.

There are long-standing hurdles in the way of innovation that are difficult to change. Limits on who can "practice law," compensation structures of law firms, unchanged law school curricula, and professional self-preservation are all very real hurdles that can only be overcome through continued experimentation and justification for change. Any small wins are helpful in convincing others to come along on an innovation journey. Small wins also establish credibility for those driving innovation.

There is a lot of talk about legal innovation, much of which is hard to sift through. From the pontificating to the promises of legal technology, it is nearly impossible to filter out what is real and what isn't. Even once the opportunities present themselves, knowing where to start can also be overwhelming. In sum, I want to conclude with the three steps that every lawyer can start doing immediately to kick off their innovation journey.

1. Start tracking. Begin to jot down data points about the recurring work. Think about reporting on how many, what types, and how long certain aspects of the work take.
2. Imagine the process. Think about the various steps commonly taken to deliver certain pieces of legal work. Break down the concept of

"work" into a process to identify even some minor tweaks that may improve the client's experience or increase efficiencies.

3. Try something different. Get comfortable taking risks in how the work is currently done, and consider trying something that may have been publicized in the legal press. Reach out to someone who has done something innovative in their practice and learn from them.

I hope this book has provided some inspiration or sparked a little curiosity in the art of the possible. Onward on the innovation journey . . .

Appendix

The appendix contains a collection of samples, guides, and templates that I have used in my practice and operations. There are many others available online and through different industry group sites. There is no right or wrong template. The only thing that makes it right is that it works for the users.

The Buzzword Glossary and Project Management Glossary are collections of key terms that I hope will be helpful as readers orient themselves to new topics or want to dive in deeper.

NOTE ON PROJECT MANAGEMENT VISUALS

For starters, there are lots of different charts that are really great. There are documents that are used for communications plans, and templates that are used for tracking. There are many varieties, so think about what works well in your environment and with your audience. That is the most important thing. What works well for the project team may not work well for the audience that you are communicating with.

And these are just a couple of examples of what can be used, whether it is a chart for planning for stakeholders and listing them out with their different roles and responsibilities, or the actual scheduling and timeline. In fact, these are all samples that I have used in the past, and they were created by project management experts. These are not simple and are here for demonstrative purposes to give a sense of what they entail.

There are also some fantastic tools available. Some of them are more complicated than others, but many are very simple and probably available already on the desktop applications that you have. Consider checking online because choosing the right format that is comfortable for people might move the project forward more quickly and efficiently.

We spent years learning terms like *habeas corpus*, *amicus curiae*, and *certiorari*. But the rise of legal technology is keeping attorneys on their toes with a whole host of new vocabulary words.

A-C

- **Alternative Business Structure (ABS)** – An entity that, while providing regulated reserved legal activities, allows non-lawyers to own or invest in law firms.
- **Alternative Legal Service Provider (ALSP)** – Nontraditional legal service provider that performs activities directly related to the provision of legal services. Service types include electronic discovery services, document review and coding, litigation and investigation support, specialized legal services, intellectual property management, due diligence services, and legal drafting.
- **Artificial Intelligence** – the theory and development of computer systems capable of performing tasks that normally require human intelligence. Common applications include visual perception, speech recognition, decision-making, and translation between languages.
- **Blockchain** – A permissionless, distributed database that maintains a continuously growing list of transactional data records. In the legal field, blockchain is becoming increasingly common in the form of smart contracts.
- **Chief Innovation Officer (CINO)** – A person in a company or law firm who is primarily responsible for managing the process of innovation and change management within the organization.
- **Cloud Computing** – The use of various services such as software development platforms, servers, storage, and software programs over the internet, which is often referred to as the "cloud."

D-L

- **Disaggregation of Legal Services** – The fragmentation of legal service activities into discrete parts, the performance of which can be outsourced or delegated to a lower-cost resource.
- **Expert System** – A domain-specific system that uses artificial intelligence to emulate the decision-making abilities of a human expert in a specific field. Expert systems are designed to solve complex problems by reasoning through bodies of knowledge, represented mainly by if-then rules, rather than through conventional procedural code.
- **Hackathon** – A fast-paced, typically single-day event in which multi-disciplinary teams of software developers, designers, project managers, and domain experts collaborate intensively to solve a problem or build a new software tool.
- **Innovation** – Making changes in something established, especially by introducing new methods, ideas, or products.
- **Legal Operations** – A multi-disciplinary function that focuses on optimizing legal services delivery to an organization.

M-Z

- **Machine Learning** - An application of Artificial Intelligence that provides systems the ability to automatically learn and improve from experience without being explicitly programmed. It focuses on the development of computer programs that can access data and use it to learn for themselves.
- **Matter Management** – The process in which matters and related data such as type of legal work, attorneys on the case, budgets, and invoices are gathered, tracked, and reported on by the legal department through the matter lifecycle.
- **Predictive Coding** - The electronic coding, organization, and prioritization of entire sets of electronically stored information ("ESI") according to their relation to discovery responsiveness, privilege, and designated issues before and during the legal discovery process.

How to approach a legal technology implementation

Legal Technology implementations should be well thought out and methodical. This guide will help you get the most out of your next purchase or project.

1. Make sure you're ready

The work begins long before a purchase is made.

Do

* Carefully identify your problem(s) – listen to your employee's pain points.
* Start getting buy-in and find a project champion
* Begin your market research early – finding the right tool takes effort

Don't

* Forget the mission – marketing can be convincing. Think about your needs + "nice to haves" and stick to the list
* Treat your project as an after-thought – a project manager can help you stay on track

2. Map + improve your processes

Layering technology on ineffective processes only perpetuates the cycle.

- Map the *current* state, not the "ideal" or future state. Work closely with the team to capture those details.
- Trace any bottlenecks or inefficiencies to their root cause, rather than just managing the symptoms
- Evaluate your process capabilities, focusing on quality, speed, delivery, and productivity.
- Make subtle changes that affect outcomes without expensive tech, or large behavior modifications.

3. Do your research

Thoughtful questions can help you find the right technology partner.

Company

- Who makes up the business team – what is their experience in the arena and/or do they have a well-versed adviser?
- How does this tool work and what is its value proposition? What are it's strengths and limitations?

Cost

- What is the solution's cost structure? (per user/seat? flat, monthly, or annual fee? cost per feature or module?)
- Are there other costs associated with implementation and maintenance?
- After understanding all costs – does this actually save money or offer some other intangible benefit?

Implementation

- What is the on-boarding process like? (time, costs, support level)
- What have other customers implementing this tool struggled with most?
- Is the company open to co-creation of features that more closely match your needs?

4. Put it into action

Making big changes can be hard work.

Do

- Have a clear but flexible approach to implementation
- Make sure your team is involved in executing your plan; give them a sense of ownership
- Invest up front in training

Don't

- Expect perfection; change is iterative and may come with some resistance
- Force adoption – incentivize and encourage it
- Forget to measure impact over time; compare against the benchmarks you set with your initial process evaluation

RUNNING AN RFP

Define Requirements

- Must have functions/skills
- Future needs and capabilities
- Minimal requirements to go-live (without this, you might as well stick with what you have)
- Involve stakeholders

Vendor List

- Market research: what's available?
- References from peer companies
- Older, stable companies vs new entrants

Proposal Review

- Send standard template to all vendors
- Set clear timelines
- Involve stakeholders

Negotiate

- Minimal terms and conditions
- Approval of security, data protection, IT and other subject matter experts
- Pricing based on identical feature-sets or skill-sets (try to compare apples to apples)

Select

- Establish objective criteria
- Define weight/importance of each criteria
- Set expectations for post go-live support & engagement

Sample timeline developed by www.uplevelops.com.

RUNNING AN RFP

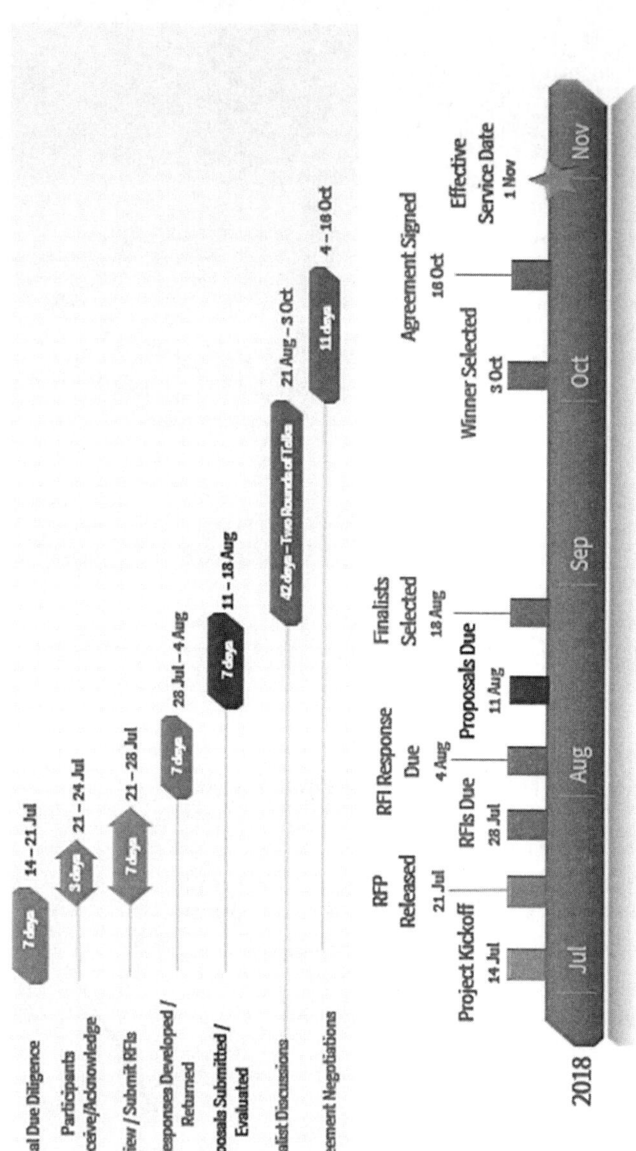

Project managers have their own lingo and terms of art.
I feel a little smarter around them when I can use these basic terms correctly.

Key Concepts Translated

- **Adoption** – Are they using what you implemented, the way intended
- **Assumptions** – If these things don't happen, the project may fail
- **Budget** – How much has been approved to spend on the project
- **Charter** – Summary of the project goals, scope, cost, timeline, and vision
- **Champions** – Who can be counted on to socialize the benefits of the project
- **Change Management** – Getting people to prepare for and actually adopt a new way of doing something
- **Communication Plan** – What to say, to whom, when, and in what medium
- **Deliverables** – Tangible output, usually a document or piece of software
- **Governance** – How to resolve problems and who is the decision-maker
- **Issues** – Known problems or challenges in the project
- **Milestones** – Key dates for deliverables or actions to be completed
- **Program** – Combination of projects, and ongoing activities
- **RACI** – Chart that sets out who is responsible, accountable, must be informed, and consulted on the project
- **Risks** – List of things that may happen, and if they do, could impact the project
- **Scope** – Detailed description of what is included in the goals of the project
- **Scope Creep** – When scope grows beyond the initial expectations
- **Stakeholders** – Comprehensive list of people impacted by the project
- **User Testing** – Scripted activities to be performed in the system by future users

PROJECT CHARTER

Guiding Principles		
Business Opportunity		
Objectives		
•		

Milestones & Deliverables	**Target Date**
1.	
2.	
3.	
4.	
5.	

Success Metrics		
Goal Area	**As Is**	**To Be**
TBD	TBD	TBD
TBD	TBD	TBD
TBD	TBD	TBD

In Scope	**Out of Scope**
TBD	TBD
TBD	TBD
TBD	TBD

Team	
Executive Sponsor(s)	**Working Group Managers / Leaders**
Contributing Resources/Personnel	
Legal:	
IT:	
Sales/Procurement:	
HR:	
Finance:	
Meetings, Communications & Reporting	
Bi-Monthly Working Group Meeting – {date, time}	
Quarterly Steering Committee Meeting – {date, time}	
Status Report Distribution – {date, time}	
Document Management & Collaboration Location(s)	
< insert link to online content >	

PROJECT CHARTER - TIMELINE

Phase	No.	Key Tasks	Task Owner(s)	Other Task, or Dependencies	Deliverables	Due Date	Status
Phase 1: Initiate	**1.0**	**TBD**	**TBD**				
	1.1	TBD					
	2.0	**TBD**	**TBD**				
	2.1	TBD					
	3.0	**TBD**	**TBD**				
	3.1	TBD					
Phase 2: Plan	**4.0**	**TBD**	**TBD**				
	4.1	TBD					
	5.0	**TBD**	**TBD**				
	5.1	TBD					
	6.0	**TBD**	**TBD**				
	6.1	TBD					
	7.0	**TBD**	**TBD**				
	7.1	TBD					
Phase 3: Execute	**8.0**	**TBD**	**TBD**				
	8.1	TBD					
	8.2	TBD					
	8.3	TBD					
Phase 4: Maintain	**9.0**	**TBD**	**TBD**				
	9.1	TBD					
	9.2	TBD					
	9.3	TBD					

Key: **⮉/On Track:** Progressing toward successful completion **➲/At Risk:** Potential risk to successful completion (Mitigate) **⮋/Behind:** Blocking issue impacting successful completion (Escalate)

ACTIVITY TRACKER

#	Topic / Task	For	Deliverable Format(s)	Deliverable Review?	% Complete	Due Date	Complexity/ Effort	Priority	Comments
1							High	High	
2							High	High	
3							Medium	Medium	
4							Medium	Medium	
5							Low	Medium	
6							Low	Low	
7							Medium	Low	
8									
9									
10									
OTHER									
1									
2									
3									
4									
5									
COMPLETED									
1									
2									
3									
4									
5									

Communications Plan

Communication Area	Project Area	Status	Due Date	Event/Message	Key Message(s)	Attachments
		Legend: Not Started (NS); In Progress (IP); Closed/ Delivered (C/D)	*A date or set of dates that the communication/ event/process is due. If it is an 'ongoing' event, this could be blank or N/A.*	*Note the event or message that is driving the communication need*	*List the purpose(s) and activities associated with the Message Content Ideas.*	*List the documents that will be attached or included in the communication.*
Topic						
Topic						
Topic						
Topic						
Topic						
Topic						

udience(s)	Method/Vehicle	Developed by	Sent/Delivered By	Schedule/Frequency	Comments
ist of individuals, groups, teams, takeholder groups, roles, rganizations, etc. that will receive he communication or participate in he event/process.	*Provide information on how the communication/ event/process will be delivered to the audience (via email, memo, meeting, group event, etc.)*	*List of individuals, groups, teams, stakeholder groups, roles, organizations, etc. that will develop the communication or facilitate the event/process.*	*List of individuals, groups, teams, stakeholder groups, roles, organizations, etc. that will deliver the communication or facilitate the event/process.*	*A schedule listing the frequency of this communication/event/process, such as how often it is delivered or the recurring schdedule of the event (like a status meeting).*	*Additional notes associated to the communication/event/process that may be needed to complete the task. This includes listing perhaps the desired results, the person responsible for building the communication (if different for the "Sender") and other relevant information.*

Stakeholder Analysis

Project Area	Stakeholder Group	Description	Sub-teams or Individuals	Unique Characteristics	Overall Risk	Impact	Current Adoption Level	Future Adoption Level	Adoption Gap	Comments
	A group of people with common interests in the change, both in what matters to them and how the change will affect them. Stakeholders are specific to an organization and the particular change	*Describe the members of this stakeholder group or the criteria for people to be considered in this group*	*Individual stakeholders who belong to this group.*	*Describe why this group should be treated differently from other stakeholder groups, whether it is specific communications, types of training, their level of involvement, etc.*	*Level of overall risk to the **project** due to **resistance** from this stakeholder group (L, M, H)*	*Impact is the degree to which the change will affect each stakeholder group (L, M, H)*	*Unaware, Aware, Understand, Buy In, Own / Adopt*	*Unaware, Aware, Understand, Buy In, Own / Adopt*	*Gap between current and future adoption level*	
Example	Help	Production support *Line One (Routing/Error Triage) *Line Two (Error Validation/Offshore & Outsourced) *Line Three (Troubleshoot & Own Resolution)	*Person1 (Line 1) *Person2 (Line 3)	*Receives high-level information. *Person1 is best contact.	Low	Low	Unaware	Aware	1	
									0	
									0	
									0	
									0	
									0	
									0	
									0	
									0	
									0	
									0	

Governance RACI

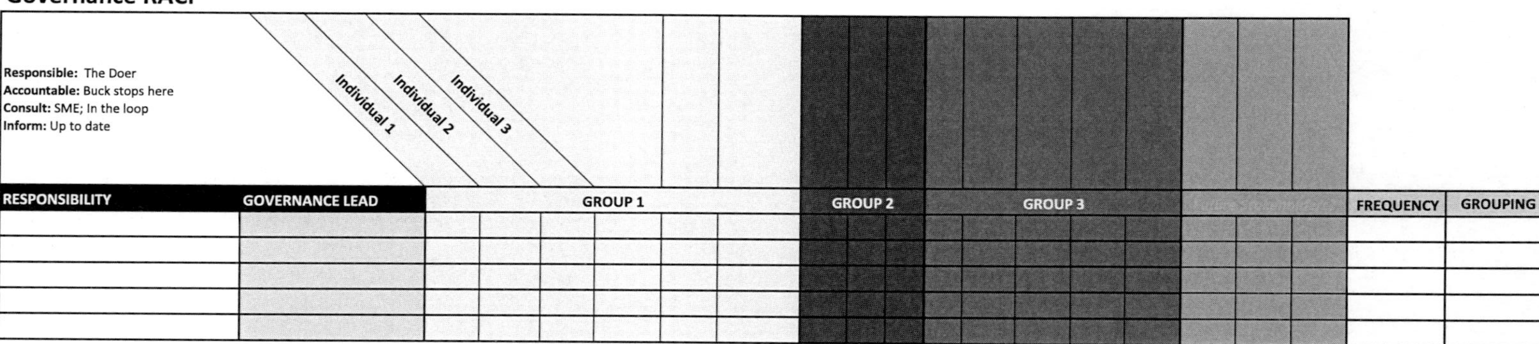

Responsible: The Doer
Accountable: Buck stops here
Consult: SME; In the loop
Inform: Up to date

RESPONSIBILITY	GOVERNANCE LEAD	GROUP 1						GROUP 2			GROUP 3								FREQUENCY	GROUPING
		Individual 1	Individual 2	Individual 3																

Functional RACI Matrix

Responsible: The Doer
Accountable: Buck stops here
Consult: SME; In the loop
Inform: Up to date

Function	Responsible Resource	GROUP 1								GROUP 2		GROUP 3		GROUP 4			GROUP 5					
		Individual 1	Individual 2	Individual 3																		
Category 1																						
Category 2																						
Category 3																						

Endnotes

1. See Mark Ross and Lucy Bassli, *LPO and the Future of Contracting: 4 Tips*, CORPORATE COUNSEL, May 12, 2015.
2. See Appendix "Legal Press Summary."
3. The first article is very representative: https://www.mcca.com/wp-content/uploads/2017/10/Managing-a-Multigenerational-Workforce.pdf. Others to review (original source has been archived on THE AMERICAN LAWYER): https://www.law.com/americanlawyer/almID/1202749825654/; http://www.lawfuel.com/blog/5-millennial-changes-generation-bringing-law-firms/; https://press.pwc.com/News-Releases/nextgen-global-generational-study/s/376ce2a9-1769-46f2-a228-8b97d252f660; http://www.legalteam-news.net/news12/docs/Thomson-Reuters-Millenials-report.pdf.
4. Content in this section is adapted from Lucy Endel Bassli, *The Legal Ecosystem: Boulders, Hurdles & Glass Ceilings In-House (Part 8)*, THOMSON REUTERS, November 28, 2018, THOMSON REUTERS, *available at* http://www.legalexecutiveinstitute.com/legal-ecosystem-glass-ceilings-part-8/.
5. I dedicated an entire subchapter on this topic in chapter 7.
6. *The Alternative Legal Service Providers 2019: Fast Growth, Expanding Use and Increasing Opportunity Report*, THOMSON REUTERS, *available at* https://legal.thomsonreuters.com/en/insights/reports/alternative-legal-service-provider-study-2019?cid=9008178&sfdccampaignid=7011B000002OF6AQAW&chl=pr; *see also* www.abajournal.com/news/article/alternative-legal-service-providers-worth-over-10-billion-come-into-their-own-says-new-report/.
7. For details, see the Intersoft Consulting site: https://gdpr-info.eu/.
8. Washington State Bar Association, *Limited License Legal Technicians*, *available at* https://www.wsba.org/for-legal-professionals/join-the-legal-profession-in-wa/limited-license-legal-technicians.
9. Lorelei Laird, *Despite Kinks in Program, Nonlawyers Successfully Providing Some Legal Services in Washington State*, ABA JOURNAL, March 29, 2017, *available at* http://www.abajournal.com/news/article/despite_kinks_in_program_nonlawyers_are_successfully_providing_some_legal_s/.

10. The Big 4 accounting firms are Deloitte Touche Tohmatsu Limited, Pricewater houseCoopers (PwC), Ernst & Young (E&Y), and Klynveld Peat Marwick Goerdeler (KPMG).

11. Lucy Endel Bassli, *The Legal Ecosystem: Law Firms—In Defense of the Institutions (Part 4)*, THOMSON REUTERS, July 23, 2018, *available at* http://www.legalexecutiveinstitute.com/legal-ecosystem-law-firms-part-4/.

12. Lucy Endel Bassli, *The Legal Ecosystem: Alternative Providers Are Not Alternative Anymore (Part 5)*, THOMSON REUTERS, August 15, 2018, *available at* http://www.legalexecutiveinstitute.com/legal-ecosystem-alternative-providers-part-5/.

13. *Washington State Bar Association, Op. Cit.*

14. The Association of Corporate Counsel (ACC) is a professional association serving the business interests of attorneys who practice in the legal departments of corporations, associations, and other private-sector organizations. ACC states that it has more than forty thousand members employed by more than ten thousand organizations in eighty-five countries (http://www.acc.com/).

15. CLOC has identified core competencies representing the focus areas that "every legal department must manage to have a disciplined, efficient, and effective legal function." See the CLOC website: https://cloc.org/.

16. Technology is addressed with more depth in chapter 5, and practical uses and tips are provided in chapter 7.

17. Note that the names of these people and teams will vary widely across corporate legal departments, but the functions and capabilities will tend to be similar.

18. Practical guidance on project management can be found in chapter 7.

19. Commission on the Future of Legal Services, *Report on the Future of Legal Services in the United States*, 2016, *available at* https://s3-us-west-2.amazonaws.com/mcf-redesign-assets/multimedia/Report-on-the-Future-of-Legal-Services-in-the-US-2016.pdf?mtime=20170117133354.

20. *See Discover the 2019 Best Law Schools*, US NEWS AND WORLD REPORT, March 19, 2018, *available at* https://www.usnews.com/education/best-graduate-schools/articles/slideshows/us-news-best-law-schools.

21. The millennial generation is defined as those born between 1980 and the early 2000s, the first generation to come of age in the new millennium. *See* http://www.pewresearch.org/topics/millennials/.

22. Jane Croft, *Law School Admissions Collapse Continues*, FINANCIAL TIMES, November 20, 2016, *available at* https://www.ft.com/content/4ddb437e-9ace-11e6-8f9b-70e3cabccfae.

23. Mike Stetz, *Enrollment Up At Some Schools, But Is That Good or Bad?*, THE NATIONAL JURIST, September 4, 2018, *available at* http://www.nationaljurist.com/national-jurist-magazine/enrollment-some-schools-good-or-bad.

24. Sally Kane, *Learn About Non-Lawyer Careers in a Law Firm*, THEBALANCE CAREERS, July 6, 2018, *available at* https://www.thebalancecareers.com/legal-jobs-part-ii-non-lawyer-careers-in-a-law-firm-2164538.

25. *See* Codex, The Stanford Center for Legal Informatics, *available at* https://law.stanford.edu/codex-the-stanford-center-for-legal-informatics/.
26. *See* Harvard Law School Center on the Legal Profession, *available at* https://clp.law.harvard.edu/mission/.
27. Suffolk University Boston, Institute on Legal Innovation & Technology, *available at* https://sites.suffolk.edu/legaltech/.
28. Law School Innovation Index, 1/02/2017 Prototype, *available at* https://www.legaltechinnovation.com/law-school-index/.
29. Northwestern Pritzker School of Law, Center for Practice Engagement and Innovation, *available at* http://www.law.northwestern.edu/research-faculty/practice-engagement/.
30. Chicago-Kent College of Law, J.D. Certificate Program in Legal Innovation + Technology, *available at* https://www.kentlaw.iit.edu/academics/jd-program/certificate-programs/legal-innovation-and-technology.
31. Duke Law, Law & Entrepreneurship, *available at* https://www.law.duke.edu/llmle/.
32. Miriam R. Albert, *Ten Tips for a Successful Transition from Law School to Law Practice*, May 19, 2011, *available at* http://apps.americanbar.org/buslaw/blt/content/2011/05/training-for-tomorrow.shtml.
33. Lisa A. Grigg, *The Mandatory Continuing Legal Education (MCLE) Debate: Is it Improving Lawyer Competence or Just Busy Work?,* 12 BYU J. Pub. L. 417 (1998), *available at* https://digitalcommons.law.byu.edu/jpl/vol12/iss2/11.
34. Rocio T. Aliaga, *Framing the Debate on Mandatory Continuing Legal Education (MCLE): The District of Columbia Bar's Consideration of MCLE*, 8 Geo. J. Legal Ethics 1145, 1145 n.l (1995), *in* Chris Ziegler and Justin Kuhn's: *Is MCLE A Good Thing? An Inquiry Into MCLE and Attorney Discipline*, *available at* https://www.clereg.org/assets/pdf/Is_MCLE_A_Good_Thing.pdf.
35. *See* Lawline.com, *available at* https://www.lawline.com/cle-requirements/rhode-island.
36. *See* the American Bar Association's CLE website, *available at* https://www.americanbar.org/cle/mandatory_cle/mcle_states/states_p-z/washington_state.html.
37. Based on research from various online CLE course providers (for example, lawline.com), the American Bar Association CLE site and individual state bar associations.
38. Robert Ambrogi, *Tech Competence,* LawSites, *available at* https://www.lawsitesblog.com/tech-competence/.
39. Tad Simons, *For a Lawyer, What Does Tech Competence Really Mean?* Thomson Reuters, *available at* http://www.legalexecutiveinstitute.com/lawyers-technological-competence/.
40. *See* The Florida Bar Continuing Legal Education (https://www.floridabar.org/member/cle/), The Resource Center of the Florida Bar (https://www.legalfuel.com/category/technology/), and Lawline (https://www.lawline.com/).

41. *See* LexisNexis University, *available at* https://www.lexisnexis.com/university/Course.aspx?classInfo=Crs~686~25379&str=t.

42. *See* Hotshot (https://www.hotshotlegal.com/) and Consero (https://consero.com/).

43. *See* the SLS CodeX Techindex, *available at* https://techindex.law.stanford.edu/.

44. In chapter 7's subchapter on technology there is a definition of AI provided by a software engineer. The definitions are similar, and I have heard other varieties. It does not really matter what the precise definition is, as long as everyone is clear on what the tech solution actually does. The misuse of the term "AI" in marketing hype by legal tech providers is a whole other issue.

45. *See* Thomson Reuters Legal for more information, *available at* https://legal.thomsonreuters.com/en/products/westlaw.

46. See LawGeex site, *available at* https://www.lawgeex.com/ (disclaimer: at time of publication, I served as an advisor to LawGeex).

47. Steve O'Hear, *LawGeex Raises $12M for Its AI-Powered Contract Review Technology*, TheCrunch, April 17, 2018.

48. *McCann FitzGerald Launches Credit Reporting Compliance App*, McCann FitzGerald Knowledge, June 25, 2018, *available at* https://www.mccannfitzgerald.com/knowledge/briefings/mccann-fitzgerald-launches-credit-reporting-compliance-app.

49. *Norton Rose Fulbright Launches First Australian Law Firm Chatbot to Help Manage Data Breach*, December 13, 2017, *available at* http://www.nortonrosefulbright.com/news/159704/norton-rose-fulbright-launches-first-australian-law-firm-chatbot-to-help-manage-data-breach.

50. *See* Norton Rose Fulbright, *Contractor Check, available at* http://www.nortonrosefulbright.com/knowledge/online-services-resources-and-tools/contractorcheck/.

51. *See* the Lex Machina website at https://lexmachina.com/.

52. Premonition also calls itself the "the world's largest litigation database." *See* https://premonition.ai/.

53. Avvo has ratings, reviews, and disciplinary records for lawyers in every state. *See* https://www.google.com/search?q=AVVO&oq=AVVO&aqs=chrome..69i57.11859j0j7&sourceid=chrome&ie=UTF-8.

54. LegalZoom website is at https://www.legalzoom.com/.

55. Legal Services Corporation, *2017 Justice Gap Report: Measuring the Civil Legal Needs of Low-Income Americans, available at* https://www.lsc.gov/media-center/publications/2017-justice-gap-report.

56. For more details, see the ABA website at https://www.americanbar.org/groups/professional_responsibility/publications/model_rules_of_professional_conduct/rule_1_1_competence/comment_on_rule_1_1/.

57. Memorandum of Opinion, Gloria James v. National Financial LLC, and Loan Till Payday LLC, December 5, 2014, *available at* https://courts.delaware.gov/opinions/download.aspx?ID=215820.

58. Natalie Runyon, *The 'Delta' Lawyer Competency Model Discovered through LegalRnD Workshop*, THOMSON REUTERS, June 14, 2018, *available at* http://www.legalexecutiveinstitute.com/delta-lawyer-competency-model/.

59. American Bar Association, *A Current Glance at Women in the Law*, January 2018, *available at* https://www.americanbar.org/content/dam/aba/administrative/women/a-current-glance-at-women-in-the-law-jan-2018.pdf.

60. National Association for Law Placement Inc., *2018 Report on Diversity in U.S. Law Firms*, January 2019, *available at* https://www.nalp.org/uploads/2018NALPReportonDiversityinUSLawFirms_FINAL.pdf.

61. LawGeex.com, *The 2019 General Counsel Landscape*, *available at* https://www.lawgeex.com/resources/gclandscape/.

62. Definition from Oxford English Dictionary, *available at* https://en.oxforddictionaries.com/definition/innovate.

63. Varun Warrier et al, *Genome-Wide Analyses of Self-Reported Empathy: Correlations with Autism, Schizophrenia, and Anorexia Nervosa*, NATURE, March 12, 2018, *available at* https://www.nature.com/articles/s41398-017-0082-6; *see also* Tereza Pultarova, *Genes Can't Explain Why Men Are Less Empathetic Than Women*, LIVE SCIENCE, March 12, 2018, *available at* https://www.livescience.com/61987-empathy-women-men.html; Justin Bariso, *Emotional Intelligence at Work: How Men and Women Interpret Feedback Differently*, INC., *available at* https://www.inc.com/justin-bariso/emotional-intelligence-at-work-how-men-and-women-interpret-feedback-differently.html; Erin Gabriel, *Understanding Emotional Intelligence and Its Effects on Your Life*, CNN.com, July 26, 2018, *available at* https://www.cnn.com/2018/04/11/health/improve-emotional-intelligence/index.html.

64. Gender and the Economy, *Gender and Perceived Creativity*, *available at* https://www.gendereconomy.org/gender-and-creativity/; *see also* Devon Proudfoot et al, *A Gender Bias in the Attribution of Creativity: Archival and Experimental Evidence for the Perceived Association Between Masculinity and Creative Thinking*, PSYCHOLOGICAL SCIENCE, September 18, 2015, *available at* https://journals.sagepub.com/doi/abs/10.1177/0956797615598739.

65. Kate Adams, *Even Women Think Men Are More Creative*, HARVARD BUSINESS REVIEW, December 2015, *available at* https://hbr.org/2015/12/even-women-think-men-are-more-creative.

66. Vivian Hunt, Dennis Layton, and Sara Prince, *Why Diversity Matters*, McKinsey & Company, January 2015, *available at* https://www.mckinsey.com/business-functions/organization/our-insights/why-diversity-matters. *See also* Credit Suisse Research Institute, *Large-Cap Companies with at Least One Woman on the Board Have Outperformed Their Peer Group with No Women on the Board by 26% Over the Last Six Years, According to a Report*, July 31, 2012, *available at* https://journals.sagepub.com/doi/abs/10.1177/0956797615598739; *see also* Rocío Lorenzo et al, *The Mix That Matters: Innovation Through Diversity*, BCG, April 26, 2017, *available at* https://www.bcg.com/en-us/publications/2017/people-organization-leadership-talent-innovation-through-diversity-mix-that-matters.aspx.

67. Nadella references it in his book *Hit Refresh: The Quest to Rediscover Microsoft's Soul and Imagine a Better Future for Everyone* (New York, NY: HarperCollins, 2017).

68. This *New York Times* article by David Brooks discusses a book that argues this same theory that I share: *Why Men Fail*, September 10, 2012, *available at* https://www.nytimes.com/2012/09/11/opinion/brooks-why-men-fail.html.

69. Paula Alsher, *Innovation and Change Management: The People Side of Implementing a Great Strategy*, IMA, April 6, 2017, *available at* https://www.imaworldwide.com/blog/innovation-and-change-management-the-people-side-of-implementing-a-great-strategy.

70. Kimberly Fitch and Sangeeta Agrawal, *Female Bosses Are More Engaging Than Male Bosses*, GALLUP, May 7, 2015, *available at* https://news.gallup.com/businessjournal/183026/female-bosses-engaging-male-bosses.aspx.

71. Many of these concepts were covered in an online course I taught for Suffolk University Law School's Legal Tech Certification Program simply titled "Legal Operations," first delivered in Summer of 2018 (https://www.legaltechcertificate.com/courses/).

72. Content in this section is adapted from LinkedIn posts by Lucy Bassli: "Can Law Firms Lead the [R]evolution?," published June 3, 2017, and "3 Simple Steps to Law Firm Innovation," published on July 12, 2018. LinkedIn posts available at https://www.linkedin.com/pulse/can-law-firms-lead-revolution-lucy-endel-bassli/ and https://www.linkedin.com/pulse/3-simple-steps-law-firm-innovation-lucy-endel-bassli/.

73. Definition from Oxford English Dictionary, *available at* https://en.oxforddictionaries.com/definition/innovate.

74. A good place to start is the Association of Corporate Counsel website: https://www.acc.com/?csModule=security/getfile&pageid=1432511&page=/valuechallenge/index.cfm&qstring=&title=Unless%20You%20Ask:%20A%20Guide%20to%20Law%20Departments%20to%20Get%20More%20From%20External%20Relationships&recorded=1#.

75. There are many tools and approaches to project management. Readers should take aspects that make sense in their practice and not feel constrained that there is one right way.

76. *See* the appendix for project management glossary of terms.

77. *See* the appendix for sample charters and other types of templates used to keep projects organized and stakeholders informed.

78. RACI is an acronym that stands for responsible, accountable, consulted, and informed. According to CIO.com, "a RACI matrix is the simplest, most effective means for defining and documenting project roles and responsibilities. Knowing exactly who is responsible, who is accountable, who needs to be consulted, and who must be kept informed at every step will significantly improve your chances of project success." *See* Bob Kantor, *The RACI matrix: Your blueprint for project success*," CIO, January 30, 2018, *available at* https://www.cio.com/article/2395825/project-management-how-to-design-a-successful-raci-project-plan.html.

79. Content in this section is revised and adapted from Lucy Bassli, *Process is Not a Four-Letter Word*, LEGAL BUSINESS WORLD, January 4, 2018.

80. Content in this section is adapted from Suffolk Law course transcriptions and articles for Thomson Reuters.

81. Valentin Pivovarow, *713% Growth: Legal Tech Set An Investment Record in 2008*, Forbes.com, *available at* https://www.forbes.com/sites/valentinpivovarov/2019/01/15/legaltechinvestment2018/#5a5d18957c2b.

82. "2004 Legal Technology Evaluation," Continuing Education of the Bar (CEB).

83. Material adapted from Lucy Endel Bassli, *The Legal Ecosystem: Legal Tech's Impact on Legal—Contracting & Beyond (Part 7)*, Thomson Reuters, October 16, 2018, *available at* http://www.legalexecutiveinstitute.com/legal-ecosystem-legal-technology-part-7/.

84. Content in this section is adapted and revised from my chapter in K. Jacob, et al. (eds.) (2017) *Liquid Legal: Transforming Legal into a Business Savvy, Information Enabled and Performance Driven Industry (Management for Professionals)*, and from my Suffolk Law Legal Operations course transcript on Law Firm Management.

85. Davis Wright Tremaine LLP (Seattle, Washington) and Addleshaw Goddard LLP (London, United Kingdom) contributed their perspective.

86. Material in this section is adapted from my Suffolk Law course transcript (2017) and the following articles: Lucy Bassli, *Legal Process Outsourcing Has Grown Up*, Metropolitan Corporate Counsel, October 2017, and Mark Ross and Lucy Bassli, *LPO and the Future of Contracting: 4 Tips*, Corporate Counsel, May 12, 2015, *available at* http://www.mondaq.com/article.asp?article_id=529464&signup=true.

87. *See* Ben Seal, *The 2018 Am Law 200*, The American Lawyer, May 22, 2018, *available at* https://www.law.com/americanlawyer/2018/05/22/the-2018-am-law-200/?slreturn=20190310192114.

88. *For example, see* Miriam Rozen, *UnitedLex and LeClairRyan Announce Innovative New Law Venture*, June 13, 2018, *available at* https://www.law.com/americanlawyer/2018/06/13/unitedlex-and-leclairryan-announce-innovative-new-law-venture/?slreturn=20190321164828; *see also* Elevate, *Elevate and New Law Firm ElevateNext Formed by the Founders of Valorem Law Group Join Forces to Provide Seamless Delivery of Legal Services*, April 23, 2018, *available at* https://www.prnewswire.com/news-releases/elevate-and-new-law-firm-elevatenext-formed-by-the-founders-of-valorem-law-group-join-forces-to-provide-seamless-delivery-of-legal-services-300634534.html.

89. MiFID II is a legislative framework instituted by the European Union to regulate financial markets in the bloc and improve protections for investors with the aim of restoring confidence in the industry after the financial crisis exposed weaknesses in the system. It is a revised version of the Markets In Financial Instruments Directive, or MiFID, and was rolled out on January 3, 2018. Investopedia definition available at https://www.investopedia.com/terms/m/mifid-ii.asp.

90. This case study is based on my personal experience having conceived and implemented Microsoft's contract review outsourced model during my tenure in-house at Microsoft.

91. Content in this section is adapted and revised from Chapter 8, Data Analytics: The Foundation of Successful Legal Department published in *Legal Operations* eBook; the *LeftFoot Podcast* in 2018; and Lucy Bassli, Tami Baddeley, and Olga Masek, "Time to make legal a digital workplace,"*Microsoft Industry Blogs*, May 19, 2017, *available*

at https://cloudblogs.microsoft.com/industry-blog/uncategorized/2017/05/19/time-make-legal-digital-workplace/.

92. Content in this section is adapted from podcasts (*LeftFoot* and *Technically Legal*); a presentation by me on Millennials; and articles, including *Attorneys, Let's Take the Pledge*, LinkedIn Pulse, April 14, 2017, *available at* https://www.linkedin.com/pulse/attorneys-lets-take-pledge-lucy-endel-bassli and *Make Way for the Unicorns*, Law360, November 1, 2017, *available at* https://www.law360.com/articles/977359.

93. In the financial world, a unicorn is a privately held startup company valued at more than $1 billion. The term was coined in 2013 by venture capitalist Aileen Lee, choosing the mythical animal to represent the statistical rarity of such successful ventures. *See* https://en.wikipedia.org/wiki/Unicorn_(finance).

94. See *A Millennial Explains How Law Firms Can Attract and Keep His Generation of Lawyers* (https://www.americanbar.org/news/abanews/publications/youraba/2018/june-2018/a-millennial-explains-how-law-firms-can-attract-and-keep-his-gen/); *Law Firm Survey Says Millennial Era Is Here, But Change Has Just Begun* (https://www.law.com/americanlawyer/2018/05/18/law-firm-survey-says-millennial-era-is-here-but-change-has-just-begun/); *Millennials Force Law Firms to Shift Their Mind Set* (https://www.mlaglobal.com/en/knowledge-library/articles/millennials-force-law-firms-to-shift-their-mindset?byconsultantorauthor=alex-russell); *How Millennials are Reshaping the Practice of Law* (http://www.cobizmag.com/Trends/How-Millennials-are-Reshaping-the-Practice-of-Law/); *Millennials are Changing the Legal Profession in An Unexpected Way* (https://www.forbes.com/sites/wesgay/2017/06/28/millennials-unexpected-change-legal-profession/#226da60973ab); and *Four Ways Millennial Attorneys are Changing the Legal Profession* (https://www.lawstudies.com/article/four-ways-millennial-attorneys-are-changing-the-legal-profession/).

95. A creative event by presented by Evolve the Law, ATL's Innovation Center, was held in Chicago in April 2019 with this description: "The traditional career paths are atrophying. Not only are there fewer openings on the 2,000 annual billables "up or out" track, today's entrepreneurial and technologically fluent law graduates increasingly want no part of that grind. Technology and information abundance are rapidly disrupting every facet of our economy, and the legal industry is no different. Today, trailblazing legal professionals and employers leverage new delivery models, data analytics, process management, service design, and many other tools and approaches to create careers that look very different from the law jobs of yore. Radically new legal career paths are here. Join us at the inaugural alternative legal career fair."

96. Six Sigma is a set of techniques and tools for process improvement. It was introduced by engineer Bill Smith while working at Motorola in 1980. Jack Welch made it central to his business strategy at General Electric in 1995. A Six Sigma process is one in which 99.99966 percent of all opportunities to produce some feature of a part are statistically expected to be free of defects. Wikipedia definition available at https://en.wikipedia.org/wiki/Six_Sigma.

Index

Note: Page numbers with *f* indicate figures.

A

accounting firms, Big 4, 25–28
activity tracker, 233
Albert, Miriam R., 58
alternative fee arrangements (AFAs), 15, 119–120, 218–219
alternative legal service providers (ALSPs), 4, 21–25, 95, 104
  efficiencies with, 195
  emergence of, 168–169
  engaging, 170–172
  evolving dynamic between law firms and, 169–170
  functions of, 167–168
  governance framework for, 202–203, 203*f*
  potential savings with, 196
  requests for proposals for, 200
  resource allocation optimization and, 130–131
  scalability with, 194–195
approach, project, 115–116
approval, contract, 141
artificial intelligence (AI), 14, 49, 59, 65, 67–69, 146–149, 147*f*
Association of Corporate Counsel (ACC), 63
assumptions, issues, and risks, project, 114–115
automate branching logic decision trees, 68–69
automation, 133–136, 135*f*. See also technology
  analytics and data extraction, 139–140
  of contract drafting, 140
  contract management, 138–139, 139*f*
  contract review, 140, 174–175
  document management, 136–138
  e-discovery, 146
  IP management, 145–146
  of legal work, 134
  matter management and ebilling, 143–145
  process, 127–128
  process for buying technology for, 149–151
  task, 70–72, 94
Avvo, 72

B

back-office legal ops, 37
  technology and, 66–67
bias for experimentation, 88
Big 4 accounting firms, 25–28, 64
billing cadence, 162*f*, 162–163
blended rates, 163*f*, 163–164
blockchain technology, 65, 69–70
business intelligence (BI), 164
business-minded lawyers, 188–189
business of law, 52, 75
business strategy and planning in legal ops, 42–45, 43*f*

C

change, acceptance of, 39
change management, 112–113, 182–183
chatbots, 68–69, 71, 72
Chicago Kent College of Law, 58
chief legal officers (CLOs), 11
client questions, responding to, 98–100
Colle, Olivier, 147, 148
communication process, 117–118
communications plan, 234–235
competency, model of, 75–76
consultants, accounting firm, 25
continuing legal education (CLE), 4, 58–59, 64
  requirements for, 59–62, 60*f*
  sampling of options in, 63–64
  technology requirements in, 62–63, 74
continuous improvement, 131–132
contracting, innovation in, 100–102
contract life cycle management (CLM), 138–139, 139*f*, 142
contract management, 138–139, 139*f*
contracts
  analytics and data extraction from, 139–140
  approval and signing of, 141
  drafting of, 140
  negotiations of, 121, 140–141
  notifications regarding, 143
  review of, 140, 172–176
  storage of, 142–143
convergence programs, 212
corporate legal departments, 18–19, 104
  openness to legal tech in, 21
corporate legal management
  convergence programs in, 212
  engagement guidelines in, 212–213
  law firm services buyers and sellers in, 210–211
  managing law firm performance, 216–218
  ping pong engagement and, 209–210
  stratification of work and, 213–216
Corporate Legal Operations Consortium (CLOC), 28, 29–30
costs
  analyzing, 49–50, 96, 144
  outsourcing and saving, 196
  project timelines and, 115
culture, innovative, 85–86

D

data, 95
  for better relationship management, 178–180
  bridging the skills gap with, 182–183
  innovation using existing, 107
  and insights in legal ops, 48*f*, 48–49
  lawyers influenced by, 189–190
  for quality improvement, 180–182
  value of, 177–178
  visualization of, 51–52
data analytics, 16, 38, 49
  analyzing spend using, 49–50, 96
  analyzing transactional data, 50
  data extraction and, 139–140

data extraction, 139–140
data-influenced lawyers, 189–190
deep learning, 68, 148
defining the problem and innovation, 81*f*, 81–82
delivery of legal services, 52–53, 104. See also managed services model
design thinking, 80–85, 81*f*
disaggregation of legal process, 126–127
document management, 136–138
drafting of contracts, 140
Duke Law School, 58
Dweck, Carol, 84

E

e-billing, 143–145
e-discovery, 146
Emotional Quotient (EQ), 81
empathy, 81*f*, 81
engagement guidelines, 212–213
established trusted relationships and accounting firms, 26–27
extraction, data, 139–140

F

fill-in-the-blank management system, 40*f*, 40–41
financial benefits of managed services model, 162–165, 162–166
financial management, 118–119
flow charts, 125–126
frequently asked questions (FAQs), 98–100
front-office legal ops, 37–39
  automation and, 134–135
  technology and, 67

G

goals, clearly defined, 111, 198
governance framework for outsourcing, 202–203, 203*f*
governance RACI, 116, 237

H

Harvard Law School, 57

I

ideation and innovation, 81*f*, 82–83
implementation
  innovation, 81, 84–85
  legal technology, 226–227
industry groups, 28–29, 31
infrastructure in legal ops, 39–42, 40*f*, 119
  automation and, 134
in-house lawyers, 105, 210–211
  level of innovation by, 19
  openness to legal tech among, 20–21
innovation, 97
  aligning the right resources for, 9
  applying learning from other experts to, 8
  areas ripe for, 97–102
  Bassli's journey with, 5–11
  in contracting, 100–102
  creating opportunities for, 85–86, 108
  defining the problem and, 81*f*, 81–82
  definition of, 93
  different approaches to learning about, 3–4
  empathy and, 81*f*, 81
  encouraging, 11–12
  final pitch for, 86–89
  ideation and, 81*f*, 82–83
  implementation of, 81*f*, 84–85
  intake form, 99*f*
  legal workforce and, 184–186
  prototyping and testing in, 81*f*, 83–84
  reasons for understanding, 7

innovation (*Continued*)
in responding to client questions, 98–100
sharing, 10–11
steps to pursuing, 106–108, 221–222
technology in, 9–10, 42, 106
using data in, 6–7
who is responsible for, 102–105
women and, 80–85, 81
Integreon Managed Solutions, 168
internal policies, 47
IP management, 145–146

J

justice, technology and access to, 72–73
Justice Gap study, 72

L

law firms
benefits of managed services model for, 160–162
evolving dynamic between ALSPs and, 169–170
in the legal ecosystem, 15–18, 94
myth that managed services won't work for, 156–158
performance management in, 216–218
relationships and, 15–16, 161, 178–180
stratification of work in, 154*f*, 154–156, 156*f*, 213–216
LawGeex, 69, 146, 147*f*
law schools. See legal education
lawyers. See legal workforce
LeftFoot, 13
legal ecosystem, 13–14, 14*f*
alternative legal service providers (ALSPs) in, 4, 21–25
"Big 4" and, 25–28
corporate legal departments in, 18–19
industry groups in, 28–29, 31
law firms in, 15–18
myth busting and, 19–21
regulation of, 29–32
legal education
changes in, 16–17
continuing, 4, 58–64, 60*f*
quick look at, 55–58
Legal Fuel Resource Center, Florida Bar, 63
legal innovation. See innovation
legal market jobs, technology and, 74–75
legal ops, 19–20, 32, 52–53. See also alternative legal service providers (ALSPs)
analyzing spend and, 49–50
analyzing transactional data and, 50
back-office, 37, 66–67
business strategy and planning in, 42–45, 43*f*
data and insights in, 48*f*, 48–49
data visualization and, 51–52
defining, 35
fill-in-the-blank management system in, 40*f*, 40–41
front-office, 37–39, 67, 134–135
functions of, 36, 36*f*
growth and evolution of, 36
project and program management in, 45–48, 46*f*
solution design and implementation services in, 41
technology and infrastructure in, 39–42, 40*f*
tech system support in, 41
legal process outsourcing (LPO), 9, 21, 22, 95–96, 126, 156–157, 167. See also outsourcing
back-office services provided by, 157
emergence of, 168–169
outsourcing contract review to, 172–176

legal project management, 100
  alternative fee arrangements (AFA), 119–120
  contract negotiations, 121
  in litigation space, 120
Legal RnD Program, Michigan State University College of Law, 75
legal service provider (LSP), 167
Legal Services Corporation, 72–73
legal technology. See technology
legal workforce, 74–75, 95, 184
  business-minded lawyers in, 188–189
  changing role of attorneys in, 186–187
  data-influenced, 189–190
  innovation and, 184–186
  millennials in, 56, 95, 192–193
  process-focused, 190–191
LegalZoom, 72, 134
LexisNexis, 63, 69
Lex Machina, 71
lifecycle management, 139
Limited License Legal Technicians (LLLTs), 23, 30–31
litigation space, 120

M

machine learning, 68, 148
managed services model, 153–154
  client benefits of, 158–160
  financial benefits of, 162–165, 162–166
  key challenges to overcome in offering, 166
  law firm benefits of, 160–162
  myths about, 156–158
  opportunities for broader service offering with, 161–162
  relationship building with, 161
  stratification of work in, 154*f*, 154–156, 156*f*
management consulting, 25–26
mapping, processing, 128
matter management, 143–145
McCann FitzGerald, 71
Microsoft Access, 9
Microsoft Outlook, 145
Microsoft Research in Artificial Intelligence, 147
Microsoft Word, 7, 9
millennials, 56, 95, 192–193
Model Rules of Professional Conduct, ABA, 73
monitoring and continuous improvement, 131–132

N

Nadella, Satya, 84
negotiations, contract, 121, 140–141
neural networks, 68
non-disclosure agreements (NDAs), 101–102, 190
Northwestern Pritzker School of Law, 58, 75
Norton Rose Fulbright, 71
notifications, 143

O

opportunities for innovation, 85–86, 108
outside counsel programs, 20
outsourcing, 9, 21, 22, 95–96, 126
  best practices for successful, 204–208
  desired outcomes for, 198
  efficiencies with, 195
  governance framework for, 202–203, 203*f*
  planning before, 204–205
  post-transition activities in, 207–208
  potential savings with, 196
  reasons for, 194–196
  requests for proposals for, 200
  staying connected in, 203–204
  steps in, 197–198

outsourcing (*Continued*)
transition stage of, 205–207
transition timelines for, 200–201, 201*f*
types of work for, 196–197

P

panel programs, 20
paralegals, 47
performance management, 216–218
ping pong engagement, 209–210
post-mortem exercise, 112–113
practice of law, 24, 52
Practicing Law Institute (PLI), 63
pre-empting of recurring problems, 107
Premonition, 71
PricewaterhouseCoopers, 29
pricing, Big 4 accounting firms and predictable, 27
prioritization of work, 128–129, 129*f*
buying technology and, 149–150
process engineers, accounting firm, 26
processes, 94, 132
automation of, 127–128
disaggregation of, 126–127
managed services model and, 164–165, 165*f*
mapping exercises for, 128
monitoring and continuous improvement of, 131–132
optimizing resource allocation and, 129–131
outsourcing and, 195
prioritizing work and, 128–129, 129*f*
simple example of, 124*f*, 124–126
stigma and, 123
workflow for, 198, 199*f*
process-focused lawyers, 190–191
process optimization, 46
program management, 118–119
project charters, 8, 113–116, 231–232
project management, 16, 26, 94, 121–122
alternative fee arrangements (AFA), 119–120
attributes, 110*f*
contract negotiations, 121
core concepts in, 113–118
defined, 109–110
glossary, 230
legal, 100
in legal ops, 45–48, 46*f*
in litigation space, 120
as only the beginning of change, 112–113
power and pitfalls of, 110–112
technology for, 117
project managers (PMs), 47–48, 100
project overview, 113–114
project plan, 118
prototyping and testing in innovation, 81*f*, 83–84

Q

quality and reputation of Big 4 accounting firms, 27
quality improvement, data for, 180–182

R

RACI, 116, 237
reallocation of resources, 129–130
regulation, legal ecosystem, 29–32
relationships and law firms, 15–16, 161
data and, 178–180
request for proposals (RFP), 150, 200, 228–229
resource allocation optimization, 129–131
resource models, 9
retrieval, document, 138